"If you only have time to read one book on leadership this year, *read this!* It's a tremendous and timely work, which will become a classic in its own right, and a great gift to those of us who want to be the best leaders we can be in this time of warp-speed change."

—*Bernard DeWulf*
Chairman, Allied Holdings

"I attended the High Impact Leadership Seminar offered by Staub-Peterson . . . I dived in, immersed myself, and emerged with a halo."

—Fortune *Magazine*

"Because of Dusty's programs, I have been able to identify my leadership weaknesses and position myself in a very special and unique role, which not only has improved our company's bottom line but has made me more of a role model to my colleagues and employees."

—*Edward M. Gabriel*
Ambassador to Morrocco

"Dusty has developed a practical, workable, integrated approach, based on many theories of leadership, self-awareness and self-appraisal, and group interaction. Dusty's approach shows he has his finger on a part of leadership and performance improvement others haven't discovered."

—*Harold A. Kurstedt, Jr.*
Director, College of Engineering,
Virginia Polytechnic Institute and State University

"It helped me to solidify my thinking and feeling about leadership. I highly recommend it!"

—*Richard Rodriguez, M.D.*
Medical Director,
Kaiser Permanente, Georgia Region

"*The Heart of Leadership* is a powerful tool for those who want to measure their leadership skills. Staub highlights the criteria for 21st-century leadership."

—*Jon Baker*
President, Baker McCormick Group, Inc.

"I have worked with Dusty as a colleague and friend for over 20 years. Throughout that time, I have been continuously impressed with Dusty's creativity, integrity, and energy. He is able to articulate sophisticated and complex ideas in a very usable format, and constantly offers his clients and students his compassionate heart and practical wisdom. He is a master teacher."

—*Robert "Leif" Diament*
Partner, Wellness Alliance

"Dusty Staub's *The Heart of Leadership* gets at the heart of real leadership and doesn't miss a beat. He breaks the old command and control mold of techno-managers and clears the way for the makers and enablers. Here's a book which validates that one's personal power truly comes from self-awareness, vulnerability, compassion, and grace. If you're not moved by Staub's insights and examples . . . better check your pulse!"

—*Robert A. Williams*
Area Vice President, Southeast Region,
Aetna Health Plans

"The key value of Staub's work and book, over and above other leadership programs and books, is his focus on heart. By connecting leadership issues and practices with "heart" factors, such as passion, relationships, and integrity, Staub helped me and my team develop a stronger organization, create more passion and energy toward our business goals, and achieve greater alignment of individual and group objectives. It's not another pretty cover, flashy model, or collection of buzzwords. This book really gets at the heart of leadership—what you need to know and the issues you need to think about and deal with to be effective as a person, as a leader, and as a successful enterprise."

—*David R. Richards, Ph.D.*
Director, UK Product Marketing,
Northern Telecom

THE HEART OF
LEADERSHIP

12 Practices of Courageous Leaders

8/26/00

Linda,

May you thing as you listen and challenge as a leader. May you always follow the path of heart,

ROBERT E. STAUB, II

Robert E. Staub

Executive Excellence Publishing
1344 East 1120 South
Provo, UT 84606
phone: (801) 375-4060
fax: (801) 377-5960
web: www.eep.com

Revised and updated edition, 1/2000

Printed in the United States of America
10 9 8 7 6 5 4 3

ISBN 0-9634917-3-3
Library of Congress Catalog Card Number: 96-085694

Cover design by Heather Stratford-Innes
Printed by Publishers Press

Author's Statement of Purpose

What I hope to create in this revised and updated version of my book is a focus on wholehearted leadership. I am firmly convinced that what we have seen has been halfhearted leadership attempts and models for those in senior levels of management or leadership roles. What do I mean by halfhearted? I mean those who only focus on their business life and neglect their personal life, their health, and their family. It is true that many have sacrificed their families and even their health and their relationships on the altar of financial success. But the truly great and lasting leaders have modeled a more wholehearted approach, in which they have found a way to create meaningful and lasting relationships both outside and within the workplace, all while achieving substantial and even remarkable results. It is precisely because of their focus on the whole of the human heart in themselves and others that they are able to draw out the very best in creativity, innovation, talent, ability, and, ultimately, bottom-line results. What I have discovered follows.

This book represents more than five and a half years of research, and over 27 years of professional work with people at all levels of society, both public and private. Having worked with many families, thousands of executives, large and small organizations, and teams (both community based and industrial based) I have come to the following set of conclusions:

- The key to lasting success, both personally and professionally, is found in the willingness we have to go more deeply into the details that surround us, to go more deeply into the meaning of the events which surround us, and to go more deeply into our own heart and into the hearts of those who work with us.

- Each of our lives is bigger than any job or any company. There are many problems that emerge when we shrink our lives down to only one task or one job or one company. If we remember just how big our lives are, it allows us to bring a much faster sense of perspective and greater levels of innovation and creativity, as well as passion and energy, to whatever task we are doing, to whatever job must be accomplished, to whatever process must be completed, to whatever company we are forming, creating, partnering in, or helping to develop and grow.
- Without courage, it all fails. Without courage, there can be no leadership. In fact, there can be no lasting sense of joy or ultimate success in our lives, either personally or professionally. I have personally witnessed what comes about when executives fail to exercise their courage, as well as when individuals fail to exercise courage in their private lives, in their relationships, and in their families.

This book is my attempt to articulate a simple philosophy of powerful and effective leadership and leading. I hope that as you read, you will be able to diagnose where you have strengths, where you may have weaknesses, and how you can systematically develop and cultivate a more powerful, effective, and lasting leadership impact, both in your personal life and in your professional life.

I hope you will enjoy the book and find a way to take it deeper. For those wishing to go more deeply into personal mastery and to develop greater depths of courage beyond the scope of this book, you might want to check out *Seven Acts of Courage: Bold Leadership for Wholehearted Life.*

—Robert E. Staub II

Leadership Is . . .

Leadership is the courage to put oneself at risk.
Leadership is the courage to be open to new ideas.
Leadership is being dissatisfied with the current reality.
Leadership is taking responsibility while others
                    are making excuses.
Leadership is seeing the possibilities in a situation
                    while others are seeing the limitations.
Leadership is evoking in others the capacity to dream.
Leadership is inspiring others with a vision
                    of what they can contribute.
Leadership is your heart speaking to the hearts of others.
Leadership is the integration of heart, head, and soul.
Leadership is the power of the one made many
                    and the many made one.
Leadership is the capacity to care, and in caring, to liberate
                    the ideas, energy, and capacities of others.
Leadership is the willingness to stand out in a crowd.
Leadership is the ability to submerge your ego
                    for the sake of what is best.
Leadership is, above all, courageous.
Leadership is an open mind and an open heart.
Leadership is the dream made flesh.

Acknowledgments

I wish to express deep appreciation to a number of people without whose help and influence this book would not have occurred. First, I thank all the clients I have worked with over the years and the senior executives who allowed me to interview them and who are quoted liberally in this book.

I also thank Dr. Martin Groder for his guidance and supervision from a clinical point of view, as well as his wonderful friendship and guiding wisdom.

I owe a profound thank you to Dr. Richard Moss, the most powerful teacher with whom I have worked.

I wish to thank Dr. James Farr, one of the pioneers in leadership training, who supported my leadership development, and also Tony Speed for his friendship and support. I also wish to thank Robert "Leif" Diament, best friend and wonderful advisor. I also owe a very special thanks to Kirtland "Cat" Peterson, co-founder of Staub-Peterson and a brilliant advisor.

I wish to thank the outstanding staff at Staub-Peterson for all they do and the difference they make in the individual lives of our clients and the complex systems called organizations.

To Victoria Laing-Peterson: thanks for the continuing partnership and all your creativity.

To Tracey Simmons: thanks to the greatest marketing partner any organization could ever want.

I would like to give a special thanks to Laurie McLain for her editorial support, the frequent calls to agents and publishers, and the miracles she has wrought. I would also like to remember and thank Catherine Sharp for her energy, excitement, and belief that a book would be created so many years ago.

Thanks is also due to Mike Hammer for his editing, advice, and particularly his passion to make this book more available and enticing to the reader. I feel a debt of gratitude and appreciation to Trent Price, my agent, for his unfailing optimism, and to Ken Shelton, my publisher at Executive Excellence, for his faith in this book and in its message.

There are literally dozens of others I could thank, but the list would take pages. For all of you who have offered encouragement, feedback, and support, thank you.

Finally, I owe a most special appreciation to Dr. Christine E. Staub: friend, healer, mate, spouse, best friend. Tina, thanks for the patience, inspiration, support, and forgiveness.

Finally, to Sean, Kendra, and Chamberlain, my beloved children, may the future you inherit be one that is created with love.

Contents

Dedicated to Lieutenant Colonel "Bob" Staub,
April 1925–July 1992:
Father, Teacher, Leader

Dad, almost too late I came to know you and found a
man of courage, vision, and heart. Thanks for the
lessons, and especially your laughter. You have
become the star by which I steer.

Foreword

I enjoy the writing of Robert "Dusty" Staub for its refreshing candor and creativity on the age-old topic of leadership. This book is a prime example of his ability to "dust off" the clichés and catch phrases (so popular in the consultant trade) and shed real light and add genuine insight.

I also appreciate his value base. The courage to lead, in his book, comes from one's moral convictions and willing observance of the timeless principles of leading other people effectively. The heart of leadership is, in a real sense, the human heart—that passionate, emotional, and moral center of the person. In this context, the standard list of leadership subtopics—such as vision and motivation—are seen in a new light.

So, too, is followership. Within the stewardship of authentic leaders, no one is abused or taken for granted. On this point, Dusty and I agree. I have long argued that counterfeit leadership breeds false followership and "plantation management," meaning the employment of people solely for the economic benefit of the owners. Authentic leaders liberate people from various forms of prejudice, abuse, exploitation, and ignorance. And enlightened self-leadership seeks emancipation from self-defeating habits, relationships, contracts, and controls. Emancipation of the human mind, heart, and soul, then, is one of the first and sweetest fruits of authentic leadership.

The curse of counterfeit leadership is the often subtle subjugation of people and human rights. In his *Letter from Birmingham Jail*, Martin Luther King, Jr. writes: "Injustice anywhere is a threat to justice everywhere. Freedom is never voluntarily given by the oppressor: It must be demanded by the oppressed. Segregation distorts the soul and damages the personality. It gives the segregator a false sense of superiority and the segregated a false sense of inferiority."

The false sense of self—on the part of both leaders and followers—is the stuff counterfeits are made of. On one side of the coin, the "superiors" practice the sort of communications and public relations described by Aldous Huxley in *Propaganda under a Dictatorship*: "Thanks to modern methods of communication, it is possible to mechanize or condition the lower leadership. Today the art of mind control is becoming a science. The first principle is a value judgment: The masses are utterly contemptible. To make them more mass-like, the counterfeit leader assembles them by the thousands in vast halls and arenas where individuals can lose their personal identity, even their elementary humanity, and be merged with the crowd. Mindlessness and moral idiocy are not characteristically human attributes; they are symptoms of herd-poisoning." Huxley noted that marching "diverts or kills thoughts, makes an end of individuality, and is the indispensable magic stroke performed in order to accustom the people to a mechanical quasi-ritualistic activity." Network television now accomplishes the same thing much more efficiently.

On the other side of the coin, the "inferiors" struggle with their sense of self-worth and identity. They are often self-contradictory, having both a positive and negative pole. "Two souls are lodged within my breast that struggle there for undivided reign," said Goethe. H. G. Wells noted: "I am not a man but a mob." Mark Twain observed: "Every man is like a moon, having both a dark side and light side." And in Robert Sherwood's play, Abraham Lincoln says of himself: "You talk about a civil war: There seems to be one going on inside of me all of the time. One of these days I may just split asunder and part company with myself."

Each person must develop his or her own leadership, as leadership can't be conferred, inherited, or transferred. Though it can be modeled, it is acquired only by each individual gaining mastery over attitudes, ideas, and actions.

Would-be leaders must either leave the "plantation" or change the nature of their roles and relationships in order to gain the degree of freedom and identity needed to progress.

The cure for plantation management and counterfeit leadership often starts with an overdose of the drug, a nose rub, a tough loss, a slap in the face, a cold-water shower, a citation, a summons, a shock—or with objective feedback, accurate assessment, or an early morning wake-up call for improved performance.

The laws of motion apply to leadership: A body at rest, or at a low level of motion or achievement, tends to remain at rest unless acted upon by some outside force; conversely, a body with motion and momentum tends to remain in that state unless blocked and stopped. To move from one state to the next, we sometimes need a wake-up call or a mentor.

Enter Robert "Dusty" Staub, a Quixote of sorts. Does it take a madman, a Don Quixote, to see Dulcinea in Aldonza? It certainly takes a visionary. And then, to get from here to there, it takes a talented team to deal intelligently with all the messy realities—to pull up anchor (what has been) and set sail for what might be takes a courageous Columbus and crew and a belief in something beyond "me and mine," "here and now."

The quirks of Quixote—his poor eyesight and romantic mind-set—made him the perfect candidate for leading man and change agent. For who in his "right" mind would dismiss "the resumé" and look into the eyes and heart of another human being and say, "You're hired"? Who would dismiss the past—with its grades and degrees, credit reports and medical history? Who would trust a criminal? Who would believe an outcast?

To get the most benefit from this book, you will need to act on the constructive feelings or impressions you have as you read. Like Don Quixote, you will need to believe in something—in natural laws, timeless principles, and in yourself and other people. You will need to work effectively, with faith, to create authentic models and environments—and to make those "impossible" dreams come true.

The "heart of leadership," after all, is simply the visionary faith and courage necessary to lead for tomorrow.

—Ken Shelton

"It's never too late to be what you might have been."
—George Eliot

PREFACE

Courage to Lead for Tomorrow

Being a leader

means having the

courage to engage

the hearts and minds

of those who

would follow.

In early April 1945, near the end of World War II, the American Third Army was within striking distance of the infamous concentration camp Buchenwald. The brilliant and bold leader of that army was General Patton. Patton knew that a mere three-hour delay in liberating the camp could mean the deaths of thousands of inmates. Against the rules of caution and strategy, he mounted an enveloping armored attack on the hill, cutting the SS guards off from the camp, coincidentally just after they had been issued orders to blow up the buildings and exterminate all prisoners! His leadership cut through the normal pathways and strategies, striking at the essential heart of the matter before him. This leadership made the difference between life and death for thousands. If he had just been "managing," then yet another tragedy would have played itself out.

Leadership is a word widely used and, generally, poorly, understood. The synonyms for "leading" are "piloting, guiding, offering direction, influencing, effecting, heading up, showing the way by going in front . . . " What most of us lack in our personal lives and in our professional work is that quality of "leading" or piloting.

We have grown up in a society which, for the past 100 years, has prized following directions, being obedient, and maintaining the status quo in our schooling and work environments. Management has been the "science" of running a business, and an MBA is both a status symbol and the ticket to success. We have looked for a few leaders at the top, expecting everyone else to be a manager or a worker.

The challenge before us is not more and better management. It is more honest and courageous leadership at all levels of society and organizations. Leadership cuts through the assumptions, the status quo, the certainty, the rigid structures of what has been. Leaders thrive in the shades of gray and the ambiguities of rapid change and the complexities change brings. Indeed, the ability to navigate the uncharted and roiling waters of today's business environment and the complex global realities around us requires the very skills and ways of thinking and relating found in effective leaders.

What is a good model for understanding this quality of leadership? Are there any similarities to be found in science or mathematics for the kind of leadership we now need?

Mathematical Model

A mathematical model for such an approach does exist and is, in fact, finding its way into the next wave of consumer products: "fuzzy logic." Fuzzy-logic engineering allows for smoother transitions, more accurate readings of reality, increased precision, and greater flexibility. It deals with approximations versus the hard and fast world of binary logic. Lofti Zadeh developed it in 1965. A Danish company was the first to use this new tool in the early '80s, when it created a fuel-intake process for a rotating kiln used to make cement. Hitachi next used it in the Sendai City subways, eliminating jerky or abrupt motions in starts and stops.

In 1994 Whirlpool won a multimillion-dollar contest to design a new, highly efficient refrigerator. One of the key components of that winning design was a fuzzy-logic chip that saves energy in defrosting by reading the environment and defrosting only when necessary. Other new advances include vacuum cleaners that change suctioning power depending on the surface being swept; washing machines that judge the load size and materials to be cleaned; and ovens that cook according to taste preferences. Fuzzy logic may very well be more than the new word in consumer electronics. It also has direct application to the new leadership paradigm.

Fuzzy logic is different from the old absolutes of digital: on or off, right or wrong, yes or no, true or false, black or white. It recognizes and makes use of the vast shades of gray between the rigid poles of the binary model. Most of our world, our social and management systems, and our politics have been designed around the digital approach. However, this older model is not one that lends itself to great flexibility, or even to great intelligence. There is a hard, fairly rigid approach to problems and to life. This limits the responsiveness of individuals and systems to changing conditions and shifting paradigms. It is an approach that lacks the capacity to adapt or change quickly and smoothly. This way of thinking and managing is a critical part of how we have been failing. We have a way of thinking and living that makes it extremely difficult for grace to appear or life to flourish since it constricts us emotionally, conceptually, and creatively.

Fuzzy logic is an approach of approximations. A crude example is the difference between a regular light switch, which turns a light on or off (digital), and a dimmer switch, which allows a light to vary in degrees of brightness (fuzzy logic). This allows for a greater range of responses and therefore flexibility to the requirements of the environment and even the "mood" or ambiance desired. So too, in real life, the range of options can be extended to many more iterations between the two fixed positions of off or on, right or wrong, black or white. This means that the environment can be read with greater precision and the responses to that environment calibrated with much more flexibility and appropriateness.

This has led to a saying we have coined at Staub-Peterson: "In approaching the challenges of our complex world, it is important to remember that while white matters and black matters, where it really counts is in gray matter(s)." It is really in the shades of gray that we find innovation, creativity, fresh perspectives, and the ambiguity necessary to challenge and check our paradigms. Fuzzy logic excels at, and exists in, the realm of the gray. Great leadership thrives in and utilizes the shades of gray to find new approaches, new opportunities, more options, and fruitful behaviors and actions.

The Duke of Wellington, Napoleon's bane, used this kind of thinking to out-innovate the French emperor, creating new initiatives and possibilities. The power of this kind of thinking in upgrading leadership effectiveness is illustrated very powerfully in his three-year campaign to free the Iberian peninsula. It was in this setting that he successfully wielded a force of 60,000 men to best 340,000 Frenchmen, using unheard-of tactics, such as fighting an aggressively offensive battle from a defensive position!

We are beginning to see and know that in our complex world value is found less and less in the positions of either/or, or for/against, and more in the position of "and." It is this *and* that, true *and* false, right *and* wrong. It is the ability to synthesize and integrate disparate and different viewpoints, which adds value in an increasingly complex global marketplace.

Canon of Japan used this approach when it was trying to crack the American marketplace for copiers by out-thinking and out-innovating the formidable Xerox organization. It essentially saw the opportunities in the shades of gray, seized a niche, and exploited it. Xerox was too powerful to compete with head to head, so Canon developed a strategic path designed to "surround" a larger, better financed, and supremely positioned opponent. The answer: use Xerox's strengths and positioning against itself, forcing it to cannibalize its most profitable advantages to respond to Canon. Canon built smaller, inexpensive copiers that could be sold by office supply shops, had replaceable cartridges, and needed less servicing. Xerox, heavily wedded to its rental of large, expensive copiers with extensive servicing agreements and its extensive sales force, hesitated for five years before formulating a coherent response. By then Canon was well-established and off to the races.

This kind of leadership encompasses logic and ambiguity—is willing to hold both positions and looks for answers within conflict instead of trying to eliminate it. Such leadership requires tremendous flexibility and openness. To be that flexible and open—especially within the confines of our prevailing digital cultural paradigm—requires great courage, the courage to remain open. Staying open to creative tension, to criticism, and to new possibilities is at the very core of what is required of those who wish to be leaders today. The ability to use the tension between the need for certainty, predictability, order, and alignment versus ambiguity, empowerment, and innovation is at the core of effective change efforts, forming the backbone of lasting leadership.

The fuzzy logic concept can be applied to empowerment and the leadership skills required to move us successfully into the 21st century. The old logic of precision and rigid controls, known as "command and control management," was powerful, but it could only take a culture and work force so far. It worked well when long factory runs were the norm and production was the greatest concern; when the world moved more slowly and the customer was less demanding; when competition was localized and not global; when the pace of technological breakthroughs and innovation was measured in decades and not in quarters.

Command and control leadership and management created powerful movement, but in the new world we live in that same system works with a lot of jerky starts and stops. It leaves an organization ill-prepared to respond rapidly and flexibly; it also limits work groups' responsiveness and adaptability. A more responsive organization requires greater freedom and more applied intelligence. The power of approximations in team communications and work processes means more allowances for—and even a cultivation of—intuition, loose-knit organizational relationships, and multiple, yet integrated and aligned choices from moment to moment.

We cannot have just a few leaders at the very top of an enterprise. My dad used to say that in peacetime an army can get by with some leadership at the top and just managers at the other levels. In a war, however, or when faced with complex and rapidly changing conditions, that same army must now have leaders and leadership initiatives at every level capable of interacting with an effective, coordinating chain of command. As he so colorfully put it, "Leadership is a simple task, really, just like drinking and whistling at the same time!"

Like it or not, we are in a "war" environment: constant challenges, unrelenting competition, shifting scenarios, chaos, and tremendous ferment. We now need leaders at every level of business and government, and throughout our communities. Without this texturing and layering of leadership throughout society, we will be seriously, if not mortally, disadvantaged. Our old command and control paradigm has left us ill-prepared and ill-equipped to generate pervasive, powerful leadership. For several generations we have essentially created and taught the assumption that we need just one good leader supported by strong managers and management practices. This is the path to failure in our current global environment.

We need the courage to challenge the old assumptions and to ask tough questions about our ways of interacting, thinking, and living. Then we need the courage to take in new data and act on it. And we must find the courage to be interdependent, knowing that none of us is as smart as all of us. We must dream and dream again, while putting our dreams into play by committing to make them realities. We must have the courage to challenge much of what we have learned and to open ourselves to learning anew in a never-ending process of discovery, engagement, practice, measurement, and then rediscovery.

The combination of binary or linear logic and fuzzy logic principles allows for greater precision, power, and learning to occur. It allows for flexible, responsive mind-sets and categories. Then the critical questions arise:

- How effective is your leadership?
- What are you doing to create a more powerful and effective team?
- Where are you limiting your team due to the hardening of your categories?
- What is your vision for your life? Your enterprise? Your leadership impact?
- What are the principles and assumptions inherent in your actions?
- What have you been afraid to see and/or change?
- What will you need to do differently to meet the challenges before you?
- What are the essential forces that impact your enterprise, your work, your mission? What will you do not only to respond, but to proactively get in front of those forces?

One of the key tasks of leaders in this age is to ask meaningful and provocative questions, causing all concerned in an enterprise to reevaluate and rethink their assumptions. It engenders a creative orientation, developing and enhancing operational and conceptual capabilities. What are some of these critical questions? Here are a few:

Critical Leadership Questions
- Who are we?
- What business are we in? How do we rank in that business?
- What do we wish to become?
- Since society and industry continually evolve, what do we foresee that we will become? What kind of work environment do we want to create?
- What are our guiding principles and values? How do we wish to treat each other?
- Are we focused upon the right things? Where are we going and why? What is our strategic path?
- Who are our customers? Our potential customers? How do we define our customers? What are our values around our customers?
- What kind of leadership do we need to develop? What will be required of our leadership system by the global market?
- What skills are necessary for the new leadership paradigm?
- What are the leadership actions and processes that create a high, value-added impact?
- What skill sets must leaders orchestrate within their teams?

- How effective is our communication and feedback system?
- If everything we see in our organization is a manifestation of what we reward and maintain in our conscious and unconscious systems, what systemic analyses and changes do we need to explore and engage?

Questions like these are being asked more and more often by the most successful leaders today. They are essential if we are to thrive and have a dynamic future.

Max DePree, former chairman and CEO of the Herman Miller Corporation, had a long and successful tenure at its helm. In his book, *Leadership Is an Art,* he reflects that leadership is about intimacy, "intimacy with the marketplace and intimacy with the substance of the work." A few prominent examples, such as Jack Welch at GE, Andy Grove at Intel, and Bernie Marcus at Home Depot, demonstrate the power of intimacy, not only with customers and the substance of the work, but also with those who do the work.

If DePree writes about the "soul" of leadership, then this book is about its heart and how to strengthen the muscle of that heart, engaging and liberating the profound inner powers of self and others. It fleshes out the importance of intimacy, as well as the other three core drivers of leadership.

Leadership, by definition, requires followership. You create followers when you know what is important to those you want to follow you and when you engender trust. The paradox of leading is that in order to lead, you must first follow, demonstrating your ability to understand and listen to the needs of those around you. To generate that followership, much is required. It is a path that requires at least one key characteristic: courage—the courage to face yourself; the courage to face your fears; the courage to move forward in the face of uncertainty and disapproval; the courage to tell the truth with candor; the courage to be open, even vulnerable, to others' ideas and strengths; and the courage to change beliefs, old rules and formulas of success, your behavior, and your mind.

It requires the courage to admit when you are wrong, the courage to focus on what you can change and influence, rather than simply excusing yourself by focusing on what you are concerned about but you cannot change or influence. We need the courage to be students again as well as the courage to be models and teachers. We need the courage to ask for help and to use that help with gratitude. We need the courage to grieve for losses as well as the courage to celebrate successes.

What is required is simply the courage to invite those engaged in your enterprise to bring their hearts and souls to that enterprise. It really means the courage to live out of your greater self and to pursue your highest aspirations. I want to help address this courage of heart and spirit by providing you with some examples, setting out 12 practices that generate powerful results through leadership initiatives and development. It is meant for those who are courageous enough to change and lead today, for today's sake and for the shifting challenge of tomorrow.

> *"I do not believe in a fate
> that falls on men however
> they act; but I do believe
> in a fate that falls on them
> unless they act."*
> –G. K. Chesterton

INTRODUCTION

The Imperatives of Leadership

Leadership is about

cultivating and

liberating meaningful

power for yourself

and others.

It is about change.

Leadership, practiced at its best, is the art and science of calling to the hearts and minds of others. It is engaging others in an enterprise of sound strategic focus, where they can experience a sense of ownership, of making a difference, of being valued and adding value.

The most effective way of leading, over time, is to lead from the heart. The secret to lasting leadership success is a willingness to go more deeply into the substance of the work, as well as into the relationships of those who are supporting that work, whether they be vendors, customers, employees, family members, or strategic alliances. It is the willingness to come from the depths of who I am to speak to the depths of who you are. At its very best, leadership calls people to a higher plan of performing, acting, and relating. Great leaders know about power and how to access and use it.

Consider the story of the woman who woke up in the hold of a ship. She knew she was in the hold of a ship because of the movement and the sound of waves. She went up on deck and saw icebergs. Seeking the captain of the vessel, the woman went to the bridge and asked him where the ship was headed. The captain told her they were sailing north, into the cold and ice. The woman felt saddened and complained that she wished they were heading someplace warmer and more hospitable, like Tahiti. The captain simply shrugged. The woman then asked why they were sailing north. The captain replied that the direction was the one they had always sailed and continued on his northerly course. The woman went back down to the hold. She felt powerless and dejected. Yet she had forgotten something critical. She owned the ship!

This story illustrates something that lies at the very core of leadership: understanding power. Many of us are very much like that woman, having forgotten that we own our lives, our careers, our participation in organizations, and our essential direction. When this occurs, we are powerless and adrift, not knowing how to fully exert our talents and abilities. Yet we always have the power to rediscover the essential potency of choosing and redirecting our lives and our efforts. We have the innate authority and ability to change directions, to seek more worthy and rewarding ports and destinations. I firmly believe that many people in society, in our organizations, in political life, and in communities are awakening to the need for, and the potential of, the leadership spirit that lies dormant within them.

What it takes to tap this spirit is profoundly simple, yet extremely arduous. However, if we do not engage in making the effort, then we will never release the leadership spirit within, nor will we create more effective leadership. In the end, this failure will cost us dearly.

For far too long, corporate and political America has been over-managed while being seriously under-led. We cannot thrive by focusing on the parts versus the whole fabric of society and of our organizations, by emphasizing the short term over the long term. These are survival models, and by driving a survival model, we are dangerously close to forgetting thriving and an increased quality of life.

As one philosopher put it, "We must differentiate between a higher standard of living versus an increased quality of life." They are not the same thing. Many "successful" executives have failed to be successful with their families, ending up alienated from their children or estranged from their spouses. Few have achieved a sense of inner peace or even really enjoyed their success. At another level, if one family thrives while five other families suffer, then everyone has a decreased quality of life due to fear of crime, acts of frustration and anger, a diminished quality of environment, and constraints on the human psyche.

The collective failure to provide consistent and powerful leadership has brought us to an inability to deal swiftly and coherently with war within religious factions in several parts of the globe. It has brought us to a gridlock over our own financial future in America, to an impasse over trade (even among supposedly friendly trading partners), to poisoning our environment, to an epidemic of soul-deadening and meaningless work. It can be a depressing and daunting picture, to be sure, but I stress it here to add weight to the imperative that lies before us. We must have more effective and heartfelt leadership at all levels. The leadership needs to come from all of us.

Courage is the prime requirement if we are to step up to the challenge and create more powerful and effective leadership. Without the courage to dream and create new visions, we are rudderless—without a sense of direction. Without the courage to face our present reality (our own personal inventory of strengths and weaknesses, our particular constellation of beliefs and worldview, our highest aspirations, the circumstances of our business, the quality of our lives, as well as the criticisms of others), we will fail not only individually, but collectively.

This courage comes from the heart and soul of who we are; it is influenced by the intellect, but is not the product of the intellect. In truth, there is something wondrous at the core of who we are. The spirit of this core is constantly seeking to express itself in our lives and the world we have created. To touch this leadership spirit, take a moment and recall a time when you truly stretched yourself in order to go after something you deeply desired. Remember the sense of transcendence? Remember the warming flame that pulsed through you as you strove for something greater? Do you remember that along with the fear, the anxiety, and the risk there was a sense of excitement and a terrific sense of aliveness? This passion came from a deeper part of yourself, and with it came the courage to reach beyond any self-limiting beliefs, fears, and doubts, as well as the willingness to face great obstacles.

This vital sense of purpose and aliveness—along with an attendant creativity—can be awakened in each of us when we begin to be truthful about our highest aspirations while letting ourselves clearly see the present reality around us. When we do this and have the willingness to tell the truth about both, then we touch the heart of leadership.

It is the lack of leadership, after all, not our management systems, that has failed us. Management does what it was designed to do—namely, it keeps the enterprise on a preset course, utilizing appropriate controls, policies, and procedures while focusing attention on daily operational issues and maintaining direction. Our corporate cultures have not failed us. Our technology has not failed us. We have, until recently, been the global leaders in innovation and invention.

What have failed are our leadership perspectives and initiatives, creating the wrong emphasis, focus, and practices. We have temporarily lost sight of what is most important, what constitutes real leadership. We seem to have misplaced, if not our soul, then that which nourishes our soul. Too often, it seems, to paraphrase that inveterate cynic Groucho Marx, our leaders have developed the art of looking for trouble, finding it everywhere, misdiagnosing it, and then applying the wrong remedies!

Corporate and political America, as a rule, has not invited or asked the full human being to be present at work. We have only asked for the minds and the backs of others (and just a portion of their minds at that). We have not made a place for the heart and spirit, for imagination, vision, and meaning. This is a tragic waste of invaluable resources! There are, however, more people waking up from the collective trance we have been in for the past 100 years, the trance where equipment and physical assets have been more highly prized than people. Tom Peters, for example, asked the plant manager of a large modern manufacturing facility what was the single most important asset in the plant. That man, in the spirit of true leadership, said, "The imagination of our people."

My father used to say, "Son, any fool can rent the backs and minds of others, but it takes real leadership to earn their hearts and fully engage them." If we want to have the full talent, intelligence, and creativity of those working and developing the enterprises we are engaged in, then we must earn their trust while working together to create an environment where relationships can flourish and results are celebrated, a work environment where we actively support and nurture the best possible efforts for the highest levels of performance and excellence.

Fortunately, we do have a few models before us: Max DePree of the Herman Miller Corporation; Jack Welch of GE; Mike White, mayor of Cleveland; Anita Roddick of the Body Shop; Mary Kay Ash of Mary Kay Cosmetics; and many others who are igniting the imaginations and engaging the hearts of their employees and stakeholders.

If we are to thrive as a culture and in our organizations, we must set up management and leadership processes that empower and liberate the motive energy of the entire work force. These processes must continually challenge our assumptions and paradigms, allowing for evolution and growth at many levels, from individual to team and division, up through the organization, and into the rest of society.

There are several wonderful books that illustrate approaches to the leadership challenge: *Principle-Centered Leadership* by Stephen R. Covey, *On Becoming a Leader* by Warren Bennis, *The Managerial Mystique* by Abraham Zaleznik, *Leadership Is an Art* by Max DePree,

Control Your Destiny or Someone Else Will by Noel Tichy and Stratford Sherman, *A Higher Standard of Leadership* by Keshavan Nair, as well as the diverse writings of Kotter, Deming, and Drucker, which are all seminal literature and make powerful points.

Still, there is a need for a greater synthesis and weaving of ancient wisdom with modern perspectives and practices into a coherent and accessible model. I call this model the "Living Heart of Leadership." This book will provide practical and powerful insights, tools, and methodologies for anyone wishing to develop, improve, and enhance his or her leadership abilities. It integrates and fleshes out the best thinking on leadership, providing a coherent, highly practical model for generating success. It also provides clear practices that serve to build the critical interpersonal relationships necessary for long-term success, while also focusing on the actions required to achieve outstanding results (successfully whistling and drinking at the same time, as my dad would put it!).

Our current reality is extremely challenging. We live in an age of accelerating change and a rapidly evolving global marketplace. Collapsing time frames; continuous, rapid, technological changes; environmental challenges; and globalization are the norm. The game has been changed forever. If we are to thrive as a culture and successfully compete, we need to develop more powerful and effective leadership. The best place to start is with ourselves by looking in the mirror and seeing the powerful potential leaders within.

Thriving in this age of rapid change, competitive challenge, and global economy requires powerful and effective leadership at all levels of organization and society.

The good news is that effective and powerful leadership can be developed. Leadership is not a mysterious substance. It's a mixture of science and art. In our companies and our society, we must learn how to develop and nurture quality leadership.

The need for a new perspective and a revamping of our traditional management and leadership approaches comes from the increasing failure of the old methods. Some painful examples of this leadership failure come all too easily to mind: IBM, Sears, GM, Eastern Airlines, Drexel Burnham Lambert, E. F. Hutton, The Manville Corporation, Westinghouse, etc. The list is frightfully long. On the political front, the list is equally long: Nixon and the Watergate cover-up, Bush and his failure to articulate a vision for the domestic front, Carter and his micromanagement, Clinton and his failure to articulate and act on a set of principles, and so on.

The leading edge for companies today is to be found within the para-meters of strong, effective, and creative leadership at all levels. This is the same kind of leadership we need at the governmental and commu-nity levels. Steve Ardia, the year before he retired as CEO of Goulds Pumps, put it this way during a conversation we had:

> Cultural change, the recognition that Goulds Pumps, even though it was considered, and is probably still considered, the best pump company in the world, is really not good enough as it stands—that old standard is simply not good enough. We need to be improving; we need to be raising our performance levels at an increasingly rapid rate.
>
> For us, the resistance came from the people who felt we were the best. They asked, "Why do we have to change?" The fact is, the world is changing at a very rapid rate, and if we don't accelerate our rate of progress, we will quickly fall behind. One of my first messages to our people was that in spite of our 140-plus years of success, the survival of our company was at stake. We either met customer expectations and improved our perfor-mance, or within 10 years we would no longer be an independent company and the death spiral would begin.

Yet to generate the kind of changes Steve wanted to create within his organization, he had to find a way to generate more leadership impact both for himself and the people within the company. This required a shift in perspective and an understanding of what real power is all about.

Real power comes from within you. It cannot be given by someone else, nor can it be taken away. It starts by having a high level of intima-cy with yourself, being able to touch your dreams, aspirations, core val-ues, and principles. This power exists in everyone around you, though in most people it is latent and sleeping. Awakening this power is the key to both individual and organizational resilience in the face of rapid change and daunting challenges.

This is a book about leadership, about the cultivation and liberation of meaningful power for self and others. It is, therefore, a book about change, about the inevitability and necessity of dealing with change. Leaders are change masters, responding to and anticipating the demands of a rapidly changing world. The critical cognitive maps and principled orientation, along with the skills and practices that effective leaders must have, are presented in these chapters. Be forewarned—it takes courage to tread this path. However, I have found that this courage leads to a profound sense of wholeness, fulfillment, and accomplishment. Society, communities, and corporations desperately need this courage in the exercise of true leadership. This book is about unlocking that courage and about the practices that give life to the exercise of powerful and highly effective leadership.

Part One

THE HEART OF LEADERSHIP

> *"The first job of a leader is to define reality, the last to say thank you, and in between, to be a debtor and servant."*
>
> —Max DePree

The Task and Path of Leadership

Leaders must

courageously pursue

five tasks while

simultaneously

learning from the

past and looking to

the future.

What is the essence of powerful and effective leadership? What causes one person to succeed and another to fail? Scanning the past 2,000 years of recorded history reveals that leaders are ultimately known by the actions they take as well as by the practices they demonstrate. These actions are measured by bottom-line results as well as by the relationships created. Leading is really about engaging others in a unified focus that is geared at producing outstanding results (such as achieving a vision). Why are relationships so critical? In a recent issue of *Fortune* magazine (June 21, 1999) the title article was "Why CEOs Fail." The conclusion is that they did not fail because of a lack of competence or a lack of passion or a lack of political savvy. The number-one reason why these people failed was "a lack of emotional strength." They either lacked the courage to confront people problems quickly and forcefully, or they were unwilling to be confronted by others, to seek out "multiple channels," to hear the pain, difficulty, and problems within the organization. Leaders do not fail due to a lack of intellect, but because of emotional issues, such as a lack of courage—the courage to listen, to confront, or to be self-aware.

3

In other words:

$$IQ + EQ = L^2.$$

Leadership power results when the intellect is added to emotional intelligence traits, such as accessing courage.

Courage is not the absence of fear. Rather, it is the willingness to proceed and do what is necessary and important, even when it is frightening and seems dangerous to do so. Those who are fearless are not courageous. They act, but do not feel challenged by their actions. The absence of fear is either because someone is a fool or unaware of the dangers and pitfalls. True courage is found in those who see the hazards, experience anxiety or even terror, but proceed because it is the right thing to do. These people have found the heart of leadership.

Leadership requires courage—the courage to risk, to reach, to put oneself on the line. The word courage comes from the French word *coeur*, which means heart. Thus, leaders must have the heart for the task of working with and engaging others. The real leader's heart somehow speaks to the hearts of those around her or him, inspiring and touching them. In reality, leadership is high touch.

Leadership has at its center the requirement of courage. You cannot be a leader unless you find a way of developing and generating courage in yourself and then "en-couraging" others. Without it, you slip into a pattern of managing the status quo and maintaining the round of what is known. Without courage, it is easy to avoid facing the tidal wave forming behind you. This pattern of maintenance and of avoidance has proven, and will increasingly prove, to be the undoing of many a business executive, political leader, or party, as well as the enterprises and organizations they serve. The powerful fact to remember is that courage begets courage and draws others to your side. As Jefferson said, "One person with courage is a majority." The most successful leaders achieve powerful results and sustain those results by developing long-term relationships. These factors influence team effectiveness, personal development, innovation, learning, the ability to solve problems, and the ability to notice issues and make course corrections. A quick way to view this is with the graph on the following page.

Leaders are concerned with five basic tasks:

- Ensuring that the future is being planned for, anticipated, and secured;
- Serving the needs and interests of, and eliciting the support from, key constituencies;
- Keeping the team, organization, or enterprise focused on substantive results while meeting the requirements of current realities;

• Building a long-term, value-added network of relationships;
• Tying it all together strategically.

Wholehearted Leadership

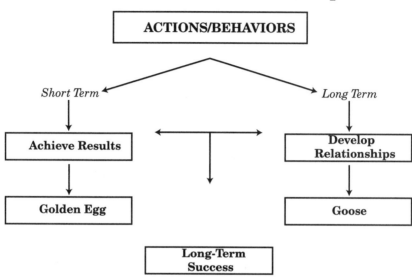

To get a sense of where courage must be applied and how these basic tasks of leadership fit together, look at the diagram on the following page.

By examining the diagram, you can see what the overall focus of leadership must be. In the bottom circle you see the past paradigms. It is critical for leaders to have a sense of the past—where we are coming from in this industry, business, organization, department, and team. This understanding provides a sense of perspective. Perspective is important since it helps a leader to identify the old assumptions, beliefs, and structures for organizing reality. It also enables him or her to see the old rules for how to succeed. This is important, to paraphrase Santayana, "Those who will not learn from the past are doomed to repeat it." Leaders learn from the past and use that knowledge to help increase effectiveness across and within groups.

The second circle from the bottom focuses on current reality, where the technology, demographics, organization, industry, department, team, and individuals stand today. It also focuses attention on where and at what level the values, morale, competitiveness, performance, team play, and values are currently functioning. The current reality of your life and organization forms the foundation on which you stand. When this foundation is not really seen, appreciated, or known, it becomes impossible to create any significant leverage to make the right things happen. Current reality is to vision as earth is to a tree. It upholds and gives you a clear sense of your position and status. Being out of touch with the current reality of your customers, employees, and industry is a dangerous state of affairs and will ultimately be very painful—if not outright fatal—to your enterprise. Even more dangerous is being out of touch with yourself, failing to have the basic self-awareness to manage yourself. (Witness the career-destructive behavior of Gary Hart, Richard Nixon, or Frank Lorenzo, former CEO of Texas Air and Eastern Airlines.)

The top circle is entitled "Anticipated Future." This is the best guess at what that vast unknown entity we call the future might look like. The future is really just a mass of potential space and time. Leaders look ahead and try to get a grasp on what is likely to be and what could happen. This is done by tracking trends, listening to others, using active imagination, searching your heart, reading far afield, and staying open and flexible. The process of outlining the potential future is a vital part of long-term leadership effectiveness. It is the essence of effective positioning and the soul of proactive business planning. (An excellent text on this aspect can be found in *Competing for the Future*, by Gary Hamel and C.K. Prahalad.)

The circle just below the anticipated future has the corporate vision (this could also be your personal vision, your family's vision, the team vision, departmental or divisional vision). This is where leadership carves out of the vast potential of the future a sense of what it wishes to own and claim. This becomes the guiding star by which an individual, team, or organization orients itself. It provides a sense of direction and coherence, a focus and aim for all efforts, energies, and tasks. Without this vision,

Future Business Success

Anticipated Future

Corporate Vision

Customers — Employees
Leadership
Stockholders

Current Reality

Past Paradigms

coherently and cogently outlined, there is a fundamental lack of cohesion. It is also impossible to create what Michael Beers, author of *The Critical Path to Corporate Renewal*, calls "task alignment."

Task alignment is the process by which all of the work and work efforts throughout the diverse functional areas of an organization are grasped, appreciated, and coordinated, forming a functional wholeness. The most astute leaders seek to have everyone engaged in an enterprise to appreciate and support the efforts of the different parts and team members. This multiplies the power and available energy of the overall system by focusing everyone on how they jointly create success while minimizing unnecessary conflict and crossed agendas.

Outlining a vision—whether it be for yourself, your family, your department, your organization, or society—is a critical practice of effective leadership. It gives everyone engaged something to shoot for and a larger context within which to plan and set strategy. It provides everyone with an essential sense of direction and purpose, whether it is which part of the market to own, or more profoundly, who and what the enterprise is striving to become.

The large circle in the middle represents the constituencies with which a leader must be concerned in order to succeed. John Kotter and James Heskett, in their wonderful book *Corporate Culture and Performance*, list three groups whose needs and agendas successful leaders in organizations must meet and balance. These groups are the customers and potential customers of the services and products being offered; the employees who serve those customers and drive the work efforts that ultimately reach the customer; and the stockholders of the company. The stockholder group can include the larger body politic and is, in fact, the community when it is a governmental unit.

Kotter and Heskett also point out that enterprises that consistently fail to satisfy all three of those groups are ones that are failing and will fail. Consider the fact that most organizations have demonstrated that they have a difficult time successfully balancing all three constituencies. All too often the customer is neglected because the organization becomes too internally driven around its own needs, agendas, and processes, while losing touch with the very group that pays the bills and salaries.

Some organizations do a great job emphasizing the customers' needs, but they somehow neglect to treat their employees in the ways they expect the employees to treat customers. This doesn't work. As Hal Rosenbluth, CEO and author, points out in his book *The Customer Comes Second*, customers ultimately end up being treated the same way the leadership and supervisory levels treat their employees. The old saying, "What goes around, comes around," truly fits.

For an enterprise to excel, for leadership to be effective for the long haul, people must be engaged, involved, inspired, and must care about their vision, goals, and agendas. Leaders generate followers, and they keep their following by paying attention to and caring about those people. They are concerned with issues such as inspiration, alignment, participation, creativity, and achieving operational excellence.

The last group, the stockholders and community, must have their needs and aspirations met or managed if the enterprise is to continue to have the financial and political support necessary to continue to function. Neglect this group and you stand to lose the capital resources required to effectively upgrade technology and processes, train and retrain employees, market and advertise, as well as develop and deliver new products and services to customers. This can be deadly. Witness what happened in mid-1995 with Royal Dutch Shell, when it underestimated public opinion concerning the planned deep-sea sinking of a used oil platform. They had to publicly back down and change course after an expensive boycott and significant loss of good will in Europe.

The diagram then, at one level, says leadership harnesses the power and energies of three important constituencies, while examining the past, clearly seeing the current reality and challenges, outlining a vision of the future, and staking a claim to that future. Leaders must have split-field vision. One part of their vision is that of looking ahead to what is likely to be, what they would like to create, and who and what they wish to become. The other part of their vision is focused upon the current reality and operational requirements—where, in fact, the enterprise is currently functioning—seeing without illusions, seeking the naked truth about how they and the system are operating today. Leaders also look, without flinching, at how well the three groups are being served and what the current state of affairs is with regard to how their different needs and interests are being balanced.

What is not so obvious in the diagram are the two fundamental, critically important gaps that leaders must traverse and bridge if they are to best leverage their talents and those of the people and enterprise they serve.

Gap 1

The first gap is between the old ways of functioning and the requirements and needs of current reality. This is the gap between what has been required and sufficient in the past and what is currently required. Leaders are not long blinded by the rules and structures of the past. They look at traditional functioning and compare that with what the best competitors are doing today, with what customers are demanding and expecting today, with the industry and marketplace today. Leaders, then, look at the gap between what is being done out of past realities and what is required in current realities.

This first gap—what I call the realm of excellence in execution—brings about improvements in the utilization of tools, resources, people time, capital, and so on. It is the area where current operational functioning can be revamped and upgraded, making an enterprise more competitive and effective in serving customers, employees, and stockholders or community. This is the marriage of good management with powerful leadership.

This gap between the way we have been functioning and the way we need to be functioning to mesh with current reality is a critical gap. It is, in Stephen R. Covey's time-matrix terminology, a "quadrant one" concern: urgent and important. If it is not bridged, the organization falls further behind and cannot successfully compete. If not addressed quickly, in our rapidly moving age of change, it can become a grievous, if not mortal, wound.

Gap 2

The second gap—what I call planning for excellence—is the gap between the vision and current reality. If this gap is not attended to, then the leader is not preparing himself or herself, the people, the systems, or the organization for the future. It is, again in Covey's time-management matrix, a "quadrant two" concern: important, but not urgent. This is the realm where a leader can excel and help a team, department, or organization secure the future. This is the gap of advanced planning, preparation, development, and proactivity. If it is studied and bridged, then an organization is preparing and planning for excellence in long-term success. If it is neglected, then the mistakes of the past are repeated, and an organization becomes caught in a permanent state of catch-up and reactiveness.

Therefore, while successful leaders appreciate the past, understand and see current realities, plan for and anticipate the future, and balance the key constituencies, they also turn their vision and attention to the tasks of analyzing and traversing the two key gaps between what was or is and what is or will be. So important is the bridging of these two gaps that at Staub-Peterson we call highly effective leaders "gap runners."

A gap runner is someone with courage, commitment, a sense of vision, and the willingness to hear and see the truth. He or she is open, curious, creative, and eager to learn. A gap runner is focused upon issues of substance, looking for results while building a network or web of relationships that will help to quicken the process of identifying gaps and closing them. All real leaders are ultimately gap runners, and they attend to the five key tasks leaders face while grasping the essentials outlined in the diagram on page 5.

Leaders, as gap runners, weave together the different needs and perceptions of others, helping them see, appreciate, and understand the significance of each gap. They then enlist, engender, and inspire the participation of others in helping to close the gaps between what was or is and what is or will be with regard to requirements, plans, needs, and operations. Like the blockade runners of the past, gap runners are courageous, adventurous, attentive, well-informed, flexible, and inventive. They generate support from many sources, scouting out the blocks and resistances of conventional thought, while planning for the next venture.

Finally, as you look at the diagram, you need to imagine a great arrow going from bottom to top with the words "Strategic Path." Think of this as illustrating that leaders function much better when they appreciate and understand the primacy of thinking and planning strategically. However, the strategies are tied into a coherent master strategy, the "strategic path." A strategic path is developed and put into place as a means of linking and moving from the past and current realities to the desired future reality. This requires an appreciation for and understanding of "systems thinking" (how everything fits together in an organization and how all work done is part of a larger, integrative process). This strategic path is overarching and lays out the framework for managing and weaving the issues of current operational needs and demands with future operational needs and requirements. It is an integral component of leadership's ability and success in driving the process of realizing the vision. Leaders link the gap analysis and issues outlined in this diagram into a coherent set of guiding strategies. This set of strategies plans for and develops marketing, operational, systems, policy, planning, financial, human resource, training, technological, and administrative initiatives.

The leaders I have been working with are recognizing the critical need not only for developing a sound business strategy, but also for developing a human-systems strategic plan. In this plan we outline how they will systematically engage all of their people and human resource systems in reinventing and renewing the culture around driving the business plan. What is more, this part of their strategic path is where they plan for and outline how they will be preparing their people in a continuous learning and growth process, operating under the assumption that change is not going to slow down. This focus helps create what has been called a "learning organization."

Leaders are the custodians of the future. They are concerned with the future and with the planning it takes to create the desired future. They know the importance of leaving a legacy and also have the courage to dream or grab hold of a good dream. They then share those dreams, engaging and enlisting others in fleshing out and working to realize the dreams. Leaders engage others with one eye on the past and present and their other eye on the future. They stand firmly on the bedrock of current reality with few illusions, seeing and appreciating the gaps that exist. They engage in actions and practices that build constituencies having a "can-do" and "want-to-do" attitude.

Leaders are concerned with strategy and sound conceptual planning, as well as followership and the overall integrity of the enterprise and its efforts. This falls into the realm of Competence, which is one of the four great chambers forming the heart of leadership. They exercise and develop this competency by building trust and enthusiasm through the way they act and the way they treat others (Intimacy), demonstrating an appreciation for past and current efforts while planning for the future.

Orson Scott Card is an internationally known science fiction writer, having won two Nebula awards, the highest honor in science fiction literature. One of his works is a trilogy called *The Tales of Alvin Maker.* It is set in colonial America, in a world that might have been. The highest accolade you can get in that world is to be called a "maker." A maker is somebody who can go out and, with his or her hands, mind, imagination, and heart, create something important. In this schemata, America is a creation, a grand "making." It took diverse people who changed their perceptions so that they saw themselves as Americans.

Alvin Maker, the chief character, grows up as a little boy who can truly "make" things happen. Leaders are the people who see themselves as makers and enablers of future makers. Those who only focus on the technical aspects of making will always be only technicians. What society needs from us, what our families need, what the corporations need, are true makers. I know that if you are a leader and you wed that to your technical abilities and knowledge, you become a maker. You cannot be a maker just being a technician. Bill Gates at Microsoft has his faults and shortcomings; however, he is a leader and a true maker, just as Jack Welch at GE and Andy Grove at Intel are "makers."

The critical difference today isn't going to be the technical expertise, because you are going to find everybody acquiring that. The difference is going to be the part you bring from your heart and soul to that process and how well you draw that out of others. Leaders ultimately have a magnetic influence on other people. They draw from others a commitment to be part of this enterprise: "I want to make a difference." Leaders enable. Leaders are willing to forge into new territory.

There is no place in the world that is really separate from us if we choose to bring our technology to bear. That means the world has gotten very small. Things happen very fast in terms of decision making. Management cannot handle that. You need good management, but you must have leaders. Only leaders know how to formulate visions, pull people together, and find a way to cut through the red tape, to make it happen in time, which today increasingly means being ahead of schedule. Leaders know how to pull out the creativity in a team and help its members be co-makers.

Chris Argyris, who has spent a lifetime studying why smart people are often so slow at learning new things, asks a potent question: "How can a group where everyone has an individual IQ of 130 get together and collectively end up with an IQ of 65?" This is functional retardation. How do we get groups of very bright people—managers in organizations, on faculties at universities—how is it that we get these people together and as a team they produce less than any one of them is capable of producing by themselves? That is where teams get a bad name. At Staub-Peterson we call them committees. You know the old saying about committees. A committee is a group that gets together to design a racehorse and produces a camel—at twice the cost while taking three times longer than budgeted.

A high-functioning team operates such that when you get people with average IQs together, they are able to produce a team IQ of 200 (genius plus). That's synergy; that's creativity, and to produce this requires leadership. It doesn't matter if you are the senior person in the hierarchy or if you are the newest hire. I've met CEOs who couldn't lead themselves out of a paper bag. I've seen people at very junior levels who show such powerful leadership that they influence the people around them, taking what would be dysfunctional teams and helping them become exceptional.

In leadership it doesn't matter what your rank is, doesn't matter how old you are, doesn't matter your sex, doesn't matter your race. It doesn't matter whether you speak the language well. If you can produce the kind of behavior that pulls teams together and generates creativity, you will add tremendous value and be a potent leader.

The challenge lies in the fact that getting a Ph.D. in engineering is simple compared to figuring out how to deal with the three-and-a-half pound universe contained within the human mind. Machines have a logic, numbers have a logic, but the human psyche has a strange kind of logic called the psyche-logic.

Now, the psyche-logic is weird, voodoo stuff. Just put a group of bright people together and watch how dumb they can act. I see it all too often in corporate teams and key relationships—just as really bright people in a marriage will often act in very dumb ways. That's psychological, and leaders have to deal with the psychological aspects of people every day.

You have to be a practical psychologist. If you don't have an appreciation for psychology—the best psychology has to offer, not some of the bull in psychology that is out there—you are going to be effectively crippled, and you will never be a true maker.

Leaders are torch bearers, holding up a torch in the darkness of the first gap, the "unseen knowable," and also lighting the way in the darkness of the second gap, the "foreseen unknown." This takes courage and conviction.

Seven Acts of Courage

There are, in fact, seven kinds of personal courage required of leaders if they are to be the best they can be. These form the base of personal mastery. They are:

1. The courage to dream and put forth that dream.
2. The courage to see current reality.
3. The courage to confront.
4. The courage to be confronted.
5. The courage to learn and grow.
6. The courage to be vulnerable.
7. The courage to act.

These acts of courage are the basis and absolute requirements if the five tasks of leadership are to be addressed and driven toward realization.

In my life and work I have had the privilege of learning from highly successful leaders, struggling leaders, and failed leaders. Based on this, my personal experience and the words of other practitioners and thinkers that ring true with my experience, I am convinced that without courage, leadership cannot exist. I have felt the power and tested the efficacy of what follows in successfully running my own leadership center and consulting firm in the setting of real-time, real-world realities. What is written here works, and where it is not applied, organizations— and ultimately people and communities—suffer.

So how do leaders deal with such a vital and ambitious agenda? They understand, at least on an intuitive level, the basics: the four critical aspects of leadership that form its heart and the 12 practices that manifest and give life to that heart. These practices work all of the five critical tasks, develop the sinews of courage, and help to navigate the essential elements illustrated in the Future Business Success diagram. The four chambers which form the heart of leadership effectiveness and the

12 practices which develop the tone of that heart will be explained and outlined in the coming chapters. All of this is done to help outline how any leader or aspiring leader can learn to be far more effective in driving current and future success, whether it be for self, family, team, department, business, school, city, state, or nation.

It is my intention to further not only the field of leadership theory and practice, but to provide you with a powerful way of organizing and focusing your leadership efforts. This will help you maximize success and more effectively leverage the talents, abilities, and intelligence within and around you. There are also some potent tools and methodologies outlined, providing you with the means to actualize your intentions and dreams.

This book is not for the timid or for those seeking easy answers. It is for those who are courageous, who are seeking to find the courage and means to make a difference. I hope you find it liberating and empowering.

The Four Drivers Forming the Heart of Leadership

Effective leaders

know that people

are their ultimate

resource.

Therefore, true

leaders are

grounded in

leadership's heart.

The usual paradigm is that leadership equals followership, or L=F. The true state of affairs is that leadership equals followership plus the creation of other leaders, or L=F+L₂. The imperative of leadership is not only to influence others and create those who are willing to follow, but to generate and encourage in others the willingness to lead. As a leader you will not only need to have followers, but you will also have to encourage others to become leaders in their own right. It is your ability to create this field of leadership in which followers and leaders interact, merge, and emerge, which will determine your legacy as a leader.

There is an old saying that there are three kinds of people in the world: those who make things happen, those who watch things happen, and those who wonder what happened! Obviously leaders fall into the first category. What is not so obvious and is often missed in understanding this saying is that the leaders are the ones who make things happen by drawing members from categories two (those who watch) and three (those who wonder what happened) into the first category (those who make things happen).

Jack Welch of GE, viewed as one of the greatest CEO's of all time, has said, "If we screw up the

15

people thing, then it is all over." Welch and the executives at GE do exceedingly well in developing and cultivating other leaders through assignments, through coaching, and by focusing on both results and relationships. However, a leader cannot appoint someone else to be a leader. It is something that is drawn out, encouraged, and created in the interaction between a leader and the people around the leader.

Leadership is not something that is hierarchical or bestowed. It flows like a magnetic current of influence from those who are willing to step up to a higher level of functioning and being. Leaders draw others along and continuously inspire them in both large and small ways. They, in essence, inspire others to function at a higher level, even drawing others to function in leadership roles themselves. At its best, this level is "spiritual" in its source and impact, connecting everyone in an inspired network of meaningful work.

Leaders define reality by laying out the scope of the enterprise at hand, helping to set a direction and velocity for movement while supporting and enabling others to accomplish the constituent tasks. Leadership, in these terms, is the vital art and science of bringing people together in meaningful relationships in order to produce outstanding results.

Quick Self Test

1. How do others perceive your performance?

2. Are you focused on bottom-line execution, figuring out how to do things better and faster?

3. Are you religiously seeking out problem areas and bad news? (Do you make a habit of seeking feedback up, down, around, and through in both informal and formal processes?)

4. How well have you aligned the key people in your organization—board members, key employees, subordinates, peers, customers, and suppliers? Are you sure they are cooperating and surfacing conflicts in order to advance what needs to be done?

5. Is your team discontented, or do you have key discontented people in your oganization or on your team?

6. Do you know the strengths and weaknesses of key subordinates? Of your superior? What are you doing to buttress them and help them be successful?

7. Do you understand your own weaknesses and limitations, as well as your strengths, and are you taking that into account in your interactions, your work, and your plans?

A powerful image that conveys the scope and requirements of leadership is that of an orchestra conductor. The conductor knows the content of what is to be played and brings to that enterprise his or her own sense of vision and passion. The different musicians all have varied tasks and assignments and bring specialized tools and skills to bear. The conductor's role is to make wise and judicious use of the multi-layered talents and specialties. He or she is concerned with timing, rhythm, interpretation, rapid response, accuracy, emotional intensity, integration, and coordination of all the efforts. The conductor, like all effective leaders, doesn't actually play the instruments; rather, she or he must be able to orchestrate the diverse people, specialties, and task-specific roles and responsibilities around the overall enterprise. In reality, a leader's role is even more complex, but the image of a conductor does provide some helpful illumination. Now take that image to another level of complexity.

Imagine, for instance, that the conductor was actually overseeing many conductors who were all simultaneously conducting different musicians forming distinct bands. Then imagine that within each of these bands were some smaller bands being conducted by yet another set of conductors. The task of each conductor would be to orchestrate the talents, timing, and playing of his or her particular group while watching for cues from the conductors around and above him or her, the grand task being the production of a coherent, cogent, and harmonious symphony. This is precisely the situation in an organization!

Part of the complexity of leadership is that there are many sub-groups and sub-levels within each group that are vital to the healthy functioning of an organization. Take this, then, and place it in the context of today, where organizations find themselves struggling with a demanding and rapidly changing world where customers, competitors, technology, employees, industries, society, and regulations keep evolving and shifting at an increasingly demanding pace. These levels of complexity and change mean that leadership must exist and function at every diverse level and that it must all link up and align around a common vision or focus and a set of integrating behaviors, a common bond.

Jim Farr taught me that there are three critical organizational systems which comprise any enterprise. The circle model on the next page gives two messages. The first is that of wholeness, in that you need to have all three systems interacting and present or you have an incomplete and failed enterprise. Second, it is an ongoing and continuous process of building an interactive relationship.

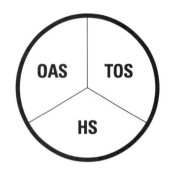

TOS stands for Technical Operating Systems—namely, all the technical systems that go into driving your enterprise: computers, forklifts, phone systems, and the like, as well as the technical expertise required by your business.

OAS stands for Organizational Administrative Systems—namely, all of the management processes, procedures, and formulas that allow you to communicate, crunch, and interpret data.

HS stands for Human Systems—namely, all of the people who are working within your organization, as well as all of the critical relationships which drive your enterprise. This comprises such interface points as agents, suppliers, customers, competitors, etc.

All three of these systems are absolutely vital and integral to the basic functioning of any organization, whether in government or business. Leave out the technical system, and you do not have the means to manufacture, deliver, produce, or communicate effectively. Leave out the administrative and organizational systems, and you do not have the means to interpret data, schedule, plan, control, focus, or communicate. Leave out the human systems, and you do not have the means of effecting or utilizing TOS or OAS systems. You also leave out the innovation, creativity, continuous improvements, problem solving, participation, flexibility, and intelligence in your enterprise.

The OAS and TOS aspects of an organization can be managed and give themselves readily to solid management practices. They are relatively predictable and work according to formula and logic. The HS aspect is also, in part, responsive to management; however, that is not enough. You can manage numbers, machines, and things. However, you can, at best, only partially manage people. It is in the province of the human system that you function as a leader. This is the only place you can lead. You do not lead machines or processes. You lead people. The interesting paradox is that you have to be able to know and manage yourself in order to successfully lead others over the long haul.

The HS component of organizations ultimately determines how effectively, efficiently, and wisely the TOS and OAS components are utilized. The human system is where the possibilities of adding intelligence, learning, innovating, and creating are lost or realized. The human system is where you get buy-in, participation, problem solving, customer relationships, coordination, energy, enthusiasm, and the basics of value-added thinking. It is also the system that receives the least amount of attention, often being taken for granted. MBA programs have historically given this vital area short shrift, leading to blue-ribbon panels' conclusion that "the students being turned out are ill-equipped and ill-prepared to function in today's organizations." It is an area we have all tended to neglect, believing leadership practices would simply be picked up on the job. What has been picked up has been far from helpful, and in many cases downright hurtful, to generating and nurturing powerful and effective human systems to drive organizational success.

Why is this so? A key part lies in understanding the different forms of logic that drive each system. Applying the wrong logic leads to utilizing the wrong approach. When looking at these three systems, it is imperative that you consider what really drives each one. The logic system of OAS is the logic of numbers. The logic system of TOS is the logic of machines and technical formulas. The logic of HS is the logic of the psyche, or the psychological.

The first two systems are predictable and follow certain laws and rules. They are logical in the traditional sense and fall into the digital form of logic discussed in the preface. This form of logic works very well in these two areas and has been applied by American managers with great success. The problem is that the very success of digital logic has been blinding us to the fact that it doesn't work very well when you attempt to use it with human beings.

Human beings are not logical in a digital way. Fuzzy logic (presented in the introduction) is much more accurate as a model for understanding how the human mind functions. The logic of the human psyche is much more complex, demanding, variable, moody, subtle, and challenging than the logic you find in machines, technical processes, or numbers. In fact, getting a Ph.D. in nuclear engineering is much easier than mastering the "soft" logic of the human mind and heart. It is in this "softer" area, though, that a leader has to play if she or he is to be effective in the long term. After all, you do not lead machines or numbers; you lead people.

Effective and powerful leadership requires the integration of head, heart, and gut in a results/relationship matrix that seeks to maximize and leverage all three systems. This is not the sum of it, however. The overall functioning of your enterprise is tremendously enhanced by upping the power of the human system. Research data indicates that while most organizations, when they are well run and working near capacity, are obtaining 80 to 90 percent of what the TOS and OAS systems can do. Yet they tend to get 30 percent or less of what the human systems are capable of doing. This cannot stand the test of today's marketplace and information-based economy.

The winning leaders of today are increasingly finding their success coming from the process of leveraging and liberating the intelligence, talents, creativity, problem solving, participation, and enthusiasm of the people comprising the human systems of their companies.

We must have effective leadership if we are to unleash the potential energies and intelligence embedded in the human system. Tapping the potential and increasing the "effective intelligence" within an enterprise is essential if we are to successfully address the challenges we currently face.

Antoine de Saint-Exupéry said, "What is essential can only be seen by the heart." I am not talking about the leadership we have been suffering under for far too long, but true, visionary leadership which is grounded in four dimensions, encompassing feeling, thinking, and behaving. These dimensions generate leadership impact, like the chambers of the human heart determine the quality of circulation for human health, strength, and longevity.

Leadership effectiveness is much like the functioning of a beating heart. The heart, to sustain life, takes in blood, sends it to be enriched by oxygen in the lungs, and then sends the energy-rich blood out to the tissues of the body. To do this, it requires four chambers of the heart working in concert with each other. If any one of the chambers is weakened or ineffective, then the heart and tissues of the body suffer, creating fatigue, malaise, illness, anemia, and even death.

Leadership, like the heart, receives input, ensures the organization is enriched and focused, and then orchestrates functional and energetic flows out to the body of the organization or enterprise. For leadership to function well and not be anemic or ultimately ineffectual, four basic aspects must work in synergy with each other. These elements form the chambers comprising the heart of leadership. These four chambers are Competence, Intimacy, Integrity, and Passion.

This simple and elegant way of thinking about leadership distills down to four words the central base of all leadership power. These four chambers undergird the five essential tasks of leadership, pumping life into them. This model integrates and explains what drives leadership effectiveness. It forms the base for real power in analyzing your own leadership challenge areas and addressing them. It integrates the best of what others have had to say about leadership, while breaking new ground. It gives a concise and potent understanding of the exercise and essence of leadership. Leave any one of these four aspects out of your leadership and you will, in the long run, fail. These chambers allow the heart of leadership to function, pumping life and effectiveness into individuals, teams, and organizations.

Head

Results / Content Focused
Competency / Integrity
What are we doing?

Heart

Relationships / Process Focused
Passion / Intimacy
How are we doing it?

Competence

This chamber has three powerful components. One is having substantive knowledge of the business, sound management practices, and/or technical issues at hand. The second is good, strategic thinking and planning. The third is having the awareness, sensitivity, and skills for good interpersonal contact. It provides for the leveraging and realization of substantive knowledge and skills while working with others in terms of driving and creating powerful results.

How many of us would like to have followed General George Armstrong Custer into the battle at Little Bighorn? His strategic competency was questionable, as well as his intelligence-gathering methodology. For leaders to be successful they must not only have competence in the substantive areas of their enterprise, but they must also have sound strategic thinking abilities or the willingness to seek out and obtain solid strategic guidance.

In the list of top 10 reasons why senior and mid-level executives fail, the No. 1 reason is a lack of competence around interpersonal, team, and relationship skills. Most teams that fail or are barely succeeding are struggling because of a failure in team learning and team working knowledge and skills. Such competence is essential to the successful orchestration of the complex system of people in a rapidly changing and challenging world.

Strategic and tactical competence are essential if an enterprise is to be positioned for the best outcomes. This aspect has to do not only with substantive knowledge and skills, but also with the capacity to innovate and respond to the unexpected. There are no examples that illustrate this form of competence better than that of Major General Joshua Lawrence Chamberlain, winner of the Congressional Medal of Honor, three-time governor of Maine, and president of Bowdoin College.

One incident speaks most powerfully to this point. Chamberlain, the hero of the battle for Little Round Top on the second day of the battle of Gettysburg, was then a colonel. His force, having fiercely repulsed numerous Confederate attempts to flank the Union army, was almost completely out of ammunition and outnumbered more than two to one. As the Confederate forces began their final charge up the slope, Colonel Chamberlain realized that if his troops stood their ground they would perish; however, if they retreated, then the army of the Potomac would be flanked. He improvised, using an obscure military maneuver and called upon his men to perform the insane act of fixing bayonets and preparing to charge.

In his own words, "Five minutes more of such a defensive and the last roll-call would sound for us! I stepped to the colors. One word was enough—*'Bayonet!'* It caught like fire and swept along the ranks. Down into the faces of half a thousand! Two hundred men! . . . It was a great right wheel. Our left swung first. The advancing foe stopped, tried to make a stand amidst the trees and boulders, but the frenzied bayonets pressing through every space forced a constant settling to the rear . . . It turned into a full retreat."

Our experience tells us that most of the senior and mid-level executives who fail do so not because of technical deficiencies, but because of a lack of competence either in strategic thinking or interpersonal, team, and relationship awareness skills. In fact, a little book entitled *The Ten Reasons People Fail* supports this, stating that research indicates that 60 percent of failures occur precisely because of poor skills in these areas. Most teams that fail or are barely succeeding are struggling because they don't have the knowledge and skills required to generate team learning and team working. This level of competence is essential to the successful orchestration of complex tasks in a complex system of people in a complex world.

Yet which of us has been systematically trained in team working and facilitation skills? Who has been prepared and coached in highly effective interpersonal dynamics? Who has been trained in giving and receiving feedback? Few, if any, have had that kind of training and preparation. The technical competencies of financial deal making and manufacturing are taught and developed. The "soft" competencies of interpersonal dynamics, effective listening, giving and receiving feedback, team working, and facilitation skills have been neglected. They are key competencies.

Integrity

This is the chamber not only of honesty and principled behavior, but also of self-awareness and honest self-appraisal. This is the dimension of principles and values along with a strong faithfulness quotient. Without integrity, there can be no long-term, meaningful relationships. Lacking integrity, a leader cannot really create or maintain trust. Without trust or effective relationships, the ability and willingness of people to believe in and follow is either absent or creates a passive resistance to direction and change.

Integrity is the commitment to a vision and to one's deepest values. It is the courage to make the tough choices and to forego what is easy and comfortable. An enterprise based on leadership that lacks integrity will ultimately fail.

In interpersonal terms, integrity is the truthfulness and honesty experienced by others when dealing with you that creates a sense of trust and belief. It is the sense that "I know where you stand and that your words and actions have a high level of consistency." It is the sense of someone being aligned with an internally consistent and externally modeled set of principles or standards. We tend to know this through the practices and demonstrated actions of the person, team, or organization in question.

Integrity forms the faithfulness quotient of an individual, team, department, or organization. Organizational integrity, for instance, has to do with how faithfully the leadership system adheres to the corporate vision, core values, and essential needs of the organization with regard to long-term viability. My experience is that there are four constituencies with which leaders must be concerned: employees, customers, stockholders, and suppliers. Leaders must keep faith with these four groups. If they keep that faith, they demonstrate integrity and generate an immense reservoir of good will. The tough part about this in our day and age is that often, in order to keep the faith, you have to take risks and court the temporary displeasure of one or more of the constituencies.

Intimacy

This is the chamber of profound knowledge—a deep knowledge of the customer, of the people engaged in the work at hand, of the task and purpose of the work, of one's self. Without intimacy there exists only superficial contact, only token leadership. Intimacy has to do with the dimension of relating with the capacity to forge and develop strong relationships. It also has to do with deep insight and understanding of customers, employees, and competitors, as well as an appreciation for the need to study the basics of human nature.

One brief example of it in leadership: General Patton walked and talked with the soldiers of the Third Army as they marched farther, fought more battles, and captured more prisoners in less time than any other army in history. Compare this to Napoleon, riding in an isolated carriage, aloof and apart from his men, even abandoning the army on the march from Moscow. Taken further, Patton read Rommel's book on tank warfare and made a deep study of his enemy. Contrast this with Napoleon, who, at breakfast before the battle of Waterloo, told his generals, "This battle will not last long; Wellington is not much of a general." Yet Wellington used the same tactics to defeat Napoleon that the British used in Spain to defeat the French force nearly a year before! More recently we have seen Boris Yeltsin and the Russian military leadership failing at intimacy as well as at strategic competence in their attempt to rapidly subdue Chechnya, precisely because of a failure to understand their enemy and to have learned from history.

More than 2,000 years ago, the great Chinese general Sun Tzu, in *The Art of War*, wrote, "Know not your enemy or yourself, and you will lose every battle you fight. Know your enemy but know not yourself, and you will lose every other battle you fight. Know yourself and know your enemy, and you need not fear the outcome of a hundred battles."

The enemy of intimacy is not the competition, nor the changing world; both of these can be seen and understood as goads for change and grist for the mill of excellence. The real enemy of intimacy is to be found in the tyrannical threesome: ego, fear and impatience. Real leaders know this three-headed dragon and face it down with self-awareness and courage.

• *Ego* makes us unwilling to learn from others, and even from our own mistakes. Our ego would rather blame others than take a look at what we have done to contribute to the problem. It can also take the path of excusing ourselves by saying we aren't capable of something, which begs off by deflating our confidence to learn and change the quality of our lives or environment. Leaders who make a positive difference have learned to manage their egos and to pursue their vision rather than the dictates of a limited self-definition. Hand and hand with this is the fact that they have developed the skills and capacity to work with the ego issues of those around them.

• *Fear* is the emotion of paralysis. It forces us to be unduly prudent, holding back and waiting for someone else to act. The poet William Blake said, "Prudence is an old maid, courted by incapacity." Fear can cause us to feel incapable of acting while life passes us by. Out of our emotion of fear, we can shrink to a tenth of our true size, engaging in actions of which we are not worthy, or refraining from taking the actions which are in keeping with our highest aspirations. In reaction to our fears we can attack or undermine others. Fear can also cause us not to listen, to fail to provide the needed feedback as well as receive it. Leaders feel fear, but they act on what they most aspire to, using the fear as raw energy to keep them humble but focused. The fear becomes an ally and not a limiting factor.

• *Impatience* is the unwillingness to allow events and processes to mature and unfold. Processes require time and effort. Impatience can also lead to aborting a process or program because the results are not immediate. There is an old joke that a Russian military commander in a paroxysm of patriotism exclaimed that whatever the Americans could do the Russians could do better and faster. One wise and diplomatic American officer spoke up and, in the spirit of looking for common ground, remarked that pregnancy was something that took everyone nine months. The Russian commander, in his patriotic enthusiasm, exclaimed,

"In America you have one woman produce a child in nine months. In Russia we have surpassed that; we take nine women and in one month we have a baby!" Obviously, no matter how many people or even how much money you throw at a project, some things are developmental and can be rushed only up to a point. Leaders know when to be patient.

Passion

Passion refers to the drive to make a contribution and to create something meaningful and worthy. It is akin to a fire that ignites the hearts and minds of those with whom it comes in contact. It is sometimes called "enthusiasm," a word meaning "to be filled with God." This is the sense of mission and inspiration that drives someone to stretch beyond himself or herself and draws others similarly to go beyond their expected limitations. Emerson said it well: "Nothing great was ever achieved without enthusiasm."

Passion is the spark that shines out of the work habits and ways of relating found in exceptional leaders. It is contagious and sets many secondary sparks, eventually generating a blaze of excellence. Passion calls out to others and draws the passion from their hearts. It is a force that can burn its way through the fog of mediocrity, confusion, and cynicism. It is the dimension of commitment.

Steve Bachand, CEO of Canadian Tire, finds his passion comes from two primary sources:

> I am motivated and driven by several factors. One is the desire to leap-frog the competition—to be setting the pace, not just matching it. Another is the sense of tremendous responsibility for the people in our organization—I work for them. It's a heavy responsibility. That's the most important thing that motivates me. That means having a plan for the future—a clear strategic path—and doing the things that help us compete more successfully.

The four chambers forming the heart of leadership are like an energy matrix, feeding and expanding the power base and effective range of a leader. When they are recognized and made a part of the developmental focus of the leadership system, a geometric process of growth in capabilities and effectiveness begins unfolding. They provide a means of measuring and focusing attention and empowerment at the individual, one-on-one, team, organizational, and even societal levels. These dimensions are revealed as being either present or absent through the actions and practices of the individual, team, or organization.

A way of conceptualizing and seeing how these four fundamentals undergird and flow into the five basic tasks of leadership can be seen in the diagram to the right.

Without integrity, it is impossible to secure the future and to fully focus upon and serve the needs and interests of the three key constituencies outlined in chapter one's model. Without competence, there is a lack of clear strategy and planning for the enterprise and a neglect of future needs. Without intimacy, there is either a dangerous gap or a lack of depth and understanding of the four key groups: customers, employees, stock and stakeholders, and suppliers. There is a fundamental lack of contact and awareness. Additionally, lacking the capacity for intimacy, would-be leaders are out of touch with themselves and therefore lack the personal mastery required to learn, grow, adapt, evolve, and change. Without passion and the commitment it communicates, it is impossible to fully engage others and build a lasting network of relationships as well as drive a substantive focus on results. All great leadership is based on the core of these four dimensions working together synergistically and the five basic tasks they support.

We have had enough—more than enough—of the calculating management and short-term decision making that has been all too characteristic of the past two or three decades. As Stephen R. Covey has so eloquently put it, we need to go beyond fads and personality characteristics and focus upon basic principles. I would add that we need principles and solid practices. We need leaders who, in the words of Herman Miller CEO Max DePree, "develop conventional relationships" with community, stockholders, management, employees, customers, and suppliers. In a world of dross, a little gold will really stand out. My experience tells me that there is gold in every human heart. With most, we need only invite them to strip away the dross and reveal the gold waiting just below the surface. To do this, we must be willing to mine the gold of our own heart and spirit.

We desperately need the gold of inspired and inspiring leadership. From experience, I know that this kind of leadership is something you can learn. It also engenders the kind of results, relationship, and behaviors that are contagious—creating a way of leading and being that is fundamentally and intrinsically potent and energizing.

Where do we find examples of this four-dimensional gold, consisting of intimacy, competency, integrity, and passion? Some famous names and companies, are apparent: Anita Roddick of the Body Shop, Jack Welch of GE, David Glass (and before him, Sam Walton) of Wal-Mart, Mary Kay Ash of Mary Kay Cosmetics, Max DePree of Herman Miller, and Tom Watson, Jr., retired chairman of IBM. Less-famous companies, or at least less-familiar names, include Gene Kaczmarski of Medaphis, Alf Andreason and Tom Brooks of AT&T, Steve Ardia of Gould Pumps, and Kitty Green of CMS. There is a revolution occurring in leadership, and it is based on principles firmly centered in the four dimensions forming the central chambers of the heart of leadership.

There are a few great truths known at an intuitive level by the most effective long-term leaders. These truths flow directly out of one or more of the four dimensions and inform and enlighten their power.

TRUTHS ABOUT PEOPLE

- People would rather make it better than make it worse. Given an opportunity and a clear choice to make it better, people will choose wisely.

- People seek out pleasure and do not seek out unnecessary pain, but are willing to go through pain if it will create greater good down the road.

- People want to feel that they make a difference, that they matter.

- People want to feel appreciated and valued.

- If leaders provide meaningful direction, a vision that inspires and touches their aspirations, people will follow with enthusiasm.

- What is sown is what you will ultimately reap in business and in relationships.

- In the long run, invitation is infinitely more powerful than coercion.

- Everyone is doing the best they know how, based upon how they have it figured out.

- We want to trust and believe in others, and we want them to trust and believe in us. All we need to do is give them an excuse to do so.

- People come first. Leadership is high touch.

The four drivers of competence, passion, intimacy, and integrity contain these truths and find their embodiment in 12 practices that empower and give muscle to them. They are the means to express and develop these four drivers, building the heart muscle of leadership. These principles and practices are introduced in the next chapter.

If you wish to be a powerful leader who succeeds on a long-term basis, you must be willing to become more effective. These 12 practices provide a systematic way of developing your leadership effectiveness. They provide a means for addressing the fundamental spiritual law governing the development of great leadership: *In order to become more effective, you must allow yourself and those around you to become bigger, to be more.*

If you wish to be more, then allow and invite those around you to be more. Being more, stretching beyond one's limitations, entering into the creative field of possibility and the engaged aliveness it brings is what great leadership is ultimately all about.

Understand this one truth—that to be a leader, you must challenge and support yourself and others in being bigger—and use the 12 practices, and you will experience a profound enhancement of your leadership capabilities and overall effectiveness.

For over 23 years I have been working with individuals, families, and organizations. In that time, I have observed and studied what creates effective leadership. I have also read more than 50 books on leadership and more than 150 articles, finding six representative writers who are kindred souls. While not laying out the concept of the four chambers of the heart in their writing, what they say can be folded into that framework. The four chambers bring it all together in a cogent and focused set.

Warren Bennis, in his insightful book *On Becoming a Leader,* indicates that all leaders share certain characteristics. Among those he mentions are a sense of mission, courage, optimism, curiosity, and compassion. Max DePree, in *Leadership Is an Art,* refers to the act of leadership as being one of honoring and liberating the gifts of one's fellow workers. Abraham Zaleznick, in *The Managerial Mystique,* refers to the wisdom which comes from suffering and the courage to challenge limitations. Stephen R. Covey, in *The Seven Habits of Highly Effective People* and *Principle-Centered Leadership,* lays out a foundation of seven habits for long-term success in business and for a meaningful life. John Kotter, in his numerous writings on leadership, is incisive and brings great clarity, demonstrating the difference between management and leadership.

These writers all point to the responsibilities of real, value-added leadership, as well as the extraordinary impact such leaders can have in changing their companies, their communities, and the lives of the people around them. I am firmly convinced that the kind of leadership we need will come not from the chosen few, but from the many of us who are hungry for more meaningful work and eager to create a better world. It will come from an understanding that if you focus upon the four fundamental chambers of the heart of leadership, while keeping in mind 12 guiding practices that develop those four chambers, you can fundamentally empower both yourself and those around you to create some wonderful outcomes.

To understand the power of this "spiritual" leadership, it is important to pause and consider our history when it comes to leadership. The leadership paradigm, our governing model on how to be an effective leader, comes from the success of our military in World War II. In our communities and in our organizations, especially in corporate America, we have emulated this hierarchical, vertically integrated, command-and-control structure. And this model served us fairly well when we were the sole manufacturing power after World War II. It was an effective model when capacity was our greatest concern, and we could not build it fast enough to meet demand. However, not only does it not serve us now, it breaks down and fails us in the present reality.

When the market became global and the competition worldwide, when the "consumers" became sophisticated and demanding "customers," when the technology began to mutate and change at an ever-accelerating velocity, when the employees began to wither because their souls and hearts were left unengaged, when time became the critical component to success and ever-increasing quality became merely the entry fee to have the privilege of competing—in other words, when the predictable world we knew changed forever—the old command and control paradigm failed us.

Managing Versus Leading

The world has changed forever, and what is needed now, in the words of Rosabeth Moss Kanter, former editor of *The Harvard Business Review*, is to be focused, flexible, fast, and friendly. Or, in the words of Jack Welch, chairman and CEO of General Electric Co.: "We need speed, simplicity, and self-confidence." The old command-and-control model fails miserably here. It is not one of flexibility, nor is it able to change and adapt quickly, nor is it very friendly. It was a model that fit another reality but is sadly out of date and ill-equipped for the rapidly evolving global marketplace of today.

What is this new model of leadership, and why is it necessary? To understand the scope of the change, it is important to take a look at the characteristics and focus of each of the two. Jack Welch says:

A manager has come to mean someone who controls rather than facilitates, complicates rather than simplifies, acts more like a governor than an accelerator . . . what we are trying to develop is an effervescent culture that crackles with creativity. We are trying to become a $60 billion global company with the fire and zest, the heart and soul, of a start-up.

Let's now look at the shifting paradigm for the requisite leadership:

Management/Command and Control		Effective Leadership
control	vs.	trust, empowerment
authority/hierarchy	vs.	alignment and expertise
rank	vs.	expertise
discrete tasks	vs.	focus on mission
one-way communication	vs.	communication rich, candor
fear of risk	vs.	experimentation
dominating perspective	vs.	inviting multiple perspectives
one decision maker	vs.	flexible, team decisions
measurement	vs.	personal accountability
quick decision making	vs.	ensuring wise decisions
tried and true	vs.	innovation
director	vs.	coach and counselor

Leadership thus becomes a critical competency; in fact, it is the crown jewel of all the core competencies we need to develop and maintain if we are to have a healthy society and successful enterprises.

The good news is that this kind of leadership can be developed, helping those who are committed become more effective and powerful. Experience demonstrates that effective leaders are not born; they are made. Leadership itself is not wholly a mysterious substance. It is a learnable mixture of science and art. A crucial task that we face, in both our companies and society, is learning how to nurture, develop, and support high-quality leadership. A place to begin is with a sound understanding of what undergirds leadership.

Assumptions

First, it is important to be aware of some assumptions that I make, based upon experience, research, and a deep intuition. The 12 practices flow out of and build on these assumptions.

- We all have the capacity to make a difference, for good or for ill; we can make a qualitative and quantifiable difference.
- We all count. Each one of us matters. Every human life is intrinsically valuable.
- The greatest asset you have with regard to your capacity to be a leader is yourself.
- The greatest liability you have with regard to your leadership is yourself.
- The most potent tool available for a leader is self-mastery. Self-mastery rests upon a foundation of self-awareness.
- True leadership is "spiritual" in its appeal and its impact. (It calls us to a higher plane of living and acting.)
- Leadership is predicated upon followership. The quality of your followers is the quality of your leadership.
- Leadership contains four drivers: integrity, competence, intimacy, and passion. Leave one out and leadership ultimately fails.
- Outstanding leaders tap 12 guiding practices and utilize, at least intuitively, 12 guiding practices.
- There are only three great barriers to your becoming a more powerful and effective leader. They have to do with self-awareness and self-management, and are ego, fear, and impatience.

The greatest barriers to becoming a more effective leader, of being able to achieve long-term, meaningful, and sustainable results while crafting relationships to maintain and accelerate those results, are to be found entirely within the leader. The barriers are the barriers we all must face if we are to develop the kind of leadership our world and our century are crying for.

Leaders are learners and curious about the world. They manage their egos, fears, and impatience in order to try new things, achieve better results, and create stronger relationships. Leaders demonstrate and develop the virtue of courage, inspiring others to rise above their own issues around ego, fear, and impatience to produce the actions which, in turn, produce results and make dreams come true.

Having studied the books and articles on leadership, I've counted more than 350 traits that effective leaders must have. At that rate, no one would qualify. General Patton did not follow a recipe book, nor did Catherine the Great, Anita Roddick, Tom Watson, Jr., Andrew Carnegie, or Jack Welch. Looking at the histories of truly effective leaders and analyzing the leaders I have worked with over the years, I find only one common way to determine effective leadership and only two ways to measure it.

Effective leaders are known solely by the actions they take and the practices they demonstrate. These actions are measured by the results they achieve and by the relationships they forge. It is as simple as that. We know leaders by the actions that flow from them and by the actions they inspire others to take. We then measure the success of those actions by what they generate in terms of results and relationships.

Results center upon and emerge from the vision or direction set by a leader. These are measured and known by the quality of the services, products, and overall coordination of tasks that shape the work environment.

Relationships center upon cultivating and improving the willingness, commitment, and abilities of those around the leader to keep producing and enhancing the desired products and services.

General Patton was a highly effective leader because of the results he achieved in getting others to perform beyond what others thought was possible. He was successful because of the quality and caliber of the relationships he forged with those around him. He was able to somehow touch the drives, motivations, and aspirations of those whom he led. It helped that he was a brilliant strategist, as well as a willing student of history and of other leaders. But that brilliance alone would not have made him a leader. The quality of leadership demonstrated itself in the followership he engendered and in what he was able to help his followers achieve. He was of the command-and-control school, but he had the flex-ibility of mind, the passion of spirit, and the deep appreciation of his men that allowed him to lead them to incredible results. He also surrounded himself with an excellent general staff.

This boils down to the two essential measurements: results and rela-tionships. The power and legacy of these results and relationships are dependent upon the four chambers forming the heart of leadership: inti-macy, integrity, competence, and passion. These are integrated and ulti-mately driven by courage.

What many seem to miss in the discussion of leadership is that a leader cannot achieve results without forging meaningful, powerful, and ongoing relationships. If we want to develop more effective leadership, we need to look at the quality of the actions taken by the leaders, and at how those actions shape relationships and propel the system and the people within the system to produce meaningful results. However, we are talking about long-term results, not just short-term ones. Leaders are willing to make mistakes en route to the desired results, and they do not allow themselves or their followers to despair on the journey.

Leadership, if it is concerned with relationships and long-term results, must then have a means of envisioning the desired future out-come, communicating that vision, and building the team spirit required to act on that vision and move toward its fruition. Leaders, if they are to continue to produce results, must build and maintain meaningful rela-tionships. They must have a capacity to touch the hearts of others.

Let's take a look at leadership by examining its dark side through a quick view of Hitler. Hitler achieved some amazing results in his war machine and the rebuilding of Germany. He also led the German people into the most disastrous war ever fought and created a horrific new age of barbarism—truly an apocalypse.

Hitler forged his leadership by reaching out and touching the aspira-tions of the suffering and demoralized German people. He also touched the shadow portion of their psyche: ego, inflation, prejudice, fear, hatred, scapegoating, and so on. He forged powerful relationships with a core group of followers, and he acted in such a way that many were eager and willing to follow him, doing their utmost to bring to fruition the dream of a greater Germany and a thousand-year reign of a pure Teutonic race. His results were both astounding and hideously flawed.

The greatest flaw seems to have been a terrible lack of empathy and a fractured and poorly developed self-awareness. He knew little of the demons within his own psyche and was therefore under their control. Still, Hitler was a leader in terms of actions: results and relationships.

The key point is that his long-term results were disastrous precisely because he was a flawed leader; his dreams had the seeds of destruction within them because of a failed or flawed relationship with himself.

Long-term, successful leadership requires a high level of self-understanding. It also must ultimately offer a positive vision of the future that does not scapegoat or shift the blame onto anyone else.

This great principle of self-relationship is best reflected in the words of one of the greatest masters of leadership strategy, the venerable Chinese general of a thousand years ago, Sun Tzu. In his classic text, *The Art of War,* he consistently spoke of the need for awareness and the knowledge of environment, self, and others.

Studies of long-term, successful leaders point to the conclusion that their actions in achieving results and building relationships are based upon a healthy level of self-understanding and a feeling for others, i.e. intimacy. This makes for long-term strength and provides a level of strategic insight unmatched by someone who is the victim of his or her drives and ambitions. The capacity for empathy allows for a deeper and more penetrating understanding of human nature and, consequently, the world. The mistakes of overreaching, of creating scapegoats, of backing down to a bully, of bullying, or of short-term gains at the expense of the future are those of the individual who lacks insight into his or her own nature and the nature of people.

To summarize: Leaders are known by the actions they take and by the relationships they forge. They are known by the actions they inspire others to take and by the quality of the relationships which form around them. They are practical visionaries and invite others to share in and develop that vision. They are engaged in helping others produce outstanding outcomes. They are focused and cause others to focus upon issues of substance and relevance. They have a high level of self-awareness and skillfully manage the dangerous and wondrous dynamics of fear, ego, and impatience.

Effective leaders remember and act upon the fact that all work is done ultimately by people, with people, through people, and for people. Leaders function by creating alignment around tasks, inspiring and relating to people. Leadership is high touch. It is grounded in the four chambers of leadership's heart: intimacy, integrity, passion, and competence.

Leadership itself is a critical and vital resource and one which is known and shaped by actions. We are all called on to contribute to the revitalization of our organizations and society through an intelligent, compassionate focus upon the vectors of results and relationships, which rest upon the base of four drivers and are driven by 12 fundamental practices.

The Four Great Elephants
Shaping Our World

A friend of mine, David Harris of NationsBank, was backpacking in the Rockies. He was walking up a mountain road and saw a large brown boulder on the path. When he was within 50 yards, the boulder moved! What appeared to be an enormous grizzly roused itself and raised its head. David froze in his tracks until the bear settled back into its nap. He then spent the next hour walking silently backward down the trail!

A maxim in big-game hunting states that the larger an animal is, the harder it is to see. At first, this seems like a ridiculous statement, but it stands up to scrutiny when you take the science of perception into account. There is a strong tendency for the mind to turn a large, obvious entity into something familiar, blending it into the natural background. The animal is so obvious that it "disappears" or is mistaken for something benign and familiar. A large grizzly at first glance or two might be taken to be a large bush or boulder. The hardest animal to see is an elephant!

It has been my experience in over 20 years of professional observation and work with individuals, families, teams, and organizations that you don't have to be a big-game hunter to miss or overlook the obvious. Most of the time we are blind to the obvious, failing to see the forces that are actively shaping our ability to compete and succeed both today and tomorrow. We tend to be blinded by our expectations, assumptions, beliefs, and patterned ways of seeing and thinking. This leaves us vulnerable to being mauled by the obvious yet unexpected.

Highly effective leaders are masters at observing and acting upon the obvious. They note the commonplace trends and changes going on in their world and galvanize their teams and organizations to think and act upon them. These trends are like great waves of change, sweeping in and impacting all in their path. Leaders are the ones coaching and preparing themselves and the people around them to ride the waves. The choice, as they well know, is to ride the waves or be swept under by them. What are the great sweeping trends and changes that leaders need to see and act upon? To capture this, let's look at an analogy from big-game hunting.

There are four megatrends that have been increasing in their impact upon our lives, our culture, and our commerce. These four trends are so much with us, so intertwined with our lifestyles, and so obvious, that few of us actually see them clearly, let alone act on that vision. Executives in the training sessions at Staub-Peterson recognize the trends when we list them, but only a few can say that they consciously keep them in mind and use them in planning how to be more competitive.

These ubiquitous trends are the largest and most obvious, so I call them the Four Elephants. The premise is simple: We either begin to actively see these elephants, planning and living accordingly, or we will be trampled by them. The trends are:

I. The Elephant of the Global Marketplace

We exist now and will increasingly exist in a global marketplace. The competition is not from across town or even the next state; it is from Bonn, Seoul, Peking, Tokyo, London, New Delhi . . . and, in the not-too-distant future, Warsaw, Moscow, and other cities. We are increasingly affected by global capital markets, vast and inexpensive labor pools, and the flow of technological know-how. Our challenges, competition, and advantages are global in scope, whether they be technological, financial, environmental, organizational, transportation and communication oriented, or whatever.

Today, the astute leader knows that planning globally and working to be world class is critically important. As Jack Welch put it when he assumed the helm at GE: "We will be No. 1 or 2 in every business and industry we compete in globally, or we will not be in the business." (In 1994 GE ranked No. 1 or 2 globally in 12 businesses.)

II. The Elephant of Collapsing Time

Speed is becoming more and more the vital competitive edge and determining factor in success. The ability to move faster and get more done in less time with fewer resources is increasingly a critical factor. Have you noticed that we are now expected to accomplish in one day what used to take three or four? This is becoming the norm. Product-development cycle times of three to four years used to be the norm, but now that is fatally slow. The new cycle times are one to two years. The wonderful book *Time Wars*, by Jeremy Rifkin, points out the paradoxical reality that the more labor-saving devices we develop, the less time we seem to have. We are now taking phone calls in our cars, faxing from the beach, and squeezing more and more productivity out of our "free" time. The pace is accelerating and the race does indeed seem to be going to the swift. As Tom Peters has observed, "Get fast or go broke!"

Steve Ardia, CEO of Goulds Pumps, says this about speed:

> The fact is that everything is changing at such a rapid rate that you just can't accept the performance standards of the past. What would have been a good goal and objective three years ago may not be good enough anymore, and even though you've committed so much to getting there, you may have to say: We've just reached here, and now we've got to go even harder and faster and higher. Everyone is getting better, and if you want to be the winner, you've got to be getting better at an even faster pace than everyone you're competing with, and that's a bit daunting.
>
> We've had a commitment to what we call the war on waste, which then focused on traditional cost reducing. We are going to add another element to it next year, which is going to be the war on time. We are going to try to focus on the fact that if we can do things faster, we can reduce cycle times. That saves us money and actually makes us more responsive to the customers. Where we're trying to get some breakthroughs is in our ability to make proposals, which is how we quote our equipment to our industrial customers. That process has traditionally taken two to three weeks. We are looking to reduce that cycle time to probably 48 hours. Then, the customer will get us the inquiry, and we will ideally overnight something out to him in two days. We are going to be trying to use time as a competitive weapon in the future as well.

III. The Elephant of Universal Access and Proximity

We are transforming the world into a "global village," making national borders less and less relevant for commerce, capital flow, and organizations. We can be in contact with any place on earth instantaneously, watching the bombing of Baghdad as it is occurring in real-time, seeing Yeltsin standing on a tank defying the coup plotters at the same moment as the people standing beside him in Moscow are seeing him. This means that the "nervous system" of the world has finally been wired in.

We are networked into the most remote habitats. This means that work can be done anywhere on the planet for anyone else on the other side of the earth. We have not even begun to really comprehend or make use of what this means. It is transforming our whole concept of the workplace and challenging the total manner in which we conduct our businesses, collect taxes, invest in infrastructure, and so on.

IV. The Elephant of Accelerating Change

Change is accelerating and will continue to accelerate as technologies, manufacturing methodologies, educational tools, culture, and the like all move through increasingly rapid transformations. Our technological innovations and breakthroughs are like some rapidly mutating and evolving organism.

A simple fact brings home the scope and pace of change: There is more information contained in one Sunday edition of the *New York Times* than the average individual of the 16th century was exposed to in an entire lifetime!

The only constant is rapid change. This requires a flexibility and willingness to learn and adapt that is unprecedented. Lifelong employment with any organization is becoming a distant memory, and the requirements for long-term success are continuous, lifelong learning, flexible thinking, and the ability to deal with constant disequilibrium and readjustments.

These "elephants" are obvious, yet the wisdom and perspective that they shed on our lives and the ways we conduct our business are seldom utilized. Leaders are the ones who will see these obvious megatrends and prepare themselves and those around them to live with and make use of the trends learning how to ride the megatrends instead of being trampled.

In a similar vein, the leadership we need for the future is the kind that, as Buckminster Fuller points out, can transform the world. The ability to do this rests firmly in the continued practice of observing and acting upon the obvious. This requires the use of fuzzy logic and even more effective use of the potential intelligence embedded in the human system of most organizations. It also means developing ongoing networks of information and meaningful relationships orchestrated around more rapid and effective learning.

An old joke I heard at a convention fits the situation well: It so happened that the President of the United States, an aged priest, a mountain climber, and the world's smartest man were riding in a private jet when the jet developed engine trouble. The pilot ran through the cabin yelling, "We're going to crash. Save yourselves." The pilot jumped out of the plane, activating his parachute. The four men looked around but could only find three parachutes. The president took one, leaped out, and yelled, "I must save myself for the sake of national security." The world's smartest man grabbed one, proclaiming, "I am an invaluable national resource and must preserve my intellect," whereupon he leaped out. The aged priest turned to the young mountain climber and said, "Save yourself, laddie; I'm 40 years in the Lord's service and not afraid to meet my maker." The young mountain climber promptly handed a chute to the priest and picked one up for himself, saying, "No sweat, padre; the world's smartest man just jumped out with my knapsack!"

The point is self-evident. No amount of intelligence or knowledge can save a business, a career, or a society if the obvious is overlooked or missed. Like the world's smartest man, we mistake one thing for another and end up having a very unpleasant landing! This is even more true in leadership actions and behaviors.

What is obvious? Primarily that leaders lead people, that they achieve results through people, and that they forge (and inspire others to forge) long-term relationships. The quality of the success of leaders, therefore, rests in their grounding in the four drivers outlined in the previous chapter: intimacy, integrity, competence, and passion.

Twelve Practices

Stephen R. Covey's *Seven Habits of Highly Successful People* includes principle-based ways of living that fold into these four drivers, a means of orienting oneself in the complexity of our current life. Yet even these well-articulated habits do not adequately prepare and develop the kind of heart tone and mental skills required to ride the wild elephants. There are 12 key practices that, like the four elephants, make instant sense when articulated, but are not seen or utilized unless pointed out. They fundamentally empower anyone who wishes to become more effective in a leadership role and its five great tasks.

The four drivers of leadership—integrity, intimacy, competence, and passion—and the five tasks of leadership they support are realized and given power by the 12 practices. These 12 practices are the exercises that enable us to strengthen our heart of leadership.

Each practice has a primary function that enables the human system to achieve high-level results and excellence. Accompanying each function is a primary emotional energy that provides motivational force. The practices are synergistic. It is the interaction of the 12 that creates real leadership impact and power. Each practice falls into one or two of the four drivers. These practices are practical and highly effective ways of preparing yourself and others to master and, indeed, ride all of the elephants of change.

Those wishing to develop outstanding leadership impact must grasp the essence of the four drivers and utilize the 12 practices in order to create, develop, and maintain a powerful leadership heart. This heart then calls to and draws upon the hearts and imaginations of others, generating a powerful current of influence and focused intent.

What is new here is not only the listing of distilled leadership practices, concerns, and behaviors. It is the awareness of and focus on the interaction and energetic emotional flow between practices, along with the successive impact of that flow. This allows for analysis, quality improvement, and precision, as well as a faster, richer, and more thorough process of learning and developing highly effective leadership.

The human system is, after all, a system composed of people. Leadership itself is chiefly concerned with people issues such as aligning

forces, inspiring others, generating trust, communicating, focusing, predicting, anticipating, learning, correcting, achieving, and involving. All of this relies on tapping the motivational power in the human heart and mind. This means engaging the emotions and aspirations of others, since emotion is the root of all human motivation.

Therefore, effective leaders engage in behaviors (practices) that serve key functions in generating followership. Each function is, in turn, supported by an emotional energy flow that provides all real human motivation.

Leaders are concerned with energy flows. The critical task of liberating energy, and helping to channel and amplify it, is the leader's task. The source of the energy, the emotions, is within the follower. Let's look at the flow of function and emotional energy as we look at a diagram of the 12 practices on the previous page.

We can best understand how all of these practices work when we look at the diagram on page 44. It shows that leadership starts with a foundation of vision and that out of that vision flows a function and an emotion. The function of vision, is to provide a sense of direction and meaning. The emotion that flows from this sense of direction and meaning is inspiration. Please note that each of the 12 practices has a primary function to fulfill, and that each of these functions has an emotional companion. This is important since leadership is built of critical functions and the emotional reactions of the people comprising the human system. It is the tapping, focusing, and orchestration of the emotional energy that gives the real power to leadership.

It is easy to see that vision, with its primary function of providing direction and meaning along with the emotion of inspiration, feeds into the practice of generating followership on one hand and the practice of focusing upon purpose on the other. Then you build the heart of your leadership effectiveness through the practice of focusing upon purpose and at the same time consciously working on creating followership. Each practice builds upon the foundation of vision, purpose, and followership, serving to reinforce and liberate the potential energy and talents that lie latent in the human heart and the human system.

In the following chapters, I will build upon and explain each of the practices. Each practice has a critical function that is essential to developing effective leadership. It is also essential to understand the emotional state that goes hand in hand with each function and helps drive leadership effectiveness. Each chapter also includes tools, processes, and techniques that supplement and enhance the development of greater precision in mastering each of the practices. The exercises in each chapter help in pinpointing areas where personal improvement is needed. A powerful way to read these chapters is to ask at the beginning and then at the end of each chapter how effectively you apply the practice and whether you have realized the importance of each one in increasing your overall impact and in bringing more precision, focus, energy, and creativity to your enterprise and to the work of the people around you.

I know these 12 practices are essential to long-term effectiveness. Miss any one of them and your leadership and your followers will ultimately suffer. By carefully noting the ones you are not utilizing, or are under-utilizing, and then acting on them, your leadership will improve dramatically as you develop the tone of your four-chambered heart.

The valued-added kind of leadership we need for the 21st century is also needed right now. The four elephants are powerful and can overwhelm an individual, family, team, organization, and society itself if we do not prepare ourselves by utilizing sound principles along with equally sound and empowering practices.

In the next 12 chapters, I'd like to flesh out these practices, giving examples from real organizations and leaders that demonstrate their power. Each chapter also has a set of questions along with suggestions and exercises to help you develop and strengthen those practices in which you might be weak. This is not a recipe book for success, but it does tease out the artfulness of powerful leadership with some clear, action-oriented practices that have made and will make a difference.

The choice is to observe the obvious and learn to ride the elephants or be trampled by them. The issue is to name the critical elephants, learning to harness their power and seize the opportunities they present. Only the kind of empowering, liberating leadership demonstrated by those who act out of the four chambers of the heart of leadership can succeed in these tasks.

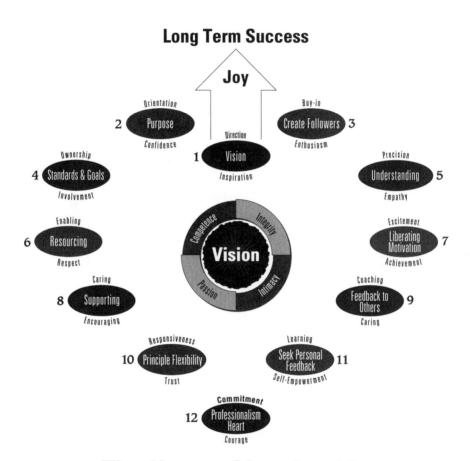

The Twelve Leadership Practices Scorecard

	The Practices	5 Point Rating	
		360°	Self
1	Offering guidance through shared vision		
2	Continual focusing and refocusing upon essential purpose		
3	Creating followership		
4	Setting standards and objectives while eliciting goals from others		
5	Working to understand people and communications: increasingly empathy and insight quotient		
6	Providing and ensuring appropriate and required resources		
7	Liberating the internal motivations of others		
8	Supporting your followers and potential followers with confrontation and caring		
9	Providing feedback on performance and vision realization		
10	Developing principled flexibility		
11	Seeking feedback on your leadership impact		
12	Being professional—having the heart to do what is required, not what is comfortable, familiar, or habitual, having the courage and persistence to challenge and push one's comfort zone		

The Core Messages of Leaders

In essence, you can summarize powerful leadership in three core messages. These messages are communicated not so much in words as they are in the way a leader interacts with and engages others. These messages invite full participation, help focus on what is essential, and systematically work the issues of achieving results while developing effective and enabling relationships for the long haul. Please pause to fill out the questions under each. How well do you communicate these messages in your interactions?

The Three Essential Messages

1. You are important/make a difference.

a) How do you convey this?

b) How does the team convey this?

c) What could you start doing to convey this more powerfully?

2. What we are doing here matters/it makes a difference.

a) How do you convey this?

b) How does the team convey this?

c) What could you start doing to convey this more powerfully?

3. Together, we can do the extraordinary.

a) How do you convey this?

b) How does the team convey this?

c) What could you start doing to convey this more powerfully?

Note: Answering these questions and acting on what you write can dramatically increase your leadership power. Take the time as you read the book and reflect to come back to this page and add other things you can do to more powerfully engage the hearts and minds of others, both at home and at work.

Part Two

THE HEART OF LEADERSHIP

What follows is an outline of the four great drivers of leadership along with the clusters of practices which enable and fuel them. The three practices under each are the ones that if neglected, create the most pain and damage. Please look carefully at the practices and the chapters which correspond to each. If you are weak in two of the practices under competency, for example, then that is a serious weakness in a major driver of success. You would then want to carefully read those two chapters and outline a plan to futher develop your leadership using and building upon the strategies and skills they contain. By focusing on those practices you are least adept in, you will be developing that particular driver, whether it be competency, integrity, passion, or intimacy. You can use the following chapters as a way of addressing and working on those practices that are most essential to your next step in becoming even more powerful and effective as a leader.

Start with the driver of intimacy. Being intimate with the customer and the marketplace, as well as with the substance of the work, is essential, yet there are two other elements that are critical for long-term leadership success. The first of these is intimacy with those around you who are engaged in driving the work. This does not mean you are best friends or that you know their deepest and darkest secrets. What it does mean is that you know who they are, what their strengths and weaknesses are, and what drives and motivates them, and you have an in-depth understanding of how to best influence them and work with them. The other dimension of intimacy that is key, is being intimate with yourself. That is, having the self-awareness to know what your weaknesses and tendencies are so that you are less likely to shoot yourself in the foot or end up being blindsided. Many successful executives have seen their careers derailed, their marriages and private lives severly disrupted, and their health compromised because of a lack of self awareness and personal mastery. Therefore, the first driver at the heart of leadership is that of intimacy.

The first practice that is driven out of intimacy is that of forming a vision. If you do not have a core vision for your life, then you are at a serious disadvantage both personally and professionally. If you look at the heart of leadership diagram, you'll see that vision is at the very center with the four drivers surrounding it. This is critical because it provides a guiding star, a sense of inner balance. Like a gyroscope, it helps you find and keep your orientation, regardless of how chaotic things become. It provides an inner sense of guidance and direction to help you navigate the tasks of leadership and challenges of life, moment by moment.

If you look at the model you will also see that vision appears not only in the center of the cluster of four drivers, but also above them as a practice. One forms the vision for your life and who you are to be, while the other is about focusing a team, a project, a department, a family, or an organization.

You will also see that at the core, it is important to formulate and develop your courage quotient. Without courage, all leadership stops. It is one of the most important requirements. In fact, forming a vision for what you are about (Practice #1) and cultivating the courage to then live it (Practice #12) are, respectively, your guiding star and your ability to move toward the star. Courage helps you, moment by moment, move toward your vision, for your life and for task, team, family, and enterprise. All of the other 10 practices are enablers and specific means of moving toward your vision both personally and professionally.

There are four great areas compromising the core of powerful leadership. These four areas function synergistically, much like the four vital chambers forming the human heart. Each of these four are strengthened and toned by a set of 12 practices, practices which fundamentally drive results while also building relationships. This results/relationship focus stacks the deck in favor of success today while also developing capacity and momentum for success in the future. Focusing on the four chambers and picking the two or three practices that you most need to develop can enhance your leadership impact four-fold.

Intimacy: *The practices which most create intimacy with
self and others are:*

Practice 1:	Developing Vision
Practice 5:	Reading and Understanding Others
Practice 11:	Seeking Personal Feedback

Competency: *The three practices which most help attend to
and develop needed competencies are:*

Practice 4:	Setting Standards and Eliciting Goals
Practice 6:	Providing and Negotiating Resources
Practice 9:	Giving Performance-Based Feedback

Passion: *The practices which most focus on eliciting and
generating passion are:*

Practice 3:	Developing Followership and Other Leaders
Practice 7:	Liberating the Motivation of Others
Practice 8:	Supporting Others

Integrity: *The practices which most help develop and maintain
personal and organizational integrity are:*

Practice 2:	Focusing Upon Purpose
Practice 10:	Developing Principled Flexibility
Practice 12:	Cultivating Courage/Being a Professional

PRACTICE 1

Providing Guidance Through Shared Vision

Through vision we

give direction and

meaning, creating

the inspiration

necessary to

follow through.

An architect was puzzled and distressed. He was charged with building a large cathedral, and he had two teams of stone masons working on some of the intricate detail around a great rose window. One team was ahead of schedule; the other was struggling and making a lot of mistakes. The architect decided to investigate.

Both teams had competent journeyman supervisors, and the team members were equally skilled in both groups. In desperation, the architect decided to speak to each man individually and ask him what he was doing. In the first group, from supervisor to mason's assistant, all gave rather detailed and involved descriptions of what they were doing—cutting the stones, setting scaffolding, mortaring, etc. In the second group, from mason's assistant to supervisor, all began their answers with, "I'm building a cathedral."

Which team do you think was ahead? Not surprisingly, the team of masons who were focused on the vision of building a cathedral. The vision galvanized them and helped them coordinate their efforts. They achieved what Michael Beers calls "task alignment," wherein all members knew how all of their different tasks fed into and

supported the whole enterprise. They were but part of the greater con-
struction force involved in building something greater and larger than
their own specialized focuses. Their efforts and the focus of their team
were the vision of creating the cathedral.

One of the most common mistakes I've seen made by leaders in
teams and organizations is that of not taking the time to formulate a
vision. And even with those who do formulate a vision, they do not do
what it takes to bring that vision to life. A vision is concerned with
doing the right thing. The communication and shared sense of ownership for that vision is part of doing it right.

Why have a vision? A vision is needed to inspire, orient, and align
people. Obviously, if you are the CEO or senior executive of a division,
you are effectively crippled if you have not formulated and promulgat-
ed a vision for the collective enterprise. However, what if you are a
supervisor in some subsection of a department? Do you still need a
vision? You do, if you wish to function as a leader—someone who
makes a difference by inspiring others to make a difference.

It is my experience that your supervisory and leadership effectiveness
increases dramatically if you have developed a vision for your group
and its efforts. Of course, the vision must be consistent in terms of supporting the overall mission of the organization, but it must come from
your heart and speak to the hearts of those in your area.

Gene Kaczmarski, former president and COO of Medaphis Physician
Services Corporation, which under his tenure was No. 1 in its industry,
put it this way:

> Vision is the art of seeing the invisible. My responsibility
> as a leader is to crystallize and materialize the Medaphis
> vision in the form of strategies and tactics which can be com-
> municated throughout the organization.
>
> I believe that the single most important aspect of leading
> an organization is the communication and ownership at all
> levels of a meaningful vision. Equally important is the need
> for every person to understand how the vision will benefit
> them, not only the company.
>
> How a vision benefits each individual is more difficult to
> materialize as it is communicated through the different func-
> tional areas and levels of an organization, but it is essential
> for buy-in to occur. The task of a leader is to help bring
> everyone to a common focal point. Although different func-
> tions, departments, and levels of an organization see the

vision through a different colored lens, everyone must be focused on the same perspective. Only then can individuals within different functions start to create subvisions as to how their area of responsibility fits into the overall vision.

Tremendous power can be generated by creating multiple, reinforcing visions which serve to coordinate and powerfully align all aspects of an enterprise. One overall vision, supported by departmental visions, breathes coherence and purpose into an organization. This multiple process of interlocking visions contributes a real sense of ownership. This sense of ownership comes from the very nature of taking time to outline and link personal, team, and departmental formulations of aspirations and visions.

Without a vision there is no overall sense of coordination. More seriously, there is a lack of spirit, inspiration, and higher purpose to the work of the departments, the individuals, or the organization. No higher vantage point exists by which to mediate conflicts or turf issues.

Admiral Tom Brooks, former director of Naval Intelligence and now a senior executive at AT&T, says:

> During the Cold War, there was a sense of a guiding vision and overall mission around serving the national defense and working for a safer world. With the end of the Cold War, many agencies and not a few defense contractors were left struggling, trying to redefine their vision and their mission.

If the vision of an organization is not clearly articulated by its leadership, then it does not exist in the minds of the followers. In far too many of the organizations I have observed, people are very confused about what the organization is trying to become. This makes it nearly impossible to do effective, strategic, long-term planning since there is not a clearly articulated reference point for the organization and its constituents.

Admiral Brooks talks about his sense of the importance of vision:

> In my view, four things are fundamental to leadership:
> First, a leader must have a vision. He must be leading something; he must be leading it somewhere. And he must know the something that he is leading. It must be well-defined and understood by both the leader and the people being led. In addition to having a vision, an effective leader is able to articulate the vision.

Second, I would differentiate between being able to articulate the vision and being able to communicate it. I've known a number of "men of vision" who have indeed been able to articulate where they wanted to go, but have never been able to effectively communicate it to everyone so it's widely understood. I have known men with significant vision, drive, and "innate leadership capabilities" who, if you got 10 people from across the spectrum of their organization, you'd get three or four ideas of the direction those leaders are trying to articulate.

The third element, I would suggest, goes beyond articulation and communication. It gets into the area of motivation. For example, you might be able to articulate and effectively communicate; however, if you can't communicate with the passion that causes people to understand the vision and desire the same end result, you haven't effectively tapped the motivation required to make the vision come alive.

Having the vision isn't enough; articulating it isn't enough; communicating it isn't enough. Being able to motivate people to keep the vision is critical and requires a fourth dimension, a fourth element.

This fourth dimension I call "drive it home," for lack of a better term. This is simply the persistence, determination, and drive to constantly push people who might otherwise operate at five miles an hour to go 55 miles an hour.

You have to go that extra step of personally getting involved, making sure that everyone is on board and aligned. You're like the sheepdog who snaps around the heels of the sheep that are not quite keeping up with the pack. That's a function a leader has to do. In some cases, it's a touch of the cattle prod; often, it's coaching; and in other cases it's getting rid of people if they can't or won't keep up.

I think that if you have all those dimensions . . . if you have a person with a vision, who articulates it well, who can tap the motivations of the people, who follows up to drive it through, then pushes constantly where pushing is required—that's the secret of a successful leader.

Vision provides a sense of purpose and coherence. It is like a torch, lighting the way, illuminating the desired future. A lack of vision leaves the organization, the team, and the individual in darkness.

One of John F. Kennedy's greatest strengths was his ability to create a vision and to persuasively communicate it. One of his famous vision statements was simple yet far-reaching, galvanizing the nation's efforts and research for nearly a decade: "In this decade, we will send a man to the moon and return him again safely."

However, be forewarned. To craft a vision of power and substance always requires courage. It is a leap of faith, spanning the abyss between the known and the unknown future. There is always the possibility that the vision will not come to pass, that you have committed yourself and your team publicly to a course and to a path without any guarantees, just the bold-faced commitment.

When he formulated the vision of the moon trip, John Kennedy knew that we had neither the means, the technology, nor the infrastructure to realize the vision. However, it was an act of faith and courage, galvanizing the public's opinion and spurring the creativity that helped make the vision a reality. On July 20, 1969, Neil Armstrong became the first human being to walk on the moon.

Too many leaders fail to recognize the need for a coherent strategic plan directly tied to a vision for the future. Even fewer develop long-term plans derived from an agreed-upon strategy. There is a growing recognition that American leaders, especially in business, have been too short-sighted. One of the most effective leaders in corporate America has revitalized his organization, taking it from a $27 billion company to a $60 billion-plus company within the past 10 years. Jack Welch is his name, and the company is an American icon: General Electric.

Welch has a prescription he has been applying at GE with tremendous success. It starts with the simple yet effective articulation of part of his vision that we read in the last chapter: "We will be No. 1 or 2 in every industry we compete in globally, or we won't be in the business." This was the first phase of his vision that he began communicating back in 1981 when he took over the reins at GE; he then fleshed it out with a code of values, a list of five critical factors that cut across the diverse industries in which GE was involved, and a set of operating principles.

One of the principles was: "Develop a constant, interactive process aimed at consensus." Three key guiding values were "speed, simplicity, and self-confidence." The process for vision realization that he describes is:

- Create vision, articulate it, and passionately own it.
- Relentlessly drive the vision to completion.
- Be open and candid.
- Don't stick to established channels; go up, down, and around to reach people and obtain feedback.
- Be religiously accessible.
- Tell your story of revitalization continuously, with commitment and enthusiasm.

The result: By 1992, GE was No. 1 or No. 2 in all 12 of the businesses they compete in globally. The galvanizing effect of the vision and the passion to drive it have led to great profitability and stability. Otherwise, GE might very well have been in the same leaky vessels that GM, Sears, IBM, and others found themselves in on the stormy seas of our global marketplace.

So, a clear vision, a relentless focus upon that vision, and a passionate commitment to driving that vision are critical to long-term success. Competence without a vision to drive it and orient it becomes drudgery, dull, and uninspired. The vision must be owned and embodied.

Many organizations that Staub-Peterson Leadership Consultants have worked with have vision statements on their walls. Some even have them made into pocket cards that employees carry around with them. However, words on a wall or on a card do not make a vision. That only comes about when the vision is embodied and lives in the daily transactions of all employees. Leaders like Jack Welch, Anita Roddick of the Body Shop, Jack Stone of Umbro, and Roger Milliken of the global textile company Milliken are truly unique and rare leaders in that they push and drive the vision, communicating it continuously and measuring all behaviors against it.

This holds true for all levels within an organization. If the CEO does not live the vision and work to communicate and flesh it out throughout his or her company, then the vision means nothing and provides no sense of mission or guidance. Yet, if the CEO is the only one owning the vision, then it cannot be realized. The CEO does not do the actual day-to-day work or interact with the customers and suppliers on a regular basis. In fact, if he or she is not careful, the CEO can become isolated and out of touch with what is driving the company day to day. What is required is that the vision be owned and talked up, held up as a torch by multiple layers of leadership. The great task is to capture the imaginations and the passion of the leaders so they feel they are working on *their* vision.

There are numerous ways to generate and promulgate a vision. The most powerful way seems to be to have leaders (whether first-line supervisors, senior vice presidents, or CEOs) sit down with their team, talk about the corporate vision, and ask what it means to the team and to the individuals on the team. Critical questions need to be asked, wrestled with, and discussed. Questions such as: Why is this vision important to our jobs? What does this vision do for us? What does it mean for our customers? What does the vision say to you? How does it change the ways we work and go about doing our jobs? What difference does it make? What difference should it make? How do we feel about this vision? How do we live day by day? How will we measure our success in doing our part to make the vision a reality?

Then the questions must turn to the more intensely personal level: What is it we wish to become individually? What is our own personal vision and sense of mission? What are we aiming for in our lives? These questions become critical when you take into account Max DePree's viewpoint at Herman Miller: "Our organizations cannot become anything more than we desire them to be." Here is where Stephen R. Covey formulates the personal part of self-empowerment in urging you to define your vision and mission in *The Seven Habits of Highly Effective People.* He suggests that you clarify the key roles you play in life: parent, mentor, supervisor, spouse, and so on, and develop a sense of the mission around each of them. I suggest that this is important, and yet it is critical that you also develop an overall, integrated vision for your life. Unless we know what we truly aspire to be and what our individual sense of purpose is, we are rudderless in the rapidly shifting currents of the modern world.

Covey talks about the need for an orientation mechanism, such as an inner compass, as opposed to a map. The terrain is changing so fast that the maps are out of date before the ink is dry. A sense of what your life is about, your own sense of mission, and some guiding principles that provide a means for orienting and directing your life, are vital to creating the life experience you desire.

This is the beginning of personal power and also real power for a leader. Covey does an excellent job of outlining these guiding habits. What is needed are some clear guiding practices that flush out and inform greater leadership development. If I, as an individual leader, consciously know and articulate my vision for working with others, a vision of the kind of person and leader I am striving to be, then I am way ahead of most managers, supervisors, and other leaders.

The kind of vision I am talking about communicates itself across the four fundamental drivers of leadership effectiveness. It conveys to others my commitment and passion. It focuses and directs my competencies while pointing to the ones I need to develop. It carries within it the roots of an uncompromising integrity, and finally, it allows for an intimacy with others and with myself that allows me to be accessible to learning and to the processes of change. Vision orchestrates and illuminates the four great chambers while forming the living heart of leadership, which drives long-term results and builds sustaining relationships.

To create real personal power, it is critical that you develop your own personal vision and a sense of your deepest longings for meaning. Try this exercise, which is one of the ones we use in our High-Impact Leadership Seminar at Staub-Peterson.

EXERCISE

Imagine you are on your deathbed. You have 20 minutes left to live, and you are reviewing your life. What does your life look like? What are you proud of? What are you disappointed in? How have you lived your life? What was the meaning of this life? What was your purpose in living the way you lived and doing the things you did? If you could go back and change any part of it, what would you change? Why? Look really hard at the values your life demonstrated. If you had to come up with an epitaph for this life, what would it be?

Now: How would you like to be living? What meaning would you like your life to have? If you could have a new lease on life and begin again, what would you choose as your guiding star? What are you really here to accomplish and to do? What vision do you have of the life you'd like to create? What is your sense of mission?

Pause for a moment and write down a brief statement of vision and mission for your life. Put down something, even if it feels incomplete. Try to capture some of the longing and deep feeling in your heart. Stop reading and just write for the next 15 minutes. Take time during the next few weeks to revisit these questions and wrestle with them. They are worth answering and critical to your development as a real leader. Revisit this exercise and think about its implications for the way you are living and working.

Leaders in today's world must be able to respond to violent and wrenching change. They need a conceptual base and a means of tapping their internal vision and sense of purpose if they are to survive.

How do you create and craft visions? Individually, the exercise above is a good way to start. The intent, at this intensely personal level, is to tap the wellspring of your soul, looking at your life and aspirations from your heart and then your head. List the most important aspects of your life: values, relationships, achievements, security, and so on. Are you living in a manner consistent with these aspects? Are you experiencing a sense of wholeness, even joy, in the way you are acting and feeling? What is it you most deeply desire and to which you aspire? Consider keeping a journal and writing out your thoughts, hopes, fears, dreams, desires and aspirations.

Writing down your vision and the attendant goals is very powerful. A 50-year longitudinal study at Harvard has looked at the people there who have been the most successful in enjoying their lives and in creating great achievements. What it found was that class rank, grade point average, and activity levels in college were not highly correlated with great success. The single most influential factor found which distinguished the most successful students from the rest, was that they had a habit of writing down their goals, aspirations, and desires and revisiting them frequently.

EXERCISE

Team or departmental vision development requires the active involvement and creative input of the team or department members. Ask each person to write down answers to the following questions: What do they most want out of the team, and what do they wish to be the true and highest aspirations of the team? What do they hope the team will be able to accomplish? What would be a team or departmental vision which challenged everyone and brought out the best they had to give? What vision would excite them and really add value to the enterprise or organization? What kind of relationships would they like to foster? What kind of work environment do they wish to create?

Then have the members, in small groups, discuss and process their answers. Have them trade sheets and let someone else read theirs. Then have that person present it as if it were their own deepest truth. This discussion process takes time and energy, yet the payoff can be tremendous. It engages the people doing the work, who are responsible for the team or department's success, in a process of dialogue. This clarifies the essential values and most value-added perspectives. It generates energy and begins to create a powerful context for excellence and integrated work efforts.

EXERCISE

Organizational vision: One method of generating a vision for the organization requires getting the departmental visions together and tying them into the senior team's best efforts to generate a worthy, powerful, and compelling vision of the organization. The vision statement needs to be supported by a core set of critical values, and it must tap the aspirations, functions, and real aim of the organization. This can be done in a matter of weeks or months, depending upon the depth, time commitment, and scope of involvement. Then you simply plug in Welch's process for driving the vision (see page 62).

EXERCISE

Another method for generating the organizational vision is for the senior leader to craft a draft and then have his or her management team draw up theirs and compare the two, discussing and exploring the two drafts. To get optimal results, it is often best to have an outside consultant or facilitator help drive this process. Then the drafts are circulated and discussed with departments and teams for their input and ideas. Later, a final draft is prepared by the CEO or executive team and published. All behaviors, performance issues, and work are then viewed in light of that vision. It is measured against, talked to, revisited, and so on.

Yet another method, but one flawed with regard to getting buy-in, is for the senior leader to draft the vision and demand sign-up and compliance. Clearly, leadership needs to be taking the lead and primary initiatives while formulating and driving the development of a vision. However, neglecting others' feedback, thoughts, and feelings in the process is usually problematic.

What if you already have a vision statement for your organization? Simple. Revisit it and ask: Is this still our vision? Does it fit who we are today and who we aspire to be tomorrow? Do you feel a sense of challenge and excitement in this vision? Does anyone "own" it? If the answers are generally yes, then reaffirm the vision and ensure that everything is measured against it. Use the vision statement! If it no longer fits, then proceed as above in generating a new one.

The importance of vision cannot be overstated for an individual, team, or organization. The vision provides a framework or context for understanding and orchestrating all of the work efforts. Without it, there is no guiding star and no overarching context for directing efforts, planning for the long term, getting perspective, and resolving fundamental priority conflicts. Taking the time to craft a personal, departmental or team, and organizational vision is time well-spent. The most effective leaders know this and make use of it in setting the tone and the standard for providing a framework for long-term success.

Let me finish this chapter with the story of Dr. Alf Andreason, who was charged with defining the guiding vision for Information Systems at Federal Systems Advanced Technologies of AT&T. When I interviewed him, he told of developing a vision in the midst of violent change.

In 1987, the organization's revenues stood at about $100 million, most of which came from the Department of Defense. Within three months, however, the first round of defense cutbacks cancelled some $50 million of those revenues. Add to that the money invested in winning the defense contracts, and the loss was a double blow. "What had been a growing business when I took it over three months earlier was gutted. At that point we went from about 900 people to about 400 people in a time frame of just a few weeks," Andreason recalled. "It was a hard way to start a new job, to have this outfit for three months and have it eviscerated."

To move beyond that, Andreason took the organization in a new direction. Instead of limiting itself to the Department of Defense, it would also do other kinds of government contracts, as well as commercial and international projects. Taking a defense contractor into non-defense arenas was a challenge laden with obstacles to overcome, not the least of which was the culture within Federal Systems itself. The environment at Federal Systems in 1988 was similar to that of Bell Systems in 1984—a culture of cooperation with the government in which competition was only vaguely understood. Andreason says:

> It was four decades of government business in which virtually all but the last few years it had been known as the Bell System. The Bell System was a special entity. Most often there were programs we were asked to take on by the administration of that time because we were considered neutral and a real partner with the government. In most

businesses, you lose more than you win. You have more
missed sales than you have wins. You have more disap-
pointments than you have victories. But a culture that has
typically had one source—where you don't even start
things that don't pan out—finds this kind of change
extremely difficult.

Andreason had to get his mistakes out of the way quickly and choose
his opportunities well. He had to be aware enough of his purpose that
he could say "no" to what seemed like good opportunities. Part of that
was knowing what he and his organization were good at. "After a while,
at least a couple of folks started to understand that we were good at a
couple of things," says Andreason. "In our case, it was communication-
system integration. We knew how to do that." Things began to accelerate. The company began to grow again and was able to partner with
organizations that used to be competitors. Key to this was having constancy of purpose and staying focused.

To inspire an entrenched culture with a new vision meant injecting that
culture with a feeling of change. "If I'd had the freedom to do it, I would
have moved all of my people into a new building, so that they would have
left their offices behind," Andreason says. "In the process of the move,
they would have shed many physical pieces of baggage, and they would
have shed a great many psychological ones." Adding new people to the
culture also helped accelerate change and energize the culture.

So it's a couple of things: constancy of vision, constancy
of how you think about it, the brutality of deciding what
you're good at, and then a constant refreshment that you
allow people to change.

All this change led to a great success story. When Andreason took
over, Federal Systems was stuck with a program that should have been
cancelled, but wasn't. Eventually it got to the point where the project
had to be a success, or those in charge of it would be disbanded. "It really wasn't the threat that unified them," Andreason says. "They were just
mightily annoyed at the notion of failure." They didn't want to be asso-
ciated with a mess. With the support of Andreason's boss, the newly
energized group made a gradual move from a 2 percent market share to
48 percent, offering lower prices and better warranties than their competitors. Notes Andreason:

> It's a wonderful success story because it didn't take a massive exit of people. It took the indignation of the organization not wanting to be associated with failure. It took the confidence of a senior to let them try. It took the diligence of a business plan that had little steps for little feet. And as we made those steps, the confidence in ourselves grew. I think the success comes from doing the homework, having a solid plan with incremental goals, having the moral indignation to not give up, and having a management structure that really hates defeat, therefore allowing you one more chance if you really, really make the case. All of that conspired to create a success.

From this experience, what could be considered Andreason's rules for visionary leadership?

> Clarify what you want to do and what you are good at doing. Have constancy of purpose. Avoid self-delusion. Break the water cooler mind-set. Communicate, communicate, communicate, communicate, and then keep communicating. It is tough because it is not in my nature to do it, but evangelism is what we're talking about, over and over again communicating how we're to think about it. The people in your organization want to be a success. They've got to understand how they can help make it so.

Leadership provides the focus and the inspiration while developing or helping to identify the leverage points for change and opportunity realization. Without a sense of vision and the passionate communication of that vision, an organization ultimately stumbles and falls. But articulating the vision and working to drive it is not enough. It is only one of 12 basic practices with which a leader needs to be concerned.

"Vision, without the continual exercise of focusing upon purpose, is like having a bike without pedals."
—Kirtland Peterson

PRACTICE 2

Focusing on Purpose

PURPOSE

Continually focusing

attention on our

sense of purpose

orients us and

generates the

confidence that

those efforts are

worthwhile.

There once was a big buggy whip factory that had just made some major improvements in their process and means of manufacturing buggy whips. They made the best quality whips, priced just right. They were getting better and better at buggy whips; in fact, they set the industry standard. Unfortunately, the leadership of the business did not give much heed to Ford and his mass manufacturing of horseless carriages. They were the best at what they did, and they were out of business in very short order.

The problem wasn't that they were not purposeful in their behavior; they had great clarity of purpose. The issue was that they mistook a means and way of doing business for their purpose and reason for being in business. Yet, if you pause to think a moment, what was the purpose of a buggy whip? The ultimate purpose of the buggy whip manufacturers was really vehicle acceleration. They forgot about the ultimate need of their customers and began to think that their purpose was more and better buggy whips, rather than better and up-to-date means of helping vehicles accelerate. They were thus left in the dust by a transformative technological revolution instead of being able to cash in on the new wave in transportation.

71

While this seems a bit outdated, consider a more modern version: IBM holding on to and being so intensely focused on its mainframe business; Sears pursuing an old agenda and formula of success that had been made obsolete by Wal-Mart; GM ignoring the "small car" companies of Japan and seeing "quality" as a quaint fad for far too long.

Futurist Joel Barker cites the example of the Swiss watchmakers, who in 1967 were in command of their industry. They accounted for a sizable share of the market and earned over 65 percent of the profits. In 10 short years, though, they plunged to just a fraction of the market share and only 10 percent of the profits. They had to lay off 50,000 skilled watchmakers out of a total workforce of 65,000. What happened was that they assumed the way they had been manufacturing and approaching watchmaking was their purpose. The shifting paradigm to the battery-operated, quartz, digital watch did them in. They lost sight of their ultimate purpose and fell in love with a means, confusing it for the purpose. What makes it even more amazing is that the Swiss themselves invented the very watch that Seiko of Japan and Texas Instruments used to undermine Swiss dominance. The Swiss watch manufacturers simply couldn't see the value of the new invention. It did not fit their beliefs and expectations about what a watch was about.

The practice of continually focusing upon the substance of what we are about in an enterprise is essential and drives the process of realizing the vision. The critical function of focusing upon the purpose is that of orienting and aligning all work efforts. The emotional state that goes with this function is one of confidence—confidence that we are doing the right things and doing them together. This means leaders must continually be ready and able to challenge their own and the organization's paradigms for success and what the business is all about.

A head architect stopped at the site of his building projects. He was impressed at how rapidly work was progressing and at the skill with which the different teams functioned. The quality of the work and the materials were top-notch. He noted the light coming through the stained glass panels, the vast spaces being enclosed, and the attention to details. To try and understand how the work could be going the way it was, he stopped and asked each person what they were doing. They proudly told him they were building a cathedral. He then called the management levels over and congratulated them on inspiring the work crews with so lofty a vision. Then he fired them all. They were supposed to be building a hospital! They had lost sight of the purpose of what they were building and had a lovely but misplaced vision.

It is not enough to simply formulate and articulate a vision. The day-to-day awareness of each and every person in the organization must be focused on that vision. This is facilitated by the development of purpose statements at both corporate and departmental levels. Such purpose statements need to be clear, focused, and user-friendly. They also must do something, rather than just say something.

The goal is for all work-related behavior to be tied to and measured against the purpose statement. A key question then becomes, "Is that action or planned action 'on purpose' with the mission we all agreed upon?" This creates a higher court of appeal and a considered, agreed-upon standard by which to make decisions and gauge actions.

As previously pointed out, it is critical to ensure that the purpose of your business is not confused with the means. Effective leaders have a vision and keep a constant focus upon the purpose of the organization; they do some up-front analysis and planning around what the ultimate purpose of their business is. For example, Coca-Cola's ultimate purpose is not about colored, flavored, sugared, or artificially flavored water. Its purpose is refreshment and a sense of well-being. If it can only remember and keep that purpose clearly in focus, the company has the talent and creativity to invent and stay current on more varied and different means of providing "the pause that refreshes."

Max DePree says one of the most valuable lessons his father passed on to him at the Herman Miller organization was a lesson about the real purpose of the company. When asked what their real business was, Max's father replied, "furniture manufacturing." The designer who worked for him replied, "The interesting thing about our business isn't furniture; it's solving people's problems."

An old saying has it that there are great business opportunities to be found in other people's problems. For Herman Miller, the real purpose is seen as helping people solve problems in space allocation, cost, function, comfort, aesthetics, flexibility, durability, and design in the utilization of office space, offices, and furniture. This purpose has taken them to a successful and profitable position in the *Fortune* 500.

Too often, companies end up suffering from a myopic or nearsighted focus, or they confuse their current products and processes with their real purpose. Powerful leaders do not make this mistake, and when they see others making that mistake they take steps to help correct these dangerous and erroneous perceptions. Railroad people, for example, fell in love with their particular way of doing business, their product and services on rails. They forgot that their ultimate purpose was really the convenient transportation of people and goods. They missed out on trucking, airlines, and the like. They changed our world and made vast sums of money, but most ended up in serious trouble and with huge losses due to a failure of leadership focus on purpose. More recently, Apple Computers has gotten itself in trouble by getting distracted and forgetting its real purpose: making the power of computing an invaluable, seamless servant in getting work done, learning accomplished, and play enhanced through the highest levels of accessibility and ease of use.

Another benefit of a clear focus on purpose is that it enables the leadership system of even the largest organization to effectively orchestrate the tasks, talents, and specialties of all constituent members. When a clearly articulated vision is absent and the purpose is not clear or kept in focus, any enterprise and its leadership are headed for serious trouble.

Gene Kaczmarski, former president of Medaphis, points out the power of having clarity of purpose and keeping it in the forefront:

> Having a vision that clearly defines where you want to go and how you plan to get there creates a consistent message that breeds strength. There is unbelievable strength in consistency of purpose and strategy. We don't have different agendas for different people. Because the message is consistent, it's easier to reinforce, and it builds trust.
>
> When people from outside Medaphis talk to employees in different functional areas, they always seem surprised to find that everyone knows the vision. They comment that they rarely see an organization where this many people are consistent in their understanding of the direction of the company. This makes me feel like we're making progress.

Too often, companies end up suffering a fate similar to that of Geneen's ITT, a *Fortune* 500 company that found itself in diversified businesses that it could neither justify nor manage in a coherent manner. The result was at least a billion dollars in losses.

As Steve Bachand, CEO of Canadian Tire, says:

> Agreement on the mission was difficult. Once there was an agreement, however, it was much easier for the organization to maintain its focus.
>
> The real challenge is conveying to all levels the necessary, detailed, job-related behavior that supports the mission. The hard work is turning the mission statement into a tactical plan that supports the mission in all respects. Making the translation into the day-to-day operation of the business is very difficult.

Another company that we have worked with, which wishes to remain anonymous, empowered its executive team to develop new business ventures. However, it was never focused on the real purpose of the corporation. Each department and business head had his or her own idea about what the company was and where it was going. Each head then vigorously pursued his or her own agenda. Each had a puzzle piece, but the pieces were, in reality, from different puzzles. The result: lost opportunities, a decline in market share, wasted energy, and a huge financial drain.

These stories are, alas, not that rare. Every day, it seems, you see a story about large companies that are spinning off acquisitions that never really fit the purpose or the competencies of the parent organization. This means more pain and losses for the membership of the organization. It also demonstrates a key lack of leadership in terms of keeping the focus on the enterprise's real purpose.

Diversification can be a highly effective business strategy. But if there is no overarching vision and constancy of ultimate purpose, bound together by clear departmental purposes, the typical result is heightened internal conflict and an ultimately destructive course of action.

Consider David Palmer. When he became the commandant at West Point, he saw that the organization needed to be revitalized and that it wasn't clearly focused on an overriding purpose. He canvassed the alumni, talked with the student body, talked with his staff and with some congressional leaders. A team sat down with him and helped to craft a powerful, simple, yet focused mission statement. The result: "The purpose of West Point is to help develop leaders of character for the common defense." This provided a focus for all efforts.

Then, using this statement of purpose as a platform and as a way of focusing and managing attention, he began to talk about it daily, with everyone. All behaviors and tasks were examined in light of this purpose. The result was a rededication and an increased level of performance through all levels of the academy. It led to a fundamental re-evaluation of practices, processes, curriculum, and training, with all actions subordinated to developing leaders of character dedicated to the common defense.

Robert Hass, when he became the CEO of Levi Strauss, saw as his first task a fundamental focus upon the core values driving the organization. This process led to in-depth discussions about the real purpose of Levi Strauss and what was important and essential to the people comprising the organization. This process electrified the company and led to revitalized and vibrant culture. Market share went up as well as profits.

Developing and Utilizing Purpose Focus

However a leader seeks to manage the focus on fundamental purpose, it is critical that it happen. The guidelines are simple:

- Ensure everybody is engaged in the task of examining purpose.

- Support, encourage, and involve all levels.

- Be honest and have the courage to ask the tough questions and hear the answers.

- Act to anchor the defined purpose and values in the living web of day-to-day interactions, measuring results and relationships against that purpose and those values.

- Live the purpose and think about it daily. Ask about actions and behaviors with regard to how they typify and support that purpose and those values.

- Invite everyone to live and play on the team according to the purpose and values.

- "By their fruits you shall know them." Ensure your reward and recognition system supports the purpose.

Be willing to release from your team anyone who is not consistently focusing on purpose and living the values, even if they produce strong results. If you look closely, you will find they are poisoning relationships and hurting the overall team.

The focus upon your enterprise's purpose and how that serves your vision is most powerful when used in conjunction with performance reviews. Such a review session begins with a review of the corporate vision and departmental purpose, thereby creating an understanding and appreciation among all employees with regard to where the company wants to go and is going. An employee's performance is then appraised against these statements. This puts teeth into the vision and mission statements, making them a very real and tangible part of daily life. This review process occurs multiple times during the course of a year, in mini-reviews with individuals and with the teams. This ensures continuity of purpose and constancy of focus.

Jack Welch has created a grid for leadership at GE. The grid focuses on two criteria: meeting commitments (results) and sharing the corporate values (purpose). In the bottom left box, you have someone who is low on results and low on values. Welch says this person falls into an easy decision. They are the ones you want to eliminate from the organization. The top right box represents someone who is high on meeting commitments and also high on shared values. This is the person you look to promote and reward.

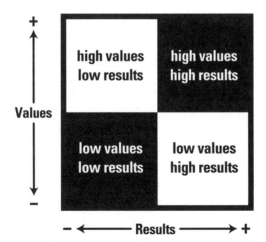

The harder choices are in the top left box (low results, high values) and the bottom right box (high results, low values). Here, discerning judgment must be used to determine if the individuals are flexible enough and capable of learning and changing. In the upper left box you might seek to coach the person on results since they already demonstrate commitment to the shared values. In the lower right box you must decide whether the individual really fits or can learn to embrace the corporate purpose and values. If not, regardless of their results, you must be willing to cut them from the team or the values lose meaning and power, diluting the organizational purpose.

As Steve Ardia, former CEO at Goulds Pumps, puts it:

> It is difficult to follow through on Welch's grid because, on the bottom line, you're getting what you want, but you know you're not getting support in those other areas, and it's those other areas that are going to sustain the long-term results. We have had to remove people who produced good results but clearly were negative in support of our values. As I look back, I say I should have removed them sooner. It would have moved the whole process forward faster. That's always difficult because you are dealing with people's lives. However, we did have some examples where people started there (not sharing and acting on the values), and we were able to coach them. They then became all-around good producers. But if we didn't remove those who only focused on results and were unwilling to focus and live the values, then the rest of the organization would have gotten confused—those sitting on the fence could actually continue to sit on the fence, and it would undermine everything we've tried to do and worked to accomplish.

A similar grid can be applied to your own life. In fact, since all of your real power as a leader comes from the inside, from the center of who you are, it is essential to clarify your life purpose and key values and evaluate whether you keep your commitments to yourself.

EXERCISE

> Take a moment and graph out your life. If you were employing yourself, where would you place yourself with regard to results and values? Now, how do you coach yourself?
>
> There is a tool you can use to help in the process of gently coaching yourself. It derives from the work of cognitive psychology and has to do with self-talk.
>
> First, take a moment and think about what your life is really about in terms of the way you spend your time. What

does that analysis tell you about your basic values and what you find to be the focus of your time? Second, when you are out of kilter with what you want or are letting anxiety and fear run you, pause and notice what you are telling yourself. What kind of self-talk are you engaged in? What are the worst things you say to yourself? Third, challenge the negative, limiting self-talk and replace it with truthful words of encouragement. Ensure the new self-talk is consistent with your personal vision and purpose. Fourth, choose to act or behave according to the new self-talk. Exercise courage.

For the organization, the guidelines flow out of the behaviors described previously. To reiterate:

- Ensure everybody is engaged in the task of examining purpose.
- Support, encourage, and involve all management levels.
- Be honest and have the courage to ask the tough questions and hear the answers.
- Act to anchor the defined purpose and values in the living web of day-to-day interactions, measuring results and relationships against that purpose and those values.
- Live the purpose and think about it daily. Ask about actions and behaviors with regard to how they typify and support that purpose and those values.
- Invite everyone to live and play on the team according to the purpose and values.
- "By their fruits you shall know them."

What gets in the way of keeping faith with the purpose of the organization, of the essential commitments, aims, and values? Again, from an interview with Steve Ardia:

My guess is that they're afraid. Afraid to take that first risky step which exposes them, or asking other people for opinions or asking other people to participate in idea generation. People fear that their authority base can be challenged, and if they don't have the self-confidence, they can feel very, very threatened. I think that fear of taking those first steps prevents people from doing it.

So you see people risk losing their job rather than go through their fear and try new behavior?
I think so—otherwise, you'd say, "Why do they have a death wish?" By the same token, there are other organizations

that don't have those same values. These people would be better situated to be working there where they don't have to face those same fears and can continue to produce results that meet their new organization's expectations.

So the essential trait required to stay focused upon the purpose and to change behaviors is really courage. Without the courage to stick to the essential purpose, values, and principles, a leader cannot persevere and move himself, herself, or others toward the realization of the vision. Somehow, leaders need to find the courage and invite the courage of others in staying true to the guiding purpose.

Purpose is to leadership as feathers are to a soaring bird. Without it, there is no possibility of staying aloft. Purpose flows from the depths of the leader's intention to realize the vision and keep a clear focus on what really matters. Knowing what really matters and keeping the attention of all involved on what matters is the essence of the practice of focusing on purpose. It is one of the foundations of great leadership.

PRACTICE 3

Creating Followership

**CREATE
FOLLOWERS**

Effectively nurturing

followers creates

buy-in for the vision

and unleashes the

enthusiasm to get

the job done.

A senior executive proudly stood at a lectern. His bank had just acquired a Florida bank with a strong franchise. He surveyed the 200 faces of the senior ranks of the acquired bank. He began by telling them what a great bank they now worked for and that his bank had a core set of values and principles that set a premium on the value of its people. They were now part of that system and would be supported and evaluated on merit. He then began to talk about the larger banking strategy, when he noticed a young man sneak in a back door and make his way down to the one empty seat. He stopped his talk and made an example of the young man's coming late, saying, "At this bank we expect people to show up for meetings on time and to keep their agreements. Take that to heart." He then resumed his talk, believing he had set a leadership example and made an important point regarding discipline and respect for authority.

What he did not know, but many in the room were aware of, was the fact that the young vice president had just rushed from the hospital where he had helped his wife deliver their first child after 28 hours of labor. He had made a

81

great effort to attend and then had been publicly flogged! More was lost by the hubris and lack of interpersonal skills of the ranking executive than he could ever realize. More than a dozen talented and gifted senior executives later shared with me that, at that moment, they decided they wanted no part of this "great" bank. They subsequently left, but many who remained had little desire to follow this high-ranking leader, no matter how many "stripes" he had.

Invitation is, in the long run, infinitely more powerful than coercion.

Leadership does not exist without followers. To be a leader means generating followership. The degree of leadership effectiveness is dependent on three things working together:

1. The enthusiasm and dedication of the followers.
2. Good plans and intelligent strategy that are supported and acted on by followers.
3. The caliber and quality of the people you draw together.

What creates followership? Faith in the leader and his or her vision is essential. People tend to follow those they respect, those they believe will enable them to achieve their own personal goals, those they trust, and those who will meet their needs. People also follow someone who touches their dreams, aspirations, and hopes—appealing to their longing or inner genius. The most successful leaders do this through a synergistic interplay of the four chambers forming the very heart of leadership: integrity (of purpose/focus and basic trustworthiness), passion (commitment and enthusiasm for the vision and purpose), competence (technical expertise and interpersonal), and intimacy (with the work, the customer, self, and others).

The function that flows from the practice of engendering followership is that of getting buy-in to the vision and direction desired. The emotive energy which flows from that is enthusiasm. Thus, the leader who realizes the importance of focusing on followers is really concerned with getting their buy-in and liberating their enthusiasm, generating a wave of energy and active participation in making things happen. This is not, however, dependent upon charisma.

Charisma is overrated as a requirement for effective leadership. There are many effective, yet non-charismatic leaders. What is more important than charisma is trustworthiness; moreover, people must have faith in the leader and the direction he or she sets for the organization.

Anyone who aspires to leadership will engender followership if they pay attention to the heart of leadership: competence, passion, integrity, and intimacy. By working on the tone of the heart, they create a level of trust as palpable as a force field. And trust, as Covey so eloquently puts it, is like water to a plant. Without water, a plant withers and dies. Without trust, followership withers and disappears.

Integrity simply reminds us that if leadership is not based on a solid ethical core, abuse of power is just around the corner. Individuals, such as Richard Nixon and Ivan Boesky, and organizations, such as E. F. Hutton and the Manville corporation, attest to the potential for abuse by leaders and to the ultimate day of reckoning they must face. Those wishing to be effective over the long term must be trustworthy.

However, integrity is not enough. There must be a capacity for openness to intimacy—intimacy which empowers and generates powerful relationships. In any enterprise, the ability to understand the customer and then to build and maintain a strong relationship is critical. The willingness to engage co-workers and employees in an ongoing relationship of increasing openness, candor, and substance-based communication is essential to long-term success. Finally, there must be an intimacy with self, understanding your own deepest aspirations, taking an inventory of strengths and weaknesses, increasing your level of self-awareness, and being open to learning more. Without intimacy in all of these forms, you are impaired in your capacity to engender on-going followership.

Competence is also required if you are to create lasting followership, formulate a vision or sense of purpose, determine the substance of the work, or engage those who know the technical essentials, as well as cultivate interpersonal and team skills. (Most middle- and senior-level managers who fail do not fail because of technical shortcomings; they fail because of weakness in the teamwork and/or interactional arenas.)

Competence also means that there must exist the proper cognitive and strategic elements or the enterprise can be in great jeopardy. Consider General George Armstrong Custer: plenty of charisma but not a very solid strategic plan! Competency also means the capacity and strength to, as Max DePree puts it, "Abandon yourself to the strengths (and talents) of others." Tom Brooks says:

> What I consider to be one of the most important characteristics and one of the most important capabilities of a leader is what I refer to as "The Brooks Leadership Technique." It works every time. The Brooks secret of successful leadership is to find the best people, surround yourself with them, let them have their head under general guidance, and share the credit for all the good things they do. It works every time.

Now, the key to this is that you take blame for the bad things they do. But if you're picking the right people—that's the key. There's no secret to the technique. The only secret is your ability to pick the right people. It works with the leader who is self-assured and feels unthreatened enough by them that he's willing to give them their head and give them credit. You come to recognize, after years in leadership positions, that even if you are standing up there and think you're getting the credit for everything your people are doing, people aren't fooled for long. And they come very quickly to realize, "Hey, that guy Brooks isn't so smart. He's got a lot of smart people working for him."

Likewise, the converse side of that: If you give your people the credit and everybody says, "Oh yeah, he's got a lot of smart people working for him," and, "Yeah, these smart people really do good things," sooner or later those people are going to say, "Yeah, that guy Brooks isn't so dumb after all. Look how effective he is, and how clever a strategy that is." So really, it's not threatening to you to surround yourself with smart people. It's threatening to you not to do that. The dumbest thing you can do is to surround yourself with people of lesser intellect than you, feeling that they don't threaten you somehow. Because you don't realize how much they really do threaten you. Everybody then identifies with that, with their collective IQ, their collective capability, as being your organization's and, therefore, your capability.

Finally, without passion there cannot be the enthusiasm, the drive, the heart to fully generate followership. Passion is the result of full commitment, intellectually and emotionally, to creating something and seeing it unfold in reality. As Emerson once said, "Nothing great was ever achieved without enthusiasm!" Passion alone calls out to the hearts of others, infecting them with a wild and wonderful fever that draws them deeply into the fires of co-creation.

Followership is the basis for all leadership, but that followership is fickle and must be maintained. Only by working on developing the tone of each chamber forming the heart of leadership can a leader ensure that he or she will continue to engage the willingness and desire of others to follow them.

The principle is obvious. Without followers, you are not a leader. Therefore, there are four simple questions which must be answered:

1. Are people following you?
2. How enthusiastically are your followers following?
3. How solid and well thought out are your plans?
4. Do you have the right people to implement the plans?

EXERCISE

On a scale of one to 10, how would you rate the degree of followership you engender in those around you—superiors, peers, and subordinates? How committed and energetic are they? How would they rate you as someone they desire to follow or as someone who they respect and are influenced by? What is creating the degree of followership you are experiencing? What inhibits it? What might you do to invite and generate more followership?

The most effective leaders are those who have already predisposed others to follow. When the time comes to initiate an action, they have a motivated group of followers already primed to follow their lead. There is a reservoir of trust and good will which the leader can tap into, an immediate connection with the followers' willingness and even desire to fulfill a request or command. This state of readiness is achieved by following the Chinese maxim of "preparing the soil for the seed."

"Preparing the soil" means that an effort has been made to cultivate relationships by building trust and good will. This is fostered primarily through the practices of understanding, supporting, and demonstrating principled flexibility (developed in later chapters). It requires that the leader or would-be leader understand that cultivating trust is an integral part of everything she or he does and that it is an ongoing, continuous process. The process of preparing the soil ties the vision, the essential mission and purpose of the organization, into central elements, such as critical competencies, essential factors, core values, standards, and goals. Gene Kaczmarski expressed it this way:

To be a true leader there must be people willing to follow. People will follow only if the vision is clear and believable, if they can see how it benefits them, and if it is communicated consistently in all parts of the organization. This builds trust, and a true leader must be trustworthy.

This approach demonstrates an integration and clarity of focus which is found in the best leaders: Jack Welch, Bob Allen, Bill Gates, Andy Grove,

Anita Roddick, Mary Kay Ash, and so on. It generates followership by providing a comprehensive picture of how all the efforts of the organization's leadership are bundled and tied together. It provides a strong sense of coherence and alignment, which is powerful in creating buy-in, commitment, and followership.

If preparing the soil is creating the context for followership, then the seed refers to the request, command, or directive of the person wishing to exert a leadership role. If the seed is to take root, the soil must be fertile and prepared to receive it. If you have not nourished and developed trust and faith in your word and intentions, then your commands and requests are less likely to be readily heeded or intelligently applied.

Preparing the soil, though, is even more subtle than this. If the trust level is properly cultivated, then the people receiving the command, directive, or request are able and willing to challenge the person making it. They will challenge the leader if they perceive that she or he is acting hastily and will focus on helping the leader realize her or his intentions, even if they must attempt to persuade the leader to change the process he or she had envisioned. The intention is to protect the leader from making a mistake and ensure that the proper strategic and tactical issues have been addressed. This is not insubordination; rather it is the highest form of loyalty and commitment. Everyone is engaged in attempting to ensure the success of the leader's initiative and intentions.

Something even more subtle with regard to this practice is often missed. Highly effective leadership requires that the leader have the capacity to follow. This means knowing how to follow the followers! No one is omniscient. The paradox of leadership is that it requires being open to and learning from the followers, realizing that sometimes they will be leading the leader. The more powerful and proactive the followers are, the more powerful and proactive the leader can be.

How are you developing and inviting the proactivity and power of your "followers" and potential followers? How well do you listen to others? How open and accessible are you?

EXERCISE

> If your direct reports could vote for the boss they wanted
> to follow, would it be someone like you? What have you done
> to inspire, to tap their motivations, to align and focus your
> fellow workers during the past month? How successful were
> those efforts? What have you planned for the next month?
> Quarter? Year? How successfully have you been following
> them? How much effort and time have you put into trying to

understand what they have been wanting you to do to help them be more successful?

The capacity to follow is a powerful secret known by the greatest leaders. It has its parallel in the martial arts of Akido and Ninjitsu. It also has a wonderful conceptual and historical base in the 2,000-year-old book by Sun Tzu called *The Art of War.*

> Those who are first on the battlefield and await the opponents are at ease; those who are last on the battlefield and head into battle get worn out. Therefore, good warriors cause others to come to them and do not go to others.

In these martial arts, the attacker is seen as the one at greatest risk. If you, as the defender, can learn to follow the attacker, meshing with the force of the attack, joining it and anticipating it, then you end up in the lead, able from that vantage point to throw, pin, and defeat the other. Here, in order to lead, you must first learn to join.

EXERCISE

A simple way to visualize this is to imagine that you are standing on a street corner. Someone grabs you around the neck from behind and starts pulling you into an alley. What is your first impulse? The natural response is to resist and try to pull away from the direction the attacker is pulling. This response, though, is dangerous since the person grabbing you expects it and is braced for it. Additionally, you are pulling away with your neck being squeezed from the two contradictory movements (you pulling forward and the attacker pulling backward).

Imagine instead that, as you are grabbed by the neck and are being pulled backward, you aggressively cooperate, stepping back swiftly and following the pull of the attacker. What happens? The same thing that happens every day in martial arts training. The person is surprised at the move and taken off balance. By following the direction of the pull, you gain leverage and a momentary loosening of the attacker's grip. This then allows you to take a leadership role and use their momentum and movements to your advantage: throwing them, breaking free, tripping them up, etc. Hence the rule: "When pulled, follow and enter. When pushed, cooperate and turn."

This "following" is not merely physical. There is a wonderful story told by an American martial arts master who had studied the art of Akido in Japan for many years. He had been working on perfecting his abilities in this martial art form for many years, but had never had an opportunity to use them in "real" life. He says he was secretly hoping to have a chance to try them out in an emergency.

One day he was riding the train from Tokyo to an outlying village. His car was only partially full when, at a stop, a giant of a man boarded his car. The man was massive, looking like he could have been a former Sumo wrestler. His appearance was uncharacteristically unshaven, his hair tousled and unkempt, his clothes soiled, and his face swollen and flushed. He carried a bottle in one hand and was obviously intoxicated.

This giant looked sullen and angry and was loud and threatening, moving menacingly towards several people. The martial arts expert thought, "This is my moment of truth," and stood up to challenge and protect. The drunken man saw the movement and bunched his fist, raising the bottle and stepping forward.

Before the American could react, both he and the giant were stopped by a high voice yelling, "Hey!" Both men turned to see an old, fragile-looking man sitting on a seat. The drunk angrily yelled out, "What do you want?" The old man merely smiled and asked, "What are you drinking?" "What's it to you?" the giant answered belligerently. "Only that I was hoping it was saki. I love to have some in the evening." The giant nodded mutely and then replied, "Yes, I have saki." The old man beamed and said, "Come then, sit here beside me. Maybe you will share a little with me. Yes, come and sit here. Rest beside me."

The giant lumbered over to the old man and held out the bottle, sitting as the old man patted the seat beside him and invited him once again to sit. Within 10 minutes the drunk was in tears, bent over his knees as the old man stroked his head and listened to the grief of having lost a wife. The martial arts expert sat quietly down, realizing he had just seen a true Akido master in action.

What transpired here, and how does this relate to following the follower? The old man followed the lead of the drunk. He spoke to the place the man was in, asking about what he was drinking and then joining with the giant in his drinking. He then gently took a different step in inviting the man to sit beside him and to reciprocate the joining behavior. Then he talked and listened, offering the man a chance to follow his lead of friendly behavior and responsiveness. This form of following and joining is at the heart of generating powerful sustained followership.

An example of this from my own consulting experience comes from work we did with the research lab of a high-tech company. We were asked to come in and roll out the initial phases of a total-quality initiative. The organization's own internal quality group and training department had attempted to do so and had been shot down in flames by the senior engineers in research labs. Knowing the importance of engaging others, we designed a comprehensive strategy. The former training had consisted of 300 view graphs and six hours of lecture. This model reinforced the old way of thinking and behaving, even as it tried to lay out a new way of thinking and approaching work.

The first thing we did was cut the 300 view graphs down to 30; we designed a two-hour training time, which had 30 minutes of presentation discussion and an hour and a half of intensive small group work sessions. The model, consistent with total quality management for this training, was the maximization of learning, interaction, and proactive listening. We effectively harnessed the imaginations, creativity, spirit of challenge, and desire to learn of the different engineering groups.

I firmly believe this is where many people fail in their attempts to be more effective in influencing others. The old image of the leader as someone who orders others about or who is always in the lead is a misleading and false image. What is often missed are the subtle steps and actions all great leaders take to ensure that the followers know the leader is really with them. To do this requires understanding, listening, keen observation, and insight about following the cues and needs of the followers. This then, as in the example above, creates an energetic dynamic between the leader and the led, a reciprocity of following.

It is a bit akin to priming the pump: In order to get water, you must first give water. Following the hoped-for follower is the priming that creates an even larger upwelling of enthusiastic followership. However, if this is used only as a technique and does not come from a desire to really understand and team with the other, then it will ultimately backfire. In this case, you are not really following; you are only trying to trick the other into believing you are interested.

Human behavior is exceedingly complex, and yet it is also sometimes obviously simple. If someone treats us with contempt, mistrust, and suspicion, we are likely to treat them the same. If someone treats us with respect, as if we were trustworthy, we tend to treat them the same way. "What ye sow is what ye shall reap." This is, however, yet another elephant (so obvious it gets overlooked) in American management. It is not an exaggeration to say that we have built into the very structure of our organizations and management systems the sense of mistrusting and being suspicious of our fellow workers!

Consider the case of the Japanese and American executives collabo-
rating on the design and setup of the Toyota/GM venture in Smyrna,
Tennessee. The plant designs did not have time clocks built into them,
and the American executives wanted to know where the time clocks
would be placed. The Japanese insisted that there would be no time
clocks. This went round and round until the Japanese spelled it out:
"Time clocks show we do not trust the workers. We trust the workers.
No time clocks." Smyrna has a system where the work teams are more
self-directed and dependent upon each member's contribution.
Someone coming late or not acting in good faith must deal with their
team members, for it is they who are being let down by that behavior.
The operation there is highly efficient and operates better without time
clocks than many other plants with time clocks.

To create followership thus requires the capacity to treat others as if
they matter and as if they are valuable contributors to the final success
of the enterprise and organization. If they are not important contributors
and are not adding value—that is, if they aren't really needed—then
they should not be on the team. Real leaders understand and recognize
the value added by others, communicating verbally and non-verbally
that they respect, trust, and value them. This is the highest form of common sense and good judgment. Even the act of attributing these values
to someone else tends to generate those behaviors.

This is known as the Rosenthal or Pygmalion effect. Rosenthal, a
psychologist, did a study in which the scores of students were altered
and then given to teachers as the students began a new school year. The
"high aptitude" and "low aptitude" scores were imaginary. Yet, at the
end of the study, the students had lived up to, and down to, the set expectations of the teachers. The teachers' expectations, based on the imaginary scores, influenced and shaped the performance of the students.

This points to a powerful shaping principle with regard to human
behavior. What we expect and believe we will get from others is what
we tend to get. They begin to resemble our belief systems about them!
What implications do you begin to see around your behavior?

EXERCISE

Take a moment and write down your basic assumptions
about human nature. What do you believe really motivates the
people around you? What levels of trust or mistrust do you communicate to others? Do you honestly believe people are trying
to do their best? What messages are you sending out about the
value, worth, and importance of others and the work they do?

Some powerful questions to ask yourself daily:

- Have I recognized the people around me for their contributions?
- Where do we stand in the areas of confidence, commitment, competence?
- Do I have confidence in my team? The people around me? If not, why not? What do I want to do about that?
- Do they have confidence in me? If not, why not? What do I want to do about that?
- What have I done today to increase the sense of control and responsibility of my team? The people around me?
- How have I demonstrated my trust in the intelligence, talents, and desires of those around me to do a great job?
- What have I done to draw forth the ideas of those around me? Are they asking for ideas and suggestions from others?
- How have I demonstrated my passion and invited theirs?
- What have I done today to focus them on the vision and mission?
- Where are we with regard to our standards? Values? Objectives and goals? Can they spell out where we are?
- Am I making the best use of my time and energy? Am I making the best use of their time and energy?
- How am I enabling them to achieve outstanding results?

Just the act of asking a few of these questions of yourself on a daily basis will begin to transform your way of thinking and acting. This, in turn, will begin to increase your leadership impact, generating more power and available energy.

Focusing on the practice of generating followership fundamentally complements and builds upon the practices of:

1. Generating the vision, and
2. Focusing on purpose.

These, in turn, develop the heart muscle, especially in the chambers of competence, integrity, and passion. It is essential to recognize the need to have followers, and this then prepares the way to work with them on Practice #4: setting standards and eliciting goals.

The practices that follow are really the applied ways of thinking and acting that serve to build the trust, faith, and enthusiasm of others around following and leading. By paying attention to preparing the soil and to the ways in which the seeds get sown, you can get a tremendous upsurge in the power and effectiveness of your capacity to influence and lead.

PRACTICE 4

Setting Standards
While Eliciting Goals

**STANDARDS
AND
GOALS**

Eliciting standards

and goals gives

followers a sense of

ownership and the

feeling of being

involved and

valued.

The chief executive officer of a hospital corporation was exasperated. He had tried for months
to get more movement and action on the broad
strategic objectives he had laid out to his senior
team. The board of directors was hot on his tail,
and the stock price had dropped over the past six
months. He held meeting after meeting with little noticeable change.

I was brought in to help him figure out how to
gain leverage in implementing the strategic plan.
The first meeting I attended went as I expected
based on the interviews I had conducted one on one
with many of his team. The meeting was his meeting and one in which he reiterated the strategy and
castigated the people in the room for lack of performance. The people listening then began to point out
how much they had done, with view graphs and
example after example of the projects they were
working on. The CEO then asked why such little
progress had been made. They had many excuses,
but overwork and too many priorities were the most
common themes. They then pledged to try harder,
and he told them that he had faith they would succeed. After three hours, the meeting broke up, and
the CEO and I remained in the board room.

93

He turned to me and said he thought he was finally getting through to them and that he hoped they had turned the corner. He asked my opinion. "I am sorry to tell you that, in my opinion, the meeting was an exercise in futility, and nothing will be different," I said. He sincerely wanted to know why I felt that way and what he could do.

"The meeting was full of holes, excuses, justifications, pontification, rationalization, and global thinking. Not once did I hear you ask them for their specific goals to begin to drive their different areas to the realization of the strategic objectives. You never asked for their specific deliverables, timelines, and accountability. They are busy pursuing tasks, but haven't prioritized those tasks by setting a series of goals and milestones by which to move the whole strategy forward. The next meeting will be a repeat of this one unless you sit down with each of them and help them to create their milestones and goals with timelines. Then ask each of them to come to your next staff meeting with a published report of what they are doing, have done, will be doing, and by when. Then let them know they will stand before their peers and be accountable. Do it with a caring tone, but be relentless about the results." He covered his eyes with both hands, let out a heartfelt sigh, and said, "How could I have missed it? You're right. I've been trying to do it through pep talks, lectures, and even haranguing. I failed to make this *their* strategic plan instead of the board's and mine!"

A leader must help set the standards for excellence by which the people working with her or him will work to fulfill the purpose. Then he or she must work at outlining the objectives that will help to provide a focus for individuals, teams, departments, divisions, and the entire organization. What gives this practice real muscle and impetus is the custom of actively eliciting specific goals from all engaged in ensuring the success of the enterprise. This helps everyone involved to own the purpose and to see how their daily tasks and efforts line up in creating something much larger and greater than what they are individually engaged in.

The critical function which flows out of this practice is creating a sense of ownership. The emotional support that goes with this sense of ownership is a feeling of being involved and valued. This practice thereby enhances and adds value to the leadership system by generating the energy around focusing on, taking responsibility for, and defining the milestones and objectives for realizing the purpose.

In most organizations, it is assumed that managers and supervisors follow this practice of setting standards and eliciting goals. That is, it is often taken for granted that managers are actively involving the workforce in running the company at higher and higher levels of performance.

This is a dangerous assumption to make. Even more dangerous (yet common) is the assumption that everyone knows what the mission is.

Gene Kaczmarski, president of Medaphis Physician Services, says:

> Identification of a business's core competencies is essential to creating strategies and tactics that support the vision. These competencies are the building blocks for departmental and functional subvisions. These subvisions can then be supported with defined strategies, tactics, and measurable achievements. It's the glue that binds the subvisions within the overall company vision.

That's the essence of what Jack Welch is getting at when he talks about his five essential factors. All 12 of GE's global businesses understand five essential factors. Everybody understands them. This makes the process of understanding, communicating, and comparing within and across diverse industries and each global business much simpler. It provides a cogent focus and standard for comparison.

Anita Roddick, the guiding force behind the phenomenal growth and success of the Body Shop, ensures that all employees of the more than 500 retail stores around the world are focused and clear on the standards and essential objectives of the company. She actively elicits their input, ideas, and goals in helping set the long-term and short-term objectives for the organization, as well as each individual retail outlet.

At Herman Miller, a *Fortune* 500 company, employee ownership and empowerment have been the norm for over 40 years. 3M is known for its creativity and active engagement of personal efficacy.

The best companies are providing better leadership through an active engagement and involvement of the hearts and the minds of the people who make up the organizations and who do the day-to-day work.

These are still, unfortunately, the exceptions. Not enough leaders clearly define the key factors or performance and quality standards; even fewer engage the intelligence and interest of their fellow workers. Fewer still actively elicit specific goals from their followers. Why should they, when the prevailing paradigm is still that of command and control, where management knows what is best and has already set the objectives and goals? In the mind-set of the past 30 years, the only task for the followers has been to steadfastly, and without question, pursue the completion or execution of senior management's plans, or of their supervisor's agenda, meeting the key objectives and outlined goals as they are laid down. Alignment and obedience, not empowerment, have been the prevailing paradigm. In an organization requiring flexibility and the capacity to adapt and change quickly, with an emphasis on superior quality, speed, and outstanding customer service, this old way of leading and managing simply doesn't work.

Why not? The reason lies in the fact that if people do not help generate the objectives and goals around the execution of their tasks, they do not really own them and cannot really bring their creativity and passion to bear. The objectives and goals feel imposed and forced upon them, and there is a subtle, yet strong resistance. Also, since they were not consulted and involved, there is no way of telling if the objectives and goals are wise or even really implementable. We have even coined sayings which capture the folly of the command and control mentality: "We never have the time to do it right, only the time to go back and do it over!" "We don't pay you to think; just do what you're told." "That's not the way we do things here." "When I want your opinion, I'll tell you what it is." "Not invented here." And perhaps the greatest folly, "If it ain't broke, don't fix it!"

The mentality that generates those sayings is pervasive and permeates all levels of American commerce, as well as all levels of government. The essence of "If it ain't broke . . . " implies that if something has been working well, we should not question it or seek to improve upon it. This flies in the face of the quality revolution sweeping the world, and it promotes a dangerous complacency. It assumes that what worked in the past will continue to work in the future and that what is working now should be left alone while we focus upon what is "broken." This may sound like sense, but at the profound level of knowledge that Deming speaks of, it is the greatest nonsense, and rather dangerous nonsense at that. In addition, it is soul deadening. That mentality disinvites participation and demotivates the employees from thinking, innovating, and putting their hearts into making the enterprise perform at higher levels of functioning.

The proper questions are: If it ain't broke, how can we make it better? If it ain't broke, when is it likely to break down? If it ain't broke now, is there an even better way? If it ain't broke now, given the rapidly changing world around us, how long will it serve? It may not be broke, but should it even be around?

These kinds of questions can help a country, a state, a company, a division, a department, or a supervisor lead others in achieving greatness. It is essential to note, however, that the answers to those questions come from the people actually doing the job! They come from the machinist, the assembly-line worker, the clerk, the secretary, the programmer—anyone whose job is on the firing line. The questions need to be asked by the leader, whether that leader be part of the hierarchy or a momentarily emergent leader. It is the act of asking the right questions of the people who must do the work that most often determines the successfulness of true leadership.

Steve Bachand, CEO of Canadian Tire, tells the following story to illustrate:

> It all starts with asking the right questions of ourselves, employees, and each other. For example, "What does being No. 1 with the customer mean for me, and what are the elements of being No. 1?" Just to give you a simple example, it can mean having on the one hand the right price, on the other hand having the right assortment. But it also goes further, all the way to being able to check out quickly. It goes to the whole service aspect; I mean, it's thinking like this: We know the customers don't like to make out their checks if it's a delay for them and for others at the cash register. That is not being No. 1 with regard to service. So I'm taking it down to the next logical level and saying, "Okay, how can we make it easier for customers to fill out their checks so they're not delayed?"
>
> It could be all the way from making it easier to write a check, to looking in the financial area: I want crisp, clear, hard-hitting, summarizing kind of information so management is not detracted from being off the sales floor and out of contact with the customer. I want management to manage their business so that part of their time is shortened, and they can spend most of their time dealing with customers. It's these kinds of examples that help the various functional areas of our company plug into the focus on being No. 1 with our customers.

God save us from those command-and-control leaders who believe the success of the enterprise relies solely upon their intelligence and experience. These "leaders" never understand the necessity of tapping into and engaging the vast latent intelligence and experience of those around them. This is a tragic mistake. In the complex, increasingly interdependent world around us, we need the energy, enthusiasm, and applied intelligence of everyone involved in our enterprise. The old saying becomes truer with each passing day: "None of us is as smart as all of us."

Yet, ego, fear, and impatience still rule the day in most of our political and commercial activities. As Rosabeth Moss Kanter puts it, we are ruled either by the "cowboy" archetype or by the "corprocrat" roles we have learned all too well.

The cowboy is the "ready, fire, aim" rugged individualist who plays to his or her own tune and wears the royal purple robes of the fiercely independent aristocrat. Capable of working alone and with little support, this kind of leader is strong, decisive, and able to confront the difficult and painful with courage. Yet he or she is seldom really listening to the ideas of others, never fully joining any team. These leaders stand aloof, invulnerable, distant, and cool. They are often some of the brightest and best our business schools produce, yet they fail more often than most would guess. Their failures are covered by the layers of management and by the slow wheels of complex, interdependent, dynamic systems (corporations, political systems, and the like).

Complex systems do not often reveal the folly of individual actions and decisions until considerable time has elapsed, often several months or even a few years. (Yet we can see these people's failures manifest themselves in the failures of their organizations: Drexel-Burnham-Lambert, Eastern and Texas Air, Manville, Westinghouse, etc.) Therefore, it is difficult for even the brightest and best to learn from their mistakes, or even for the organization to know they made any mistakes. For a wonderful exposition on this theme, please read Chris Argyris's article, "Why Smart People Fail." (Also see Peter Senge's book *The Fifth Discipline* for a wonderful discussion of how systems function and interfere with learning due to time distortion and time lag.)

The cowboy or cowgirl leader does not ever really harness the true power and intelligence of the complex systems of relationships and the diversity of people around them. They fail at what Stephen Covey calls "the task of interdependence." They are indeed the leader on the white horse, but a lot of people need to clean up after the horse!

All too often, a lot of horse manure gets taken as wise leadership, for the moment. The "great leader" is too often a loner rising and falling by his or her own strengths and weaknesses, but never really leveraging all of the different strengths of the diverse people surrounding her or him. He or she lacks the courage to depend upon others and blend talents and abilities.

The corprocrat, on the other hand, is great at joining teams and also great at subordinating his or her ego to the task. The problem is one of being too dependent and too narrowly focused. He or she remembers the Japanese proverb about what happens to the grain of wheat that stands out taller than the rest: It gets cut down! Thus the corprocrat is content to simply stay focused upon the task at hand and is really happiest when surrounded by others of like mind. There is little confrontation, little conflict, less creativity, and almost no long-term perspective. The searing issue here is the need for courage—the courage to stand out, to stand up, and to challenge, not as the cowboy might, but to challenge as an integral and caring member of the team. This kind of person needs to learn the hard and challenging balancing act of interdependence, remembering how to blend in with the team and with others while also learning how to stand apart and challenge the enclosed community, leaning upon its strengths while flexing his or her own unique powers and abilities.

The cowboy's task of courage is to learn how to listen, to ask hard questions of himself, as well as of others, and to really hear what others think and what they have to say. Then the task is to find ways of joining and validating the team or the community, practicing the immensely more difficult task of interdependence. Holding to a unique perspective, confronting, using his or her strengths, and also blending them with the strengths, abilities, and perspectives of others is the real work of transformative leadership.

Actively seeking the input of others invites discussion and allows for healthy dissent. Leaders must have the courage to bring to the surface points of conflict, misunderstanding, and confusion. This allows leadership to get an accurate read on the levels of understanding, commitment, and buy-in to the vision and purpose. There also has to be the courage to "abandon oneself to the wild ideas and strengths of others," as Max DePree, the retired chairman of Herman Miller, puts it.

The process of conferring with others takes time, but it pays off handsomely down the line. It also provides the leadership system with data about how well each organizational level understands the direction and focus of the company. This data is priceless. Moreover, the act of involving others in defining and setting goals creates buy-in and ownership almost as a by-product. People thus feel involved and that their opinions and contributions are valued. It is only here that you begin to unleash the tremendous power of the human system within your enterprise.

One company we worked with, a manufacturer of specialty equipment, had grown from 5 million to 50 million in sales within a few years. The CEO, a man of vision and charisma, had led the company during this time. He had been an expert at MBWA (management by walking about), and his active efforts to involve employees had been critical to the company's success.

However, with the increased growth and greater demands on his time, he had stopped his weekly visits to the different departments. He had assumed that his direct reports would pick up the slack and continue his behavior of eliciting goals and ideas from employees throughout the organization.

He could not have been more wrong.

Within a year, there were major conflicts raging within his organization. In large measure, this was a direct result of the rapid proliferation of goals and objectives that were in conflict with the vision and purposes of the organization.

This leader had failed to create appropriate systems—systems staffed with empowered individuals—that would ensure that goals were integrated into a coherent whole. He had also failed to lead his direct reports and to coach them effectively in how to do what he had done: involving and engaging people in setting and reaching mutual goals.

Gene Kaczmarski lays out the five elements he preaches and coaches throughout his organization and from which the standards and goals are derived:

> The first is operations. It's the foundational element and consists of all the core skills and processes necessary to provide comprehensive business management services to our clients.
>
> The second is client service and lays the framework for our commitment to high quality client service. It's a focus and dedication to service versus the services which we provide. It's a commitment to building long-term partnerships with our clients.
>
> The third component is people management. We want the people of Medaphis to be honest, ethical, and professional in all dealings. We want to help people grow, and we want to make Medaphis a place to work where, if you had a friend and there was an opening, you would be a strong recruiter. Also, life's too short to tolerate those who manage by intimidation and fear.
>
> The fourth element is technology. The company cannot progress and become more productive without technology. When you say "productivity," people generally think of working harder. But the fact is, I believe our people already work hard. I want them to work smarter. And the only way they're going to work smarter is through technology.
>
> The fifth competency is sales, developing new clients. It's the lifeblood of every business. It's the acid test—can we convince prospects to become clients?

Six Steps to Generating Standards and Goals

How do you effectively set standards and then elicit the goals and objectives of the people entrusted with your customers, your primary work processes, and ultimately your success? It boils down to six basic steps:

1. Take the time to generate your highest aspirations around service, product, customer perceptions and satisfaction, worker results, organizational outcomes, and quality standards. Do this by engaging in a process of discussing and unveiling the thoughts and aspirations of four key groups: customers, employees, suppliers, and stakeholders.

- Survey and interview your customers through qualitative and quantitative methods.
- Work and analyze the data using cross-functional teams to understand what it means for overall functioning and work processes.
- In teams, ask the employees about their reactions to the data from customers. Ensure that they understand what it means to them if the customers are not really delighted doing business with the company.
- Ask for their ideas, suggestions, and aspirations for really meeting the customers' expectations.
- Survey other stakeholders as to their expectations and hopes around company performance. Work this data into your planning and communication with employees.
- Establish and/or renegotiate overall standards of performance.
- Make the process of surveying, communicating, and planning around the data an ongoing, continuous process.

2. Finalize the standards and establish overall group performance norms in writing and in face-to-face, small-group and large-group sessions. It is critical that the rationale and necessity for these standards become clearly articulated and understood by the vast majority of people who are working within your enterprise and who are touched by that enterprise.

3. Establish the strategies and objective milestones around driving your vision, manifesting your purpose, and being faithful to your standards.

4. Sit down and review the vision, purpose, and standards with your people. Then outline the strategic path and objective milestones established.

5. Ask what they then see as their basic goals, and jointly develop, flesh out, and outline those goals. Ask them to demonstrate how these goals mesh with and empower the data shared in step four.

6. Set up a process for reviewing goal attainment with them, as well as a means of revising goals as changing conditions and plans dictate. Make this a flexible, open, and communication-rich process.

Engaging Others

Goals that are imposed are never really owned by those upon whom they are imposed. Only when the people charged with doing a particular job are actively engaged in creating and establishing their own goals do they come to really invest in those goals. This is a psychological fact, yet one that is ignored by many. If we are to establish the buy-in and full engagement of others, we must find a way to have them take a hand in setting the targets and assuming responsibility for hitting them.

How do we engage people in setting goals? How do we begin to liberate the full potential of those charged with the job done? The answer is a difficult one for any of us stuck in the command-and-control or cowboy patterns of thinking and working. The answer for any of us requires great courage, but a different form of courage than those in the two patterns above.

Means for Engaging Others

- Let them know you need them.
- Ask for their help.
- Tell them the truth about the state of business, the industry, the economy, the competition, the customers, etc.
- Tell them they can help make a difference by staying on top or getting back on track, or simply surviving, or becoming a greater success.
- Tell them just how important they are and can be.
- Ask tough, focused questions about what they think can be improved in work processes, service responses, customer relationships, team interactions, leadership performance, etc.
- Really listen to the answers to the questions asked.
- Discuss the standards; ask for their understanding of the significance of those standards. Tie it all into what your customers have to say and what they are looking for. Get them to meet with customers if possible. Demonstrate how their performance relates to the success of the enterprise.
- Revisit the vision, purpose, and strategic path. Ask them how the standards fit into that framework and serve to amplify it.
- Ask them what they think their work and performance goals need to be if the enterprise is to be successful. Ask them what they feel they would need to achieve and accomplish in order to feel really good about their contribution and efforts over a specific period of time (the next six months or the next year, for example).
- Put those goals and aspirations in writing, and post them in plain view.
- Frequently review and examine together the progress toward their goal and aspiration realization.
- Demonstrate appreciation as progress is made. Coach and counsel or redirect when progress is problematic.
- Eliminate members who consistently are off track.

It is only through the active concern of leadership that clear standards emerge and continue to guide overall performance. It is only through continuous focus that the concern and intent of leadership is felt and commitment comes to life. However, if standards are not then supported by clear goals—goals that are co-created with those charged with doing the work—then the standards fail and the enterprise falters. Powerful leadership crafts standards in dialogue with customers, suppliers, employees, and stakeholders. It also generates mutual goals by engaging the people driving the day-to-day tasks and work flow. This sets the stage for achieving outstanding results while building strong and effective relationships.

> *"The new equation*
> *in the quality age*
> *is that empathy*
> *equals power."*
> —Martin Groder

PRACTICE 5

Reading and Understanding Others

Understanding

helps us know

how to touch the

aspirations of others,

creating empathy

and stronger

relationships.

A powerful executive sat in his car, hesitant about entering the building before him. He was tired and anxious. His mind was full of business deals and work to be done. The recent failure of his marriage had brought a sense of brooding depression that even the medication his doctor prescribed hadn't eliminated, only softened into an angry melancholy. The executive sighed, remembering his promise to stop by and see what he could do to help the foundation get itself organized from a business perspective.

The executive walked up the steps and entered a large room. He saw children laughing, talking, and, in one corner, singing. Many had no hair. The chemotherapy used to treat their cancers had caused it to fall out. The executive felt a sense of irritation covering an underlying fear. "What have I gotten myself into? This is no place for me!" He stood there for a while, when suddenly he felt a tug on his sleeve. He looked down and saw a young girl. She was bald, gaunt, and walked with an IV bottle attached to a pole on wheels that she leaned on. He stared at her dumfounded. Then she said, with a look of great concern, "Mister, you look terrible. Come with

105

me, and we'll take care of you." The weight of her words and the tone of caring she expressed caused him to burst into tears. He let her lead him to a chair, and she proceeded to bring other children over, who taught him songs and told him jokes. He left, many hours later, transformed and free of his depression. He changed his life.

The little girl had taken a leadership role in seeing through the three-piece suit, the healthy, tan body, the grown-up veneer, and the aura of success the executive projected. She saw with great clarity and empathy the lost and hurting child inside the man. She spoke with compassion and direct gentleness. He followed her lead and opened his heart. Nothing was the same for him ever again, and his life became one of inner peace and joy.

A leader knows how to read people—is always seeking to understand others with regard to their desires, dreams, strengths, and internal motivators, and is always seeking a more effective way of reaching out to them. The practice of actively reading and decoding what is going on in the hearts and minds of others is the driving force behind maintaining and enhancing relationships, thereby increasing leadership effectiveness.

The practice of working to understand others has the primary function of increasing the precision with which we engage others, and the emotional flow that goes with this function is that of empathy. Empathy equates to power, since it provides insight into the thinking and behavior of those around us. It enables us to relate to others more effectively and informs our decision-making and problem-solving processes. Without empathy and the desire to understand others, we are flying blind. This practice develops the chamber of the heart called "intimacy."

There are a number of tools and techniques we can utilize to help us understand what makes others tick. However, the real power is to be found not in a set of techniques; it is to be found in developing the capacity for empathy. Empathy is the ability to feel what another is feeling and to place ourselves in their shoes. It comes from the heart, and it is cultivated by paying attention to our own heart through the development of self-awareness.

Self-awareness is critical, since the ability to learn from others and relationships can make or break a leader. As Larry Bossidy, CEO of Allied Signal, puts it, "At the end of the day, bet on people, not strategy." Lacking self-awareness, the would-be leader finds himself or herself flying blind. Lacking self-awareness, it is nearly impossible to really see and understand anyone else, no matter how hard we try. The secret to really being able to read and decipher the meaning behind the actions and behaviors of others is to be found in understanding our own hearts. This is personal power, and personal power forms the basis for all real, lasting power. As the ancient proverb says, "Master yourself and you can master anything."

What happens to would-be leaders who have little insight into their own motivations, strengths, weaknesses, and patterns? They tend to be run by unconscious, pre-programmed ways of responding. Their habits, preferences, unchecked assumptions, and beliefs have far too much dominion over their decisions and actions. This means that they are often running on automatic pilot, letting prior programming determine the course of their actions and reactions. This works fine only under two conditions:

1. There aren't any negative, destructive, or misaligned old "tapes" (beliefs, values, assumptions, prejudices, expectations, defensive patterns, and so on) that play out in their conscious minds.
2. The conditions, environment, business setting, customers, industry, competitors, and people around you are relatively static and remain similar year after year.

In my work with families, as well as consulting, coaching, and training over 10,000 executives ranging from *Fortune* 500 companies to small entrepreneurial shops (covering the spectrum of U.S. industry), I have two conclusions with regard to the points above.

First, I have met only a few people who did not have some sort of negative programming playing out consciously or, apparently, unconsciously in their personal or professional lives. And this handful of people had all engaged in a process of deep self-exploration and had come to have a compassionate sense of humor with regard to themselves and their foibles. They still had the vestiges of old, destructive patterns, but they were quick to self-correct and sensitively open to feedback.

Second, the world around us is not static, and the business environment is even more challenging and rapidly paced. Remember the great charging elephant of accelerating change! Those who think the future will be just a rehash of what has gone before are seriously out of touch with the obvious.

This means that the leaders who are counting on automatic and unconscious programming to carry them through are setting themselves (as well as their organizations and their people) up for a big fall. Remember, while it is true that you are your greatest asset, it is equally true that you are your greatest liability. Still, it is frightening to see how many of us have not really examined our lives and worked to map out our fundamental strengths and weaknesses, beliefs and assumptions, values and expectations, self-evaluations and defensive patterns. This leaves us vulnerable and heavily under the influence of psychological and emotional forces of which we have little understanding or appreciation. This makes us less conscious, less effective, and more pre-determined in our dealings with customers, fellow employees, business situations, and even with our families. This is a precarious place to be when we are in a world characterized by rapid change, globalization, universal access and proximity, and collapsing time frames.

The need for self-awareness has never been greater. With the increasing diversity of the workplace, customers, and global competition, we must have the personal mastery to know ourselves and be more conscious in our dealings with others. The more we know the workings of our own heart and our deepest values and have mapped out the less helpful or even destructive patterns in our personalities, the more self-empowered we can be. We can also be more conscious and alert in our dealings with others. This heightens our capacity to accurately assess the situation and people around us without distorting them through the filters of unconscious, automatic ways of thinking and feeling. This gives us power through clear insight into how we are put together, and from that foundation we can more clearly see how others are put together—what drives and motivates them.

The great Chinese sage, Chung Tzu, was sitting by a river watching the clouds and water. The courtiers of the emperor of China approached him, saying, "Great news, honorable one. The emperor has asked us to come and invite you to be his new grand vizier." The wise old man continued to watch the river flowing by, giving no indication that he had heard what they had said. "Perhaps he is losing his hearing," one whispered. Chung Tzu raised his head and smiled at them. "No, my hearing is fine. I was just thinking about the turtle the king has in his garden. Is it still there?" The courtiers were a bit confused with this line of questioning, but one had the wit to respond, "You mean the stuffed turtle with the emeralds and rubies embedded in its shell?" The sage smiled a gentle smile. "Yes, that very one. Tell me, do you think the turtle is happier where it is now with all of its rubies and emeralds or when it was in the mud and swimming in this river?" The men were amazed. "But what has this to do with your answer to the emperor's invitation?" they said. Smiling in a disarming way, the philosopher replied, "Tell the emperor that this old turtle prefers the freedom of the mud and the river to the restrictions and intrigue of the palace. Here I live, while there I would be but a stuffed, jeweled shell."

This was a man who had personal power! He knew what he wanted and who he was. This kind of self-awareness and personal mastery is the source of all lasting leadership power. It is the heart and soul of the man or woman engaged in a lifelong quest to be whole, to be real, to be the difference.

This search for self-understanding, knowing what is most important, what really matters, can't be underestimated in its power to transform our lives and to help us really understand where others are coming from.

EXERCISE

Take some time right now and write down your answers to the following questions. Pay attention to the ones you have difficulty answering. Taking the time to do this will repay you handsomely.

- Who are you, really?
- Where are you going?
- What is it you wish to accomplish?
- What do you most desire? Why? What will that do for you?
- What do you really desire?
- What is most important to you?
- What are your driving values?
- What are the key roles you play in your life?
- How are you living your values and playing out your roles?
- Do you feel challenged, excited, and thankful?
- What would a life well-lived mean to you?
- Where in your life do you most need courage? When will you act on that?

Working on increasing our level of self-knowledge and personal mastery prepares us for exceptional, even transformational leadership—taking us beyond normal limitations while drawing others into a similar mode of breakthrough consciousness. This willingness to engage in looking deeply at what motivates and drives us is the foundation for really coming to understand others. To successfully read others we must first learn how to read the hieroglyphics of our own heart. This consists of daily acts of courage and consistent practice.

When we really know ourselves and from that begin to read and understand others, we then have the proper focus and knowledge necessary to create alignment and effective influence. This means that we are now ready to act upon our understanding. To do this well requires that we gain perspective and check our assumptions.

Assumption Check

What allowances do you make for the diversity of talents, needs, desires, and orientations existing within the diverse group of people who work with you? What distinctions do you make about the different needs? What are your basic assumptions and beliefs about people? How are you living out of those beliefs and assumptions?

EXERCISE

To increase the capacity to understand others, list your strengths, weaknesses, preferences, and primary motivators. Now make a list of the people who report to you, your key peers, and your boss. Beside each name list the strengths, weaknesses, preferences, and primary motivators for that person. Look at the gifts, skills, and perspective each brings to the table. Where are they similar to you, and where are they different? How are you utilizing the differences to create synergies and to complement weaknesses and strengths? Where are you letting your pre-programmed patterns run the show and get in the way of working more powerfully and effectively with others?

Now answer the same questions with regard to your spouse or significant other—each of your parents, each of your children, and so on. How are you complementing or conflicting with them? What might increasing your understanding of them, their desires, aspirations, and needs do for your relationship? What is it in you and about the way you relate to them that gets in the way of creating the kind of relationships you really want?

Can you accurately outline the primary motivations of those on the list? Do you have a coherent strategy for tapping those motivations in a consistent manner? How do you treat each of them, and in what ways does that treatment reflect their needs, preferences, and motivations? How often are you simply relating to what you think, assume, and prefer versus what really motivates them?

Taking the time to answer these questions can fundamentally improve your understanding and relationship to others. To really attempt to answer them requires the willingness to see where you are not seeing or reading the realities of those around you, and then acting to discover their perceptual maps of reality. The answers and insights you begin to generate for yourself can be stunning—often blinding—glimpses of the obvious that you have been missing, mistaking your reflection in their eyes for the reality of who they are. Most of the time you will discover that you have been, in essence, seeing more of yourself, with regard to assumptions and expectations, versus seeing more of who they are.

EXERCISE

Sit down with each of your team members one on one. Ask them about their aspirations, their dreams and hopes. Ask them what they like and don't like about the way they are treated and recognized. Really involve them in a discussion about what matters most to them.

What will you do differently as a result of this information? How can you let it generate more effective ways of communicating with them?

Now, do the same with the people in your personal life who really matter to you. Take the time to ask and listen from your heart. What have you been assuming that is not accurate? What have you been missing? What does this new and expanded understanding mean for how you relate?

The principal point I wish to emphasize is that there is no limit to the motivational power within each of us. However, different things motivate and drive us. How will you cooperate with the internal motivations of those around you in order to bring out the most powerful levels of cooperation?

Covey says the fifth great habit of effective people is that of "seeking first to understand." As a daily practice it can be the "Camino Real," or royal road, to working more powerfully and accurately with others. What needs to be emphasized in this is that you must first understand yourself.

How do you cultivate and develop this capacity to understand others? It comes from three things:

1. Wanting to improve our ability to relate to others.

The attitude of wanting to improve our ability to relate to others is crucial to really understanding others. It opens the doors of perception, providing motivational energy and focus. This attitude can be as profound as realizing the awesome mystery of simply being alive, surrounded by other beings who are unique and ultimately unknowable, or it can be as obvious as simply focusing on the simple fact that trying to relate better to others gives you more power to influence and work more effectively with them. Without this attitude, or at least the awareness that cultivating such an attitude is important, it is nearly impossible to further the process of increasing the capacity to understand others.

2. Working on becoming more effective and responsive in our listening and questioning.

Working on becoming more effective and responsive in our listening is essential if we are to improve our ability to understand others. All communication between people has three components: the content of what is being said, the tone or emotional level, and the context.

Content involves what is literally being said, the actual words. "Oh, you have a great day, too!" This, surprisingly, communicates very little without the next level of tone.

Tone denotes the emotional message conveyed, which provides clues as to how to interpret the literal words or content. "Oh, you have a great day, too!" can be delivered as a gentle, caring message, as one of great sarcasm, or simply as a pro forma, empty phrase, all depending upon the coloration and shading of the emotional tone.

Context means the setting and perspective within which the message is delivered. The same message, delivered in one context with a sarcastic tone, can be a cruel and hurtful message, while in another context it's a playful exchange. The context depends upon the level of relationship, the history, the timing and place, where it falls in an exchange, and so on.

It takes all three—content, tone, and context—to successfully communicate our intentions and to understand the intentions of others. It is the intent and the skillfulness with which we listen to others that enables us to have a more complete understanding of them. Intention is important in listening because it relates to and communicates both verbally and non-verbally our interest and desire to really hear people. If the intention is just to appease or to have the right form, then no matter how skillfully we listen, that is what is ultimately seen and communicated to others. On the other hand, if the intention is to seek to understand, to really know where someone is coming from and what is important to them, then that comes across even if our listening skills need improvement.

The listening skill sets required to enhance communication through our understanding of others are fairly straightforward. They are:

A. Active Listening (skills that invite others to speak)

Silence. The capacity to be quiet, letting silence invite the other person to speak, cannot be overemphasized. Sometimes, in our attempts to listen or simply move a conversation along, we talk over someone or interrupt their thought processes. This can shut them down and limit their willingness to speak. Silence can truly be golden. It can communicate a powerful message: "I am here and focused on you. I can wait for you to think and respond." Silence can also be the place where you can hear your own intuition telling you about what is going on in the living mystery of the other person. It allows for a deeper listening to occur. What breaks the silence is our own level of discomfort with it, our anxiety and fear of what might emerge, perhaps even discomfort with our own emotions.

Reflective comments. These are a technique where the listener reflects back to the speaker what has been said. The point here is not to parrot back word for word what has been said—instead, the listener judiciously reflects upon what has been said and responds with a comment that communicates, "I've heard you, and this is, in brief, what I've heard so far." If done briefly and occasionally throughout a conversation, it invites the other to tell you more and to go more deeply into the issues at hand, as well as store their feelings and thoughts about those issues.

Clarifying questions. This skill draws out more information at the content or emotional levels by asking questions that help the speaker clarify what he or she means. If asked in ways which invite further disclosure, then the speaker can take you very deeply into understanding what is going on in his or her heart and mind. Generally, these clarifying questions are best if they are slightly indirect in tone, versus a direct, grilling, or third-degree tone. For example: "What are you feeling about that?" can be intimidating and may feel abrupt, versus "I wonder what you might be feeling as a result of this." The second question is more inviting and often moves the conversation deeper.

Clarifying questions open doors by asking the other to help you understand what is going on for them and what is important to them. They can be "big-scoop" in nature or the kind that can be answered in one word. For example: "Are you happy?" is a clarifying question, but it can be answered with a shrug or a yes or no. A big-scoop question is, "What are your thoughts and feelings about that?" or "If you were me, what would you do about this?"

Paraphrasing summary. This skill means that at certain junctures in the conversation you summarize what has been said, punctuating the points made and checking to make sure you are in sync with the speaker. Example: "What I have heard you tell me is that . . . have I got that right?" The paraphrased summary allows the speaker to hear what you have heard and provides a coherent way of checking and encapsulating what has been said. It deepens the understanding, and, if you have heard incorrectly or missed something important, the other person can, and most often will, correct you or supplement the information.

B. Empathetic Listening

Listening from the heart: What's behind the words? This form of listening requires all of the skills above and it also requires the desire to hear behind the words, the tone, and the context. It means listening with the ear within the heart. It is listening for the heart of the other by opening up and noticing what your heart is picking up. This works by paying attention to tone and context even more than the content of what is being said to get at what is going on within the other. It is intuition, patience, and compassion at its best.

Focusing on the feeling tone. What is the emotional message behind the words? What is not being said? It is inviting the other to tell more. Example: "I wonder what you feel about that?" or "I think I hear you saying you are feeling . . . Is that correct, or am I missing something?" or "I believe I hear sadness in your voice. Am I all wet, or is it something else?"

Silent positive regard. This is the practice of being still—offering acceptance and positive regard, suspending judgment, and demonstrating a desire to understand.

C. Power Questions (generate information and engage the listener)

Big-scoop questions. These are questions that, as demonstrated previously, cannot be answered with a simple yes or no. Some great big-scoop questions are:

"Tell me, if you could take a magic wand and make two things really change around here, what two things would you change and how would you change them?"

"If you could name the top two or three priorities for the company or enterprise, what would they be and why?"

"How does that impact your area and the work processes?"

"What changes would you make if you were given a free hand?"

"What do you like most about our leadership here? Least? Why?"

Questions such as these tend to engage people, and they ask for far more than questions such as "Do you like to work here?" or "Are you happy?" Big-scoop versions of the two above would be: "What is it like to work here?" and "What makes you happy?"

Opening or enabling questions. Opening questions are good beginning points, inviting the other person to open up and tell you more than they normally might. Example: "If you were totally free to speak your mind about work and what you like and dislike, what would you tell me?" or "I wonder if you would be willing to help me understand what you are feeling and thinking about this?"

Permission to explore. This is a tone, a sense of safety and receptivity, a non-defensiveness that gives permission. This is conveyed verbally and non-verbally, through eye contact, tone of voice, attentiveness, interest, and calmness. It is also generated by the use of indirect and big-scoop questions. Set this tone by generating an open mind-set, granting permission, and setting the stage for disclosure. (See mind-setting below.)

D. Context Setting and Mind-set

Connecting threads and themes. Setting the stage is what context and mind-setting are really about. We set the stage for the communication by offering a perspective on what is going to happen or what we hope will happen in the communication. This means weaving together the threads and themes into a coherent framework by which all involved can understand what we hope to accomplish and what we are looking to create with them. When this is done well, it is very powerful. It is a means of focusing attention and of inviting others to buy in and engage.

Speaking to the context within which the content sits. This simply refers to the skill of being aware of the perspective or reality frame through which the essential message is being filtered. It deals with the fact—which all great communicators remember and use—that mastering and managing the paradigms and perspectives of the audience is most critical. If I don't understand and appreciate the perspective of the other, then I will be far less effective.

Crafting mind-sets. This is the skill of establishing a framework for understanding and relates to context, as mentioned above. It is usually laid out as a prelude to listening to someone else or as a prelude to a meeting or communication from you. The practice of crafting and utilizing mind-sets may be one of the most critical skills required of leaders. It can vastly increase the power and effectiveness of a leader. The practice consists of four parts:

1. Thinking through, carefully, what the essential purpose of the meeting or session is and putting it down on paper.
2. Communicating that purpose to the team or individual in a succinct and clear manner.
3. Laying out the results desired, as well as how you want everyone to end up thinking and feeling about them.
4. Asking the person or people involved if they can buy in to the purpose, results desired, and the hoped-for cognitive and emotional reactions.

Example: "I am glad you could meet with me today. I want this meeting to be productive and helpful to both of us in identifying ways in which we can help drive the success of this project. Part of this, for me, is the hope that we will both walk out of here feeling good about this conversation and that it will help us work together more effectively. Can you buy in to this?"

3. Increasing Our Self-Awareness.

Increasing our level of self-awareness, so that we can spot the times and the ways in which we get in the way of relating more effectively, is essential. If I never see my part in the communication breakdowns—how I break the rapport and disrupt the process of listening—then I am blind. This means having a handle on my ego issues—where I am likely to throw my weight around, my insecurities and fears, my blind spots, my interpersonal and psychological defenses, my doubts, my assumptions, prejudices, beliefs, my need to control, to prove myself, to feel important, and so on. All of these ego issues can seriously harm my capacity to understand others. Controlling ego also means handling my impatience and the tendency to try to create shortcuts. Generally, shortcuts to trying to understand others do not work and actually add unnecessary pain and time to the process of really communicating effectively.

To conclude, Edwin Markham wrote a little poem a number of years ago that outlines the essence of understanding and working with others, as well as working through conflict. There are depths and profound levels of insight within it:

> *He drew a circle to shut me out,*
> *heretic, rebel, a thing to flout;*
> *but love and I had the wit to win—*
> *we drew a circle which drew him in.*

The heart of this poem is that when someone shuts us out and in essence draws a barrier between themselves and us, the best approach is to draw a larger circle (context) within which their barrier is validated and also becomes unnecessary, since we are connected in a larger, more comprehensive way.

It is a profound awareness to realize that we can invite the other person to join us in a more productive and rewarding working relationship. We can do this by creating a greater, more inclusive context that points to a mutually winning, larger frame of reference.

Does it work? It has worked well for me and for those of us who have learned it. I have used this awareness to help successfully mediate and repair marital impasses, partnership breakdowns, merger and acquisition issues, senior executive conflicts, team dysfunctions, and personality problems. It also works on the mat of the dojo in martial arts contests. The awareness is profound and, like all really profound concepts and principles, profoundly simple. I have been mining the gold in the rich seam Edwin Markham exposed in his short poem. I suggest you can do extremely well by doing the same. The message cuts across several practices and also relates powerfully to the practices of generating follower-ship, understanding others, and providing feedback.

The practice of working to understand others starts with the commit-ment to understand your own heart. It simultaneously incorporates curiosity and interest in working to appreciate the similarities and dif-ferences of others. A continuous set of actions based on listening from the heart, daily practice is essential as an integral part of leadership if the leader is to stay current with and come to more fully appreciate and understand the followers and potential followers around him or her. It allows for greater precision in working with others. It is a crucial pre-cursor to generating true synergy.

"A horse, a horse!
My kingdom for
a horse!"
—William Shakespeare

PRACTICE 6

Providing
Resources

RESOURCING

Providing resources

enables others to do

their job and gives

them a feeling of

being seen and

respected.

What good does it do if the purpose is clear, the organization is focused, and the goals are aligned, but those charged with achieving the desired ends do not have the means to do so?

It is an essential responsibility of all leaders to see that employees have the means to achieve defined goals and objectives. Resources include financing, personnel, tools, training, infrastructure, supplies, follow-through, and follow-up.

The function of resource allocation is that of enabling others to do their job. The emotion that flows from that function is one of feeling respected. To fail to provide those charged with doing the work with the tools necessary creates a sense of being profoundly disrespected. This leads to hostility, frustration, and even, at times, despair. It also can fundamentally impair the capacity to accomplish the tasks at hand, endangering or delaying the realization of the purpose.

General Patton, for example, found himself unable to bring a quick end to WWII due to a shortage of gasoline. He had the men, the equipment, the strategy, the advantage, and the focus. What he lacked was one critical resource. How many people had to die in concentration camps or in battles as a result of the war being prolonged?

119

Napoleon, in another age, found himself the victim of an inadequate food supply during his occupation of Moscow. He had achieved his military objective—occupying the capital of Russia—but he had failed to ensure an adequate supply of food. He was thus forced to withdraw and suffered disastrous consequences.

As these examples show, resources are not always readily available. Leaders need foresight, imagination, and a thorough understanding of their environments to ensure that resources are available to get the job done. They also understand that all the work being done in the enterprise is part of a system-wide process. Knowing this, they realize that real power is found by focusing upon the whole. That is, by using a systems perspective, they can create new opportunities and see new solutions to increasing efficiency and decreasing resource constraints without adding more resources—sometimes even decreasing them!

The real challenge before leaders today is that of increasing the level of production through increased efficiencies, doing more with the same, or even less, resources. This requires a fundamental change in perspective and in thinking about how resource decisions are made. The key lies in learning how to produce the same or more but consume less energy, time, and capital. In Japan, for example, the best companies can now produce the same volume of goods they produced in the mid-'60s, using 40 percent less energy and a fraction of the time. This is the elixir of success, doing more with less, enabling the organization to function at higher and more productive levels in less time. This does not come easily and requires new ways of thinking, leading, interacting, and working.

As Steve Ardia has said:

> People don't come in to work with the intention of making errors or screwing things up, and yet it happens every day. You have to look at yourself in the mirror as management and say, "It's our fault. We have not provided the tools to allow people to do things correctly."
>
> It's either that they have too much to do, they're not properly trained, they don't have the resources, or they're afraid to ask questions. All of these things contribute to the making of errors.

The wise leader—having clarified the vision, kept the purpose ever before others, set the standards, and actively elicited the goals—must now ensure that the proper resources are set before those charged with realizing the vision and fulfilling the purpose. Without the assurance of the proper tools, capital, knowledge, training, skilled co-workers, guidance, coaching, and psychological and emotional support, even the best job can result in ultimate failure. Where people are not supported, encouraged, and given the means, they are most often doomed to fail, and they fail resenting those who exhorted them to succeed. "We the unwilling, led by the incompetent, do the un-doable for the thankless" becomes the theme. This also destroys the trust of those who would follow, and it makes for an entrenched cynicism that becomes a creeping death lodged in the very soul of an organization, a deadly illness engendered by the lack of support from the leadership system.

Providing resources has many levels. It is possible, for instance, that an enterprise can succeed brilliantly despite little financial means, barely adequate tools and barely adequate expertise. But that success, in my experience, consists of a far deeper and richer form of support pumped in by the active ministrations, coaching, and even love that the leadership of that enterprise provides from their heart to the hearts of those working with them. No amount of money can ever buy this kind of success, nor can business acumen predict it. It is ineffable, flowing out of the raw will, native intelligence, and determined spirits of those engaged.

Now imagine all of that with the proper tools, the right capital, the proper training, a rich level of talent, and deep subject knowledge. You have an unbeatable organization, as IBM proved until it got lost in excessive layers of management and internal processes and lost touch with its customers as well as its sense of boldness and courage!

Resource provision is a critical function of a leader. The astute and serious leader ensures that she or he understands what the people doing the work will require if they are to succeed. How is this done? Primarily through being intimate with the substance of the work, as well as the requirements and the needs of the people charged with making it happen.

One of the most powerful ways to find out what will be required is to simply ask those who are doing the work. Then their expectations and needs are negotiated around differentiating between the "nice-to-haves" and the "got-to-haves." The astute leader must be able to sort out what is bare-bones essential from what is merely luxurious. The failure to do this well can make the difference between ultimate success and failure.

How do we ensure that the proper support is provided? How do we navigate the shoals of not enough and too much in this highly competitive world? In truth, resources are not infinite, and internal competition for finite resources can be fierce. How does leadership address this?

The best answers are to be found in dialogue. If management is the sole decision point in the allocation of resources, then there are two dangers: giving too little or giving too much. However, if the people charged with performing the day-to-day tasks that drive performance are the ones making the decision, then there are other dangers. The chief danger is that they will allocate generously to their particular area without taking into account needed resources. This can also lead to frequent running battles as each department fights to wrest assets from the others. The other danger is that there may be strategic issues requiring more investment in a particular function or department at the expense of others.

The key skill here lies in the ability to create meaningful dialogue with all parties. The dialogue orients itself through the preceding practices: vision, focus on purpose, standards, understanding others, strategies, and elicited goals. The purpose is to help all involved understand the scope of the most critical strategic business requirements for a particular period of time. This then provides a framework for mutual decision making around the current allocation of resources.

This means that in the process of discussing needs, the leadership can be assured that what is absolutely required by each unit is clearly outlined. It also means that it becomes easier to separate those things that would be nice to have from those which are really essential. This process also minimizes the prospect of ongoing conflict and destructive internal competition. It helps each area and the leadership involved create a level of cooperation and intimacy that drives more powerful results.

In the Gulf War, the general who received another star was the logistics officer who made sure that all the supplies necessary to achieve success were available to the men and women charged with winning the war. Leaders who fail to provide the requisite resources will end up as failed leaders.

Resolving Resource Conflicts

How do you best determine what the right resources are, and how do you reconcile the conflicting agendas and requests of the different parts of an organization, enterprise, or society? What process is required to make the proper allocations as well as the proper denials?

We can see the impact of conflicting agendas easily when we read the newspaper. Consider the timber industry in the Pacific Northwest and the conservationists in the spotted owl issue. Where do we put our emphasis? Where do we look to allocate resources? For the protection of an endangered species or for the livelihood of the loggers and their families? The capacity to understand the issues and to negotiate the wisest use of our resources, while critical, is not easy.

Roger Fisher and Richard Ury have written a helpful book called *Getting to Yes*. It focuses on how to negotiate and has within it the seeds and processes for wisely reconciling conflicting agendas and resource needs. There are four basic steps to negotiating resource constraints and coming up with allocation decisions:

1. Separate the people involved from the issue or problem.
2. Focus upon the needs and interests of all involved, not on the expressed positions. Really seek to understand.
3. Create agreement on some objective criteria by which to evaluate the wisdom of any agreements and decisions.
4. Create and explore alternatives using innovative problem-solving and lateral-thinking techniques and processes.

The keys to successful identification of resource needs and making wise decisions around deployment and allocation are found in these four steps. After each step is a set of tools we have developed at Staub-Peterson to actualize it.

1. Separate the people from the issue or problem at hand.

The successful leader can help the people involved step back from their personal agendas and ego issues while keeping the focus on the alignment of tasks and orchestration of priorities.

A. *Revisit the Overall Context*

The essential task here is to get everyone to the highest level of agreement about what they are fundamentally doing together. This can be as simple as reminding everyone involved of the unifying vision, getting people to agree again that they have a common context. Then the leader brings the focus back to the essential purpose of the work and the web of functions and relationships that go into the achievement of that work. The key question becomes, "Are we on purpose here in the decisions and actions we are taking?"

B. *Shift Perspective*

The leader also directs everyone by asking provocative questions that direct them to consider the issues from a different perspective. Examples of some of the best questions we have heard include:

- "Are we letting our personal needs and agendas get in the way of our essential purpose?"
- "Given the limited resources we have, what is the wisest allocation of those resources, given our standards and goals?"

- "If this were your personal business, what choices would you make to ensure that the goals we have set are achieved?"
- "A year from now, what do we have to have accomplished in order to be best positioned for continued success? How do we best allocate our resources now to get there?"

C. Use Point/Counterpoint

Have the members take the opposite viewpoint from their own and argue it. This is done to ensure that people are hearing each other and considering the viewpoint from the opposing perspective. It is amazing how powerful this simple technique can be in creating bridges between camps and beginning to separate the person from the issue.

D. Shift Position

Shift the way everyone is positioned in looking at the issues. This can be as simple as moving people together. For example, instead of having people sit across the table from each other, place everyone in a semicircle facing a flip chart on which the key issues or problems are listed. Then have them speak to the issues on the board, confronting them, not each other. This can also mean changing the sequencing of how and when materials and issues are presented.

E. Start with the End Result Clearly in Focus

Have each person share what they wish to see as the best team outcome and how they see themselves and their agendas fitting into that outcome. Get the team to stake out the desired organizational, divisional, departmental, and individual outcomes. Get general agreement around the health of the overall organizational system and how to best provide for that with regard to resources.

2. Focus on the needs and interests of all involved, not their stated positions.

A. Ask for the Principle

When someone is talking about their position and agenda, simply ask which principle they are basing their request or demand upon. Really try to understand, and help them lay out the principles by which they are engaging the group and the issues before you. This is powerful and can cut through the issues fairly quickly in terms of generating more objective criteria around needs and interests versus positions.

B. Use Active Listening

Before responding to a position or point, stop and see if you can rephrase what the other has said. Then comment on your understanding of what they meant. Ask if you have clearly heard them. Listen and clarify until they are certain you have heard them.

C. Use Power Questions

These are questions that go below the surface and dredge up the deeper issues, feelings, and needs—questions such as: "If you had unlimited resources, what would you do and why?" "If you could only get 50 percent of what you are requesting, what would you take and why?" "What do you really need, bare bones, and how do you know that what you're requesting is the bare bones?" "If you had to make the resource allocation decision by yourself for the overall good of the company, how would you do it? What would you have to know in order to do it?" "What are your people's greatest needs? Yours? Ours?" These questions begin to take the issues to a deeper level.

D. Skip Levels

Skip down to the people one or two levels below your direct reports. Ask for their input about needs. Ask for company-wide input and perceptions. Get people involved in surfacing requirements.

E. Use a Systems Perspective

It is important in examining needs and interests to keep a perspective on how each individual piece affects the ability of the whole to function. Ensure that discussion centers on how resource decisions in one area will affect how work is supplied to another area. This approach can lead to some reengineering and to some streamlining of the work processes such that resource constraints actually might improve efficiency. Make sure that the people who actually do the work in a particular area and then across areas are involved in the redesign. This has tremendous possibilities if the real needs and interests within and across areas are taken into account in the process of delivering goods and services.

3. Create objective criteria by which to evaluate the requests.

This is the powerful principle of creating agreement as to the process and means by which fair and wise decisions will be made. It requires getting the members to agree to a framework with clear criteria for making decisions and resolving conflicting agendas.

A. Ask for Examples

Help the team or individuals involved to surface examples of wise decisions in difficult or contentious settings. Have them spell out what made those decisions good. List the elements of wise decision making. Get agreement as to the principles and aspects of what makes for a good resolution.

B. Outline the Issues at Hand

With resource allocation, get all members to lay out the organizational stakes involved and then outline their issues. Compare the smaller lists to the overall list for the organization. Get discussion going about similarities, differences, points of conflict, etc. Get some sort of objective agreement as to where things converge and diverge.

C. Press for Commitment to Criteria

Get agreement as to the criteria required for wise decision making around resource allocation. Get buy-in prior to discussing the different agendas or trying to make decisions. Then refer to the criteria throughout the working process to ensure that everyone understands how the criteria are being used to make more effective decisions.

4. Explore alternatives using creative problem solving.

This is the magic of synergy, in which the pie is expanded versus merely being divided and compromised over. Resource sharing, new alternatives, process improvements, and the like usually emerge from this principle. It is a way of taking the first three steps and really beginning to increase the power available in the organization.

A. Mind-Mapping

Use this powerful tool for getting everyone involved in exploring other alternatives. It consists of getting the group into a semicircle, covering part of a wall with paper, and drawing a central circle in the paper with the key issue in the center. Then the group calls out possible ideas or solutions and a scribe records these as clusters of ideas coming off of spokes from the central bubble. Off of these sub-ideas are then other spokes as each is developed. The power of this tool is that you end up with a picture of how the ideas are related, and you get the entire team involved in throwing out ideas. Then discuss the ideas and begin to play with the alternatives and relationships suggested.

B. Paired Synergy

Break into pairs and charge each with coming up with 10 alternatives to expand the resource-base power by getting more with less. Give them only 20 minutes, and then have them present to the large group. (For real firepower and punch, pair rivals with each other.)

C. Active Imagination

Get everyone involved in imaging. This is a tool that plays with the phrase "What if . . . " Invite the participants to imagine breakthrough solutions by asking, "What if we could invent or create the best possible solution for our team and our enterprise around resource allocation? What would that look like now?" When someone offers a possible solution, ask, "What if that were ideal? What do we like most about that solution? Now, what if it is leaving out something important to the organization? What is missing from that solution?" These questions get people thinking outside the mental box that limits them to the prevailing paradigms, missing greater opportunities in the meantime.

Have the team imagine meeting their commitments with the minimum resources. How might they do that? How would that affect the others in the room who either provide information or products or receive them in the internal customer/supplier chain for your enterprise?

D. Scenario Creation

This is a wonderful tool which asks that all participants create likely near-future scenarios regarding the industry, customers, employees, and so on. The idea is to get a number of possible futures outlined and on the board. Then have the team members talk about how each of those scenarios would affect their requests and needs around resource allocation. This begins to get the focus on dangers and opportunities for the enterprise and also allows for discussion around resource allocation. Then tie the scenarios back to the first three steps to make a wise decision.

All of these ideas are but some of the possible ways of beginning to make the tough decisions around resource allocations. The keys are:

- Stay close to the people who actually do the work; involve them in being part of the decision-making process, or at least help them to understand and accommodate decisions that will affect them.
- Break out of the resource-constraint paradigm, and invite your team members to think creatively. That is, work to synergize and look for creative alternatives.

- Ensure that you look at the process from a systems perspective: How will each decision impact the whole? How does limiting resources in one area then affect the work and the speed with which they can supply to another area in the value-added chain within your enterprise?
- Make sure everyone's needs and interests are mapped out; don't get lost in the positions.
- Create objective criteria through discussion.
- Create ownership and buy-in to the decisions made, having mapped out the consequences of each decision, and then tie them to the overall systems perspective.

These steps will help any leader and leadership team create wiser, more powerful, and more enabling decisions about resource allocation. In fact, the processes used here are helpful in any discussion, not only those involving resourcing.

It is critical that leaders understand the resource needs of the people charged with doing the work. Doing this well takes all four dimensions of leadership effectiveness. First, it requires a level of intimacy with the work being done and with the people doing the work. It requires trust—the trust to be open, to question, to try new ideas and ways of working, to listen and be open to each other's needs. Second, it requires the competence to listen well—and know how to listen and question—in order to get behind the positions and get to the real needs and interests. Third, it requires the passion to want to see others succeed and the desire to ensure that they have the tools and means of doing so. Finally, it also requires the integrity to hold contradictory viewpoints and conflicting interests with the focus upon doing what is in the best interest of the overall enterprise—not doing what is politically expedient or popular.

How the decisions are made around resource allocation is a critical part of overall success. The wise leader, at whatever level he or she exists within the structure, strives to help those involved place the overall good ahead of individual agendas. She or he also works to help generate new perspectives and opportunities for operational improvements in terms of efficiency, time consumption, energy, capital, personnel, etc. This is done with an openness and willingness to forge new ties, explore new territory, and craft wiser decisions.

The leaders who will make the greatest differences are those who understand that the paradigm is now one of reducing resource consumption (including the key resource called "time") while boosting production. They do this in a way that empowers the people doing the work to perform even better and with increased understanding and power.

PRACTICE 7

Liberating Motivation

MOTIVATE

Liberating the

motivation that lies

within others enables

them to achieve and

fills them with

excitement.

A question I often ask audiences when I speak on leadership: "How many of you believe the job of a leader is to motivate others?" Nearly everyone raises their hand. However, as I make explicit to them, a leader cannot motivate anyone. It is actually rather foolish to think any of us can put motivation into anyone else. You see, all the motivation is already inside everyone we meet. The real challenge of a leader is to tap and channel the inherent motivation in others.

The traditional adage about leading a horse to water misses the point. Of course you can't make a horse drink. However, a real leader understands that the need to drink is already built into the horse—all that is required to get a horse to drink is to make sure it is thirsty!

One of the essential tasks a leader must undertake is to discover what others are thirsting for and consciously cultivate a great thirst within the potential followers, while making sure the means of slaking that thirst is to be found in fulfilling the leader's vision. This means that the vision and purpose must dovetail with the motivations and drives of others.

Leaders who can successfully do this need only be careful not to get trampled by the enthusiasm with which others follow!

The critical function that flows out of the practice of liberating motivation is that of achieving, and the emotional energy that flows from it is excitement. Liberating motivation sets the stage for achieving excellence and is tremendously exciting.

Admiral Brooks, former head of Naval Intelligence, when asked to name an inspirational leader who could liberate the motivation of others, came up with Admiral Tuttle immediately:

> One that pops into mind is a guy named Jerry Tuttle. Jerry is a naval aviator and one of the oldest vice admirals in the Navy. He is not a Naval Academy graduate and, as I recall, had not even finished college when he came into the Navy, although he subsequently finished and then went on to obtain his master's degree. He has limited technical background, but has tremendous savvy, insight, and drive. He's a fireplug of a guy with a Ross Perot crewcut and a Ross Perot approach to getting things done. By virtue of the dominance of his personality and his force, he was able to totally redesign the Navy Command, Control, and Communication system.
>
> Here was a man who didn't necessarily understand all the technical details. He was not a "computer freak." He probably had limited understanding of the technical innards of the Navy communications system. Yet he totally restructured ADP and telecommunications in the Navy because he knew how the system should work in order to support the operating forces, and he knew it didn't work that way now. He had a plain, common-sense approach to how it should be made to work. And then he refused to accept it when the technocrats came and said, "Well, we're sorry, Admiral, that's too hard. We can't do it that way." He absolutely refused to accept that, and he just left tire tracks.
>
> This was a guy with a vision: "I'm going to turn around Navy Command and Control." There wasn't anyone in the Navy who didn't know of him and what he was trying to do. They may not have understood it well because it is rather complex and technical, but they knew what he was about. He was able to effectively communicate his vision. He motivated his people, and he kept after it with persistence.

You have no idea how difficult this was. I don't know another officer (surely including myself) who could have done it. The man simply had the clarity of vision, determination of purpose, and ability to lead, motivate, communicate, and snap at the heels of the straying sheep, tossing a persistently straying sheep off the cliff when necessary. He managed to move a great, amorphous, and not always responsive organization in an entirely new direction. It took him three years. The organization will bear his mark for a decade to come.

What really motivates people? Surveys of people in the workplace have been done in which the top 10 motivators are ranked and listed. Money usually comes in fourth or fifth on the lists. In the top four, ahead of money, are variations of the following: feeling a sense of being valued and appreciated, being part of something greater, making a difference, growth and challenge.

You probably know several people who have left a higher-paying job to take a job offering more of a challenge, more personal sense of reward, or because they felt they could make more of a difference. Most of the people I know and work with have made that choice at some point in their careers. I have done so several times, and each time the money diminished initially only to come more plentifully as I pursued a path with more heart and meaning. This is neither unusual nor unique.

Each time we make that kind of choice, we have to counter the social messages and cultural taboos. It takes courage, perseverance, and determination. Not to do so, though, leaves us more lost and wounded. We lose a little bit of our soul, and our capacity to lead is diminished, for we have not even been willing to follow ourselves!

Surveys such as these, and our own experience, offer some guidance and perspective into the drives, aspirations, and motivations of others. However, the answer to what really motivates a specific person cannot be found in a survey or set of statistics. The answer is to be found in a heart-to-heart meeting and dialogue with that person.

Each of us is different, and what most strongly drives and pulls us is not always the same. The particular constellation of motivators varies in direction, focus, and intensity based upon our life situation, our past experience, our private beliefs, hopes, dreams, fears, and so on. The motivations also shift and change as we grow, develop, and age.

Scrooge's Motivation

A wonderful metaphor for understanding what drives someone and how to tap and shift the person to an even deeper set of motivations can be found in the wise book by Charles Dickens, *A Christmas Carol.*

In this story, the miser Ebenezer Scrooge is driven by the motivation of greed. He is remarkably, even cruelly, indifferent to the lives of those who work for him and those who live around him. His whole life is consumed in getting and keeping more and more wealth. He is alone and isolated, rebuffing the attempts of family and society to draw him into human contact. His heart is cold and only concerned with gold.

Then, through a remarkable event, his dead old partner, Jacob Marley, appears as a horrific apparition to warn Scrooge of impending doom. The ghost wears yards and yards of heavy chains, and every so often there are great strong boxes of iron attached. Marley labors under this hideous weight, and Scrooge asks him why he is so burdened. Marley replies that the chain is the one he wove every day of his life when he was only concerned with and focused upon commerce and gaining more wealth.

At this, Scrooge protests that Marley was always a good businessman and the ghost begins to howl in anger, replying, "Mankind was my business! And now I must eternally travel the earth, witness to what I can no longer do."

We all know what comes next. Marley tells Scrooge he will be sending him three spirits to help in Scrooge's redemption. Scrooge is terrified and tries to dissuade the ghost. The three spirits come anyway. They take the old miser on a tour of his life by visiting some Christmas scenes set in the past, the present, and the future.

It is not necessary to recap what happens with each scene and each spirit. What is essential to note is that through these spirits and the scenes he witnesses, Ebenezer Scrooge is provided a different angle, a new perspective on his life and the way he is living it.

He sees what he has sacrificed and what he has lost in his single-minded pursuit of wealth. He feels joy at times when he sees himself as a youth and feels the kindness of his sister, his first employer, his fiancée. He experiences great remorse and bitter pain as he witnesses how he has chosen gold over his love and financial gain over meaningful relationships. He sees and feels the emptiness of his life, the wasted times, the lost opportunities.

He comes to understand, with regard to the Cratchit family, what his selfishness and self-centeredness have cost the family of his employee. His cold, old heart is touched by the sweet gentleness and courageous heart of the youngest Cratchit, the crippled and sickly little child they call Tiny Tim. He finds himself asking the spirit if the boy can be helped, if he will live. The spirit replies, "If these shadows remain unaltered, I see an empty chair by the fire and the tiny crutch without an owner." Scrooge is shaken by remorse and finds he wishes to change that particular future. His heart begins to reach out to the crippled boy.

After all of these visions and more, Scrooge meets the third and final spirit, a specter of death. The spirit takes him to see two scenes. One is the grieving Cratchit family and the desperate love of the father for his lost little son. Scrooge's heart is pierced by this scene.

He then asks to see some merriment, some sign of cheer to lighten the burden of what he has just witnessed. The spirit transports him to a scene where several people are cheerfully discussing the death of someone. It is Scrooge they are laughing over. Scrooge gets to see how his own life will end, and he is terrified, begging for another chance.

In the story, the old miser awakens on Christmas morning, and his outlook on life has been utterly changed. What he has valued and the way he has been living his life appear to be some demented dream. He has awakened to a whole new way of seeing the world and his place in that world. He is full of joy, and his only thought is to surprise and delight others, using his wealth and his heart to touch others, to help.

He becomes a second father to Tiny Tim, saving the small child and, not so strangely, also saving himself. He becomes a leader in his community, honoring the relationships, the needs, and the dreams of others. He becomes a joyful and rich man for the first time in his life!

What is exceedingly wonderful in this story is the convergence of several powerful truths when it comes to understanding and liberating the motivations of others:

Appearances can be deceiving.

Scrooge appeared to be mastered solely by the motivation around acquiring and holding onto money. In truth, there were deeper, more powerful motivations buried within his heart, buried so deeply that even he could no longer feel them. Leadership is about helping others to discover what they really care about and what may be hidden even from themselves. To do this, the leader must have some insight and connection with her or his deeper aspirations and motivations. In Scrooge's case this touches on the aspirations to make a difference, to be loved, to remember what is finest and best.

The genuine need of others has the power to touch the heart and open a new way of seeing.

Scrooge saw the need of his employee's family, and he was touched by the plight of the crippled child. He saw his power to make a difference,

and it moved him. The motivating power of compassion and caring began
to flow in him.

*The courage and heart of another can open us to a new relationship
with ourselves.*

Scrooge saw the courage and joyfulness of an impoverished, crippled, sickly little child. He was touched at the strength of spirit dwelling
within that thin, small body. It called to the part of him that needed to
be courageous and needed spirit. In fact, Tiny Tim was richer and more
alive than the wealthy old man who wanted for nothing, save love and
meaningful relationships.

*Viewing the past, assessing the present reality, and imagining the
future are powerful tools for helping us get our priorities straight.*

These tools provide a sense of perspective. Scrooge got to see what
had really been significant in his past and where he had been mistaken.
He came to understand exactly where he currently stood and the price
he paid to be where he was; he came to see the mistakes he was currently making. Finally, he came to understand where he was headed and
was going to end up if he continued on his present course. These perspectives helped him get his priorities straight and make a course cor-
rection more in keeping with what he really valued.

*Once we begin to shift our perspective, our perceptions open to other
realities, and our world will never be the same.*

The old miser totally changed his life by having his paradigm and
perspective on life challenged. He began to see the world in a new way,
and with it he began to live a new life.

Our lives are inextricably linked.

We cannot make a change or take an action without affecting the lives
of those around us. What we do or do not do makes a difference for
good or ill. Scrooge did not see until that special night that his way of
living impoverished not only himself, but those around him. Conversely,
when he shifted his way of relating to himself and others, he enriched
and contributed to many lives.

*We are motivated when we can see the real costs and benefits of living
and acting in certain ways.*

These costs and benefits can best be seen in terms of the impact we have on others, the quality of our relationships, the results we achieve, and how we are experiencing ourselves from day to day.

Powerful Leadership

The power inherent in acting as a leader is the power of not only coming to understand and read others, but also of helping others to understand and see themselves better, fuller, and more richly. This is alchemy, the artfulness of great leaders.

Powerful leadership first seeks to outline and flesh out a vision and sense of mission, inviting others to join in and help flesh out that vision. Then, focusing on the fundamental purpose of the business or enterprise, leaders work to generate followership around standards and mutual goals and objectives. To help drive this, they work to understand others and the needs they have with regard to resources. This then helps the focus to sharpen around what motivates and drives others, looking with curiosity and compassion at the complex play of forces in each person and team.

Liberating the motivation of others is discovering what makes them "thirsty," or even where they already thirst for greater meaning or contribution, recognition or reward. Then the task is to demonstrate that following, working with, and pursuing your agenda, path, idea, or direction is what will help them quench that thirst. The only thing left to do, then, is to work really hard to stay slightly ahead of them, or get left behind! Going after a goal, knowing it will help satisfy a deep thirst, has a strong tendency to ignite the passion and motivation of people. You need pump nothing in. Any exhortation on your part, any motivational program at this point, is only carrying water to the ocean—a weak, futile effort in the face of the tide of inner motivation unleashed.

Removing Obstacles

The true challenge of motivation is not adding things to get people motivated. It is instead an issue of removing obstacles, the barriers to the free expression of the motivation already present but blunted or repressed.

If this is true, then what gets in the way? How is the tremendous power and corresponding emotional energy of the human system blocked? Why does this happen? How do we change it and remove the barriers so the energy can flow?

To answer this and to get a sense of perspective of what can be done, let's look to the behavioral sciences for guidance. There are three great behavioral science principles that stand the test of time. They are:

- All behavior is purposeful.
- All behavior is motivated 100 percent around key, perceived needs 100 percent of the time.
- All behavior is, at root, selfish.

All behavior is purposeful.

It is axiomatic that all behavior has a purpose behind it. Our study of nature points out that even in one-celled organisms the behavior is purposeful, moving toward nutrients, away from threats, and so on. No matter how bizarre someone may be acting, there is a purpose and intent behind the behavior. They are trying to do something: avoid pain, seek pleasure, obtain something, achieve something, prove something, connect, feel important, be safe, and so forth. There is always a purpose to the behavior, even if the behavior is that of not doing something. Leaders try to pierce the veils that often obscure a clear understanding of what the intent and purpose of someone's behavior might be. Knowing there is a purpose helps to focus, leading to uncovering or intuiting what the reasons behind the behavior might be.

All behavior is motivated by some need 100 percent of the time.

Knowing that all behavior has a purpose, the insightful leader then turns to the axiom that the behavior and its purpose are tied to meeting some need, and that the individual is motivated 100 percent to meet that need. This means that here is where you can uncover the thirst, finding out what they are really wanting and needing. The key is not to pump motivation in; rather, it is tapping the motive energy already present, and always working at 100 percent. This then leads to principle three.

All behavior is selfish.

Here the rubber hits the road. We all do what we do because it is what we most want to do. We act on meeting our needs. We are selfish. This principle usually elicits the most controversy and, initially, gives some people the most trouble. In fact, when I lay this principle out at seminars, it usually generates some angry response. One time a father of four children in college jumped up and said this wasn't true. When asked why, he went into a long, passionate rendition of how he and his wife were making great personal sacrifices to put the kids through school and that he thought this was very unselfish of them. I then asked how he felt about the fact that he was helping his children to get an education and a good start in life. He responded that he felt pleased he was being a good father. I then asked how he would feel if he were not helping his children get ahead. He said he would not be able to look himself in the face in the mirror. I then asked if he loved his children. He gave a strong affirmative answer. I then asked if he would be pained if they were suffering or not doing well. His response was the obvious one any parent would give: their pain and suffering was very hard on him, and he felt a sense of anguish wanting them to be happy and well.

After all of this, I pointed out how selfish all of those answers were. Selfish does not necessarily mean being a miser. It does mean that we do what we most want to do. That father most wanted to put his kids through school, more than he wanted a new car or a fat savings account. He and his wife were making sacrifices, and the sacrifices fit their values, sense of self, and love for their children. He got the point. Often the key to liberating the motivation of others is helping them connect to what they most want from the deeper part of themselves.

This principle, tied to the first two, indicates that the real task of the leader in liberating motivation is helping others make the connection that following your leadership initiative is in their best interest. That is, what you want them to do is seen as being intimately connected to their aspirations, needs, hopes, and desires. They come to see that following your lead is going to help them achieve what they want.

So what blocks motivation? What gets in the way of making the logical connections, understanding others, and acting on that understanding? Actually, there are a number of things, and I call them the "10 Mortal Sins":

The 10 Mortal Sins, or Guaranteed Ways to Fail as a Leader

1. **Not listening.**
   Impact: creates indifference, hostility, miscommunication.
2. **Fostering confusion** through lack of vision or clear purpose.
   Impact: poor focus, little coordination, haphazard planning.
3. **Not trusting** or believing in the capacity of others.
   Impact: creates resentment, weakens employees' self-confidence.
4. **Playing politics** versus substantive focus.
   Impact: poor cooperation, suspicion, C.Y.A., turf battles, inefficiency.
5. **Not creating time** for dialogue, sharing information.
   Impact: creates learning-disabled teams, low synergy.
6. **Not recognizing diversity.**
   Impact: treating everyone the same, imprecision in coaching and supervising, communicating poorly with others,

missed opportunities, anger, resentment, poor synergy, misunderstanding.

7. **Stealing credit** versus giving credit to others.

   Impact: generates anger and resentment, de-motivates, weakens trust.

8. **Fostering the impression that someone doesn't matter,** isn't valued.

   Impact: creates apathy, low confidence, resentment, powerlessness.

9. **If it ain't broke, don't fix it.**

   Impact: lack of passion, low aspirations, missed opportunity, poor quality focus.

10. **Perseverance poverty.**

   Impact: no "stick-to-it-ive-ness," not enough warrior to see things through, no follow-through, lack of commitment, indifference, cynicism.

Liberating the motivation of others is an essential practice of artful leadership. It means making the effort to really understand and decipher what others feel, think, and want—how they have put the world together. It requires that the leader function as a practical psychologist, taking the best that psychology has to offer and throwing out the rest. This is not theoretical in the least. It is hands-on, practical in orientation, and focused upon results. It rests on the following axioms:

Axioms of Motivation

- People feel motivated when they believe that what they do really matters, that they make a difference.
- People are motivated to do their best when they feel appreciated, valued, and respected.
- People act in their best interests as they understand them—demonstrate how their best interests are served in following your initiatives, and you will have their motivation.
- Motivation flows when people feel they are part of something larger and greater than themselves and they are contributing to its success.
- People are motivated about helping other people and knowing they have played or can play a critical role in their success.
- People are motivated when they feel needed and are asked for their help.

- People are motivated at the prospect of personal mastery, challenge, growth, self-understanding, freedom, and meaning.
- People are motivated by love, most of all—serving that which they care about.
- Motivation always has a strong emotional component.

Keeping these axioms in mind and remembering the lessons from Scrooge, you can invite and tap the powerful, motivational energy system in the people and teams around you. We all want to feel we make a difference and to feel purpose and meaning moving through our lives. It is the job of leaders to help generate the context for meaning and to provide a focus for the realization and attainment of purpose. This is emotional and even spiritual in nature. The most effective leaders tap this dimension of motivation and help model the kinds of behaviors, principles, and values which, in turn, inspire others to emulate them. Thus, leaders replicate the best of themselves, causing others to aspire to the roles of inspiring and working with the motivations of others.

"It is one of the most
beautiful compensations of
life that no man can sincerely
try to help another without
helping himself."
—Ralph Waldo Emerson

PRACTICE 8

Supporting Others

Supporting others

encourages them

in their tasks and

creates a climate

of caring.

My marketing director was in trouble. She was overwhelmed with work demands, disorganized, and trying to be all things to all people. She was great with people, exuding warmth, charm, and charisma. Yet, she was failing. Goals and targets were not being met. My partner and I were in the early days of creating Staub-Peterson, and we were very distressed. After repeated attempts to address the issues, we took drastic steps. We apologized to her! We had taken a willing, competent, and skillful salesperson and set her up to fail. In consultation with her, we scaled back her responsibilities and created a clear focus with definite goals.

We spent many hours over the next three months working through the backlog of frustration, anger, and bad habits collectively created. She didn't like that we cut her pay, changed her title, and limited her role. We spent a lot of time listening and demonstrating our commitment to her success. It was an exercise in relentless caring, asking her to stay, but being prepared for her to leave. We made it through the three-month shakedown period, and it became evident that she was being successful. She was hitting her goals, and the sales commissions began to kick in. She became elated and felt both supported and encouraged. It was a painful and joyful experience, teaching all of us the rewards of having the courage to support another. In supporting her despite her anger and resistance, both I and my partner discovered that we had grown and become more whole in our leadership. The company began to prosper in ways that were delightful.

Supporting others is a separate practice from providing resources. Supporting others cuts much deeper and requires much more from a leader. It is, in essence, the pumping of the leader's lifeblood, energy, and spirit into the veins of others.

Supporting others is the golden thread that ultimately leads to being lavishly supported by them. Unless a leader is willing to offer his or her personal support, appreciation, corrective feedback, caring confrontation, emotional awareness, and courage, then he or she can never expect to really be intimate with the real needs and concerns of others. This weakens leadership impact and undermines all of the achievements of the first practices.

The function that flows from this practice is that of encouraging others, and the emotional aspect of that is a deep sense of caring about the work being done and about those doing the work. This dynamic flow of encouragement and caring is a powerful current carrying everyone to a higher level of functioning than they had thought possible.

This practice is one of the most demanding. It requires the willingness to engage the heart and to feel the hearts of those around you. It means coming to grips with fear: the fear of failure, the fear of appearing foolish, the fear of intimacy, the fear of not being cool, the fear of commitment. Supporting others is committing to their success. It means putting ourselves on the line. It means letting ourselves really care about the needs, the fears, the problems, the hopes, and the successes of others. Without this, all of the other leadership practices ultimately fade.

It is this injection of our spirit into the work and efforts of others that communicates to them our passion. It also demonstrates the integrity we bring to the enterprise. Without the practice of supporting the people around us, we are seen as not "walking the talk," and this creates a real sense of cynicism, weakening the desire to follow us. However, to really support others requires an intimacy with the substance of work, the customers, and the people doing the work. This requires us to have the courage to be open to others: to their ideas, hopes, dreams, fears, feelings.

The power of emotions should never be underestimated. "E-motion" itself is a word standing for "energy in motion." Leaders are those who have developed the capacity to engage the energy systems of those around them. Leaders literally help set the energy in motion and then keep the energy flowing by their lavish emotional and psychological support of those around them. In the human system, emotions are the prime motivating force, and those emotions are shaped and channeled by the perceptions and mind-sets of the people involved.

Supporting others does not mean pats on the back and using encouraging words. Supporting others requires the willingness to confront them when they are off purpose and the willingness to be confronted when they see you as being off track. (Both will be explored more fully in outlining later practices on Providing Feedback and Soliciting Personal Feedback.) The capacity to understand the emotional needs and issues of others, as well as an understanding of the psychology of perception, is a vital component of successful leadership. This requires courage, meeting heart to heart, and a willingness to listen to and learn from, as well as care about, others.

Elements of Support

The elements of support are found in the work of Anita Roddick of the Body Shop, Max DePree's legacy at Herman Miller, as well as the founders of Tom's Natural Products and Starbucks Coffee, to mention a few. They typify the sense of emotional and personal support that clearly communicates they are invested in the well-being and success of their people.

At the Body Shop, Roddick has crafted a vision of saving the planet while providing healthy, pleasurable products. All of her employees have a sense of mission and a charge that they are there to help educate while serving the customer. People feel her interest and passion to make a difference. They also feel her deep belief that all of them are important, vital contributors to a great cause.

At Herman Miller, which has been around since before the Great Depression and which is consistently ranked as one of the most admired companies in America, the focus on supporting others is one of the cornerstones of success. The entire company has, since the '30s, been built around empowering, engaging, and supporting the people doing the work. The results speak for themselves. Leaders are willing to "abandon" themselves to the strengths of others and to speak from their hearts, having first listened to the hearts of those around them.

Leaders at Herman Miller focus strongly on the different gifts each person brings. The focus in the company is one of helping to honor and liberate the various abilities, strengths, talents, aspirations, and other gifts of the individuals comprising the company.

There is also a sophisticated understanding at Herman Miller that leadership is emergent and roving. That is, a leader exists in a state of potential in every person, and under the right circumstances that potential rises to the occasion. Leadership is seen as the right and power of the people doing the work, not something vested only in the management team or supervisory levels. A consistent system is in place for supporting this emergent leadership and empowerment of the human system.

Tom's Natural Products of Maine has been a wild success story of heart and principles winning out over slick marketing and financial fire power. Tom's products have developed a growing successful company with a growing and committed customer base by emphasizing quality, service, and employee involvement. The support mechanisms follow a consistent philosophy and set of core values. Everyone engaged in the business is honored for the value they bring and recognized, as well as coached, in process improvements.

Starbucks Coffee of Seattle is a rapidly growing company that has nearly tripled its stock price since its inception just a few years ago. The employees, many young and employed part-time, enjoy full medical benefits and pay/stock options. The turnover rate is 100 percent in the industry, but only 50 percent for Starbucks. The employees are lavishly trained, coached, and supported in understanding the business, the products, and customer service. Their ideas, suggestions, and dreams are elicited, listened to, and many times implemented. The results: phenomenal growth, strong customer loyalty, high employee commitment and enthusiasm, profits, strong stock appreciation, and a powerful sense of making a difference in the world of work.

Again from Steve Ardia, retired CEO of Goulds Pumps:

> I think the next level out into the future is going to be more and more empowerment of the individual worker. Give him the proper tools, give him the proper training, make sure he has your full support, and he can make the decision on the spot. Nobody actually knows the situation better than the person who is doing the job, and if we're to delight our customers, then we must give the employees the ability to make decisions and make more of them. We must commit our resources and satisfy the customer. That will be the next level of evolution we've got to achieve.

This ethic of supporting people is a source of immense power and influence. However, it must come from a sincere desire to make a difference and to help others. Used as a manipulative device, it will ultimately backfire. If the support is used with a desire to drive the organization and human system toward realizing the vision and setting up a win-win situation for all involved, then it becomes a tidal wave of good will and emotional motivation that is irresistible.

Critical Questions to Ask

When considering how to support people effectively, ask:

- What can I do that would most support you in increasing your effectiveness?
- What am I doing that you wish I would stop doing? What gets in the way of making your job easier, more effective, more stimulating?
- What am I doing that is most supportive and helpful to you in getting the job done? Why is it helpful? What else could be added to increase power and effectiveness?
- What resources are available to us that we just haven't taken advantage of?
- If you had a magic wand, what would you change about the way you get supported here in getting the job done? Why those changes? What would that do for you? How would it make it better?

A truly wise leader realizes that people do not work for him or her. In fact, it is the other way around. The leader works for his or her people. A critical component of this is the realization that "the more I can support the people around me in their ability to get the job done, the better they can perform, and the more they can support me, my purposes, and my goals."

For example, we worked with the owner of a successful regional publishing company, and he took this practice to heart. With our help, he began asking employees, "What do you need from me in order to do your job at the highest level of excellence?" He took notes.

Then, in looking over his notes, he discovered a central theme. He realized his employees needed to feel they mattered; there was a real hunger to know that they made a difference and they were recognized and appreciated.

With no extra cost to the organization, the owner set up an ongoing recognition and involvement process. Almost immediately, there was a 30 percent increase in productivity!

The owner discovered something else of extraordinary value for him-self—he discovered that running the company was a lot more fun! He began to feel supported by everyone around him in a way he had never previously experienced. This all derived from his ongoing process of questioning how and what everyone needed from him in order to func-tion at the highest level of excellence, and then his careful listening and responsiveness to their ideas and feelings.

This kind of support is priceless and can catapult the human system to a whole new order and magnitude of effective functioning. However, it comes with a price. The price is the willingness to really listen, then to act and support. The price also includes the courage to extend your-self emotionally to others. It requires not just your sweat, but some of your blood. It requires you to commit yourself to the success of others, walk the extra mile to try to understand the needs and interests of those around you, and then to act in a consistent and caring way. This is real support, and it has no equal in tapping the vast motive power that exists as potential in the human system.

Support also means ensuring that everyone in the enterprise under-stands what the critical elements for achieving success are and what the organization is trying to accomplish. This requires the analytical and rigorous review of what is really essential and then the drive and com-mitment to communicate it. Gene Kaczmarski at Medaphis put it this way in an interview with me:

> Once the vision and operational plan were created, they gave me a vehicle to communicate where Medaphis was going and how we planned to get there. Having defined the Mission, Values, Key Elements for Success, and Implementation Strategy provided a framework with which every employee in the company could relate.

Support also extends to the concept of continuous learning. In the rapidly changing and demanding world of today, wherein the four ele-phants are charging around, the only sure thing is the requirement that we keep on learning. This means that we as leaders are not only supporting others in the process of continuous learning, but that we ourselves are committed to our own ongoing education. This requires the capacity to be curious, open, and willing to challenge our beliefs and assumptions. It also means we are committed to an interactive environment where we are learning from each other more rapidly and gracefully.

The process of supporting others means a commitment to their growth and learning as well as the same commitment to ourselves. Without this, all of the other support measures will only be so much emotional feel-good-ism. We must realize that to drive toward the vision, focusing upon purpose, setting standards and goals, providing resources, and then supporting others, requires a keen appreciation of the need for and requirements of continuous learning.

Deming, in his famous 14 points about creating a total quality environment, says we "must drive out the fear." His point is that total quality can only exist in an environment in which people can learn and make continuous process improvements. This, he says, cannot occur when there is an atmosphere of fear and mistrust.

We know from all the research in sociology and the behavioral sciences that learning is retarded when either fear, intimidation, anxiety, or mistrust is high. However, these states are all too common in many workplaces in corporate and political America. It is impossible to really support others without supporting their learning processes, and it is impossible for people to learn quickly or well when they feel fear or mistrust.

What it comes down to is simple. Leaders, in order to be successful, must create ways to support others in increasing and improving their capacity to learn. This means that one of the most critical functions of leaders is that of removing the barriers to learning. This requires leaders to focus on removing whatever fear, mistrust, and sense of anxiety exist in the work environment.

If fear is the single greatest barrier to learning, then what creates fear? Potential job loss is the great fear today, and management cannot promise employees they will always have their jobs. Leaders can, however, help focus people on what they can do to ensure maximum effectiveness and skill transfer so that the necessity for layoffs is minimized, and if they do occur, the people involved have the self-leadership skills and learning tools to create greater opportunities for employment.

There is, however, an equally powerful fear that limits learning and performance enhancements, and it has little to do with job loss. It has to do with the fear of being shamed or embarrassed in front of others. I have found it to be the single greatest source of anxiety and self-limiting behavior in the workplace. The fear of being shamed, of appearing foolish, awkward, or embarrassed, is a powerful force in retarding the learning process. It is linked to our strong cultural need for approval and acceptance and the fear of being rejected or found deficient in some critical ways. For example, I was working with a senior executive in one of the divisions of AT&T when 90 of his top people were broken into nine sub-teams of 10 each. They were asked to list the top five barriers to process improvement and total quality. All nine teams independently listed "fear" in their lists. The leader was amazed and in a loud voice said, "There is no fear here!" I gently pointed out to him how his response fed the fear.

This sense of shame has its roots in any old failures, psychological and social traumas coming out of our childhood, teenage years, and young-adult experiences. Often, we have created defense mechanisms to protect us from re-experiencing such traumas again. Often, we have placed a set of self-limiting parameters on our behaviors and on our willingness to risk and try new ways of acting and being. This slows down or prevents learning, thus crippling the capacity of individuals, teams, and the over-all human system to grow, develop, and learn quickly.

What is often at the root of all this is a set of sub-vocal, nearly uncon-scious, negative self-evaluations and decisions which then have a whole host of defensive strategies and behaviors in place to protect against dis-covery or validation of what we most fear might be true about ourselves. This means that nearly everyone you meet in the workplace, and even in your social set, is running about with an entrenched set of defenses that protect them from and get in the way of having real contact, rapid learning, and an open approach to dealing with others.

In my work with individuals, teams, and organizations, I have dis-covered that it is impossible to get real traction in the change process if attention and tools are not provided to help address the self-limiting beliefs and patterns. A major aspect of our work at Staub-Peterson, especially in our five-day leadership seminar, is providing practical tools to individuals for personal mastery and team-working tools to teams and organizations for team mastery.

The job of leaders, whoever they might be and at whatever level in the organization they might exist, is then to help people counter the internal negative self-talk and self-limiting beliefs that maintain the defenses. This requires creating a sense of interpersonal safety and fostering trust.

Interpersonal safety is created when the leaders are willing to demon-strate their capacity to risk themselves by opening themselves to others. This requires courage and commitment. Interpersonal safety is created whenever people are recognized and appreciated for having taken some risks versus being called on the carpet and punished for those risks. Trust is generated when actions mesh with words and when commit-ments are kept. Trust is also fostered when the leaders offer a team of individuals a vision that counters whatever self-limiting beliefs have been prevalent. There is a sense of really believing in the capabilities, talents, intentions, and capacities of others. This sense of leaders' faith in and vision of what people are capable of achieving is a powerful antidote to the old shame-based systems and internal defenses.

All of this hinges on the commitment and willingness of the leaders to put their skin in the game and take the first steps in demonstrating the courage to risk. It also means a faithfulness to keeping our word and matching our actions to our speech. This is integrity at its best.

A powerful tool, if used from the heart, is that of attribution. Attribution is the process of holding forth or attributing certain qualities, talents, abilities, or intentions to someone else. It is an antidote to negative self-evaluation and limiting beliefs about what can be done or accomplished.

The skill required is to first sit down and write out the real or even possible qualities and talents you see in someone else or even in a collection of people, such as a team. Then you systematically communicate that vision of what they are capable of doing to them in a series of messages. You consistently look for opportunities to embed your message about their real capabilities and talents in every encounter. You are communicating in an ongoing manner that they have value. This must be done in a manner that does not imply they are currently lacking. It should be seen as having the power to multiply and add value to current valuable service.

An Example

Leaders who support others will be lavishly supported in return. Support is emotional, psychological, and even spiritual in form. It requires courage and consistent modeling. True support effectively removes the shame-based components, which induce fear and limit learning. The principles are found in five rules:

- Tell the truth and do it in a caring and consistent way.
- Model what you say and hold yourself accountable for aligning speech with actions.
- Reward and encourage risk taking in the process of learning and improving.
- Consistently offer a higher vision of what people are capable of achieving, and encourage them to step out of defensive postures through a picture of what is possible.
- Listen with empathy and support small first steps, which offer learning a movement while initially minimizing the risk.

Supporting others is the key to being supported in turn. It is a practice which must occur daily, from which flows both the function of encouraging others and the emotional companion called caring. It is a practice that builds upon the others and increases the power of followership. Supporting others in an ongoing manner creates a vortex of increasing energy and an incredible can-do attitude throughout the people making up the human system of any enterprise. Use this practice and feel its power in amplifying your influence and effectiveness, and the influence and effectiveness of the people around you.

PRACTICE 9

Providing Feedback

GIVE FEEDBACK

Providing feedback

makes you a coach,

someone who cares

about the work being

done and the people

doing it.

You don't necessarily miss feedback, unless it's non-existent, as was the case with the CFO of a $50 million company I worked with. "They don't give a flying flip about what I'm trying to do to help this company," he told me. "No one cares!" He glared at me, and yet beneath the anger I saw the fear and the hurt. "What leads you to that conclusion, John?" "They haven't given me a performance review in two years. I do not hear anything about the job I'm doing unless there's some major screwup. I just assume I must be doing OK if I don't hear anything, but I just don't know where I stand!"

As I sat there I remembered the words of the president: "John is one of the most competent people I have ever worked with. I just let him be and focus my attention on some of my 'problem children.' You'll find John to have great morale and be a font of ideas." Little did he know of the serious disconnect between his private evaluation and thoughts about John and what John did within the feedback vacuum. With some tact and coaching, the gap was closed, and John's feelings changed dramatically. Unfortunately, this failure to provide focused performance feedback is a common occurrence.

151

The critical function of providing feedback to others is that of coaching—helping them learn and become more effective. The emotional energy that flows concurrent with that function is caring—caring about the success of the work and of the people doing the work. This helps drive and empower all of the practices mentioned.

The courage to tell the truth and to tell it with compassion is found in exceptional leaders. However, they understand that the truth they tell is only the truth as they see it, seldom forgetting the relativity of perception. This is where courage comes into play. Realizing that they cannot know the total truth, they are willing to put it out there without being trapped in the rigid stance of thinking it is the total truth. Therefore, exceptional leaders are willing to put their truths out there and listen to the response, taking it into account, negotiating the gray areas, and reinforcing the aspects that seem most clear-cut.

Here is an interesting experiment to try: Go bowling, but as you approach the lane shut your eyes and do not open them. Ask someone for feedback, but forbid them to be specific. They can only say: "In the ballpark" or "way off." You can't even record the score! How much fun do you think you'll have? How quickly can you make improvements in your performance under such limited feedback?

Now review how specific and focused you are in your feedback and the system you have in place to help performance. How will you make that system and feedback more powerful and useful?

EXERCISE

> Write down six things you will do to create a powerful feedback effect. Write down how that effect will be measured (feedback on your feedback). Look at those six things and see how you might want to change them after you have read this chapter.

Leaders know that if the people in an enterprise are to thrive and perform at their best, they need to have clear and consistent feedback—feedback that focuses on communicating appreciation and course corrections. It is impossible to get anything close to the maximum power and full intelligence of the human system if there is not a rich and effective feedback process in place. To be an empowering leader requires the training, coaching, awareness expansion, and dialogue that are generated when feedback is provided in a consistent and systematic manner. To do this, a leader needs to know where the followers and potential followers are—what they feel, think, and see.

The effectiveness of the feedback process for leadership also depends upon where you are coming from when you give the feedback. If the intention is really to help the recipient be more effective and successful, then that is communicated by the manner in which the feedback is provided. If the intention is punitive or to cover your rear end, or if it comes out of fear or is merely done to manipulate, then it will ultimately backfire and be negative in impact. It really boils down to the fact that how we talk to others and what we intend in the communication really matters. It is such a primary practice, and so rudimentary to the effort of creating a truly effective employee, strong relationships, and an exceptional team, that most assume it occurs as a matter of course. As one executive once said to me, "Isn't this so axiomatic and basic that every manager does this in his or her sleep?"

No! Having consulted in all sectors of the economy and worked with thousands of people, I have been amazed at how poorly this practice is applied.

EXERCISE

Pause for a moment and think about the last time someone sat you down and really talked to you about your career and your work performance. How often does it happen? How much time and effort goes into it? How intently did the other person listen and ask searching, provocative questions? Did you feel really listened to—engaged and valued?

Now how often and to what depth does it occur with the people who report to you? How intently and carefully do you listen and reflect on what they are saying? How often does this occur among peers?

It is my experience that providing clear, focused feedback is one of the most neglected fundamentals of effective leadership.

Watch a basketball team play and notice how much communication and feedback goes on during the game. This level of intensity, support, encouragement, and corrective feedback is essential if the team is to succeed. The coach gives it; the assistant coaches give it; the players get it and give it; the officials are giving and receiving it; and on and on. It makes for tremendous learning. Then, after the game, there is a post-mortem analysis and review with additional learning and feedback occurring. This is the kind of learning and feedback that is so rare in most corporations, most divisions, most work teams, and most supervisory relationships.

True, a basketball game is not a business. But much of what goes into creating outstanding feedback and learning for the basketball team can be applied to crafting an exceptional supervisory relationship and superlative team approach. This is really lacking in the practices of most managers and leaders.

One young company we worked with had been growing at a phenomenal rate. In fact, they had become No. 1 in their industry after only eight years. In helping them address the many problems that inevitably arise during periods of rapid change, it was clear that the performance-appraisal process was ineffective, and that managers avoided it at all costs. One manager expressed his attitude this way: "I don't believe in this review bullshit. But we have to do it. So let's get it over with."

It turns out that many employees had not had a review in more than a year. Some had not had reviews in more than three years. Some said they thought they might have had a review, but they were not sure!

Employees felt angry, frustrated, and neglected. They experienced the absence of an effective review process as a lack of the company's concern and caring. Only after an effective process was put in place was management able to address the lack of trust that had spread across the company as it grew.

Unfortunately, this is not an exception. It seems to be the rule that performance feedback is provided in a very spotty and non-systematic manner. The process is not widely respected, nor is it usually effectively practiced.

Why does it not occur more frequently and more effectively? The reason given is that people just get so busy in the course of doing their jobs that they don't have the time. This is a cop-out. The reason it doesn't happen is threefold:

1. It is not valued as a vital part of the manager's job. It is not viewed as an integral part of the work process. This robs it of systems integrity.
2. It is not something most have had modeled for them; neither have they been trained or coached in doing well. They lack competency here.
3. It is emotionally difficult to really sit down and talk with depth and candor about someone's performance career—it requires interpersonal intimacy.

To provide feedback well requires courage and persistence. It is easy to let providing feedback slide. However, a great price is paid when performance feedback is not provided in a consistent and ongoing manner. As Steve Bachand, CEO of Canadian Tire, told me:

> I think the first thing is to make sure my own personal behavior is reinforcing the new direction, reinforcing the new way of thinking. I've had to be sure to be quick to compliment someone on doing something correctly. I've had to be quick to say, "Hey look, Jim, that was a mistake. Let's learn from it. Let's move on."
>
> I would say that feedback is just continuous reminders of where we want to get to.
>
> I would also say that there's no shortcut other than a lot of time and a lot of work and a lot of constant reminders of what we're trying to do, what we're trying to accomplish. Feedback is just constantly working to be sure people have the key understanding.

We spend half of our waking life at work, and a person's career is one of the defining elements of his or her life. Our successes and failures at work have a significant impact on our lives. So much is riding on how we perform: finances, family well-being, identity, self-worth, and so on. Few things we do have as much impact on our lives.

We all have a heavy investment in the work we do. Clearly, knowing where we stand and how we are doing is important. If we are doing well, it is great to be told this and to feel appreciated. If we are not performing well, it is critical that we become aware of this, learn how to correct it, and know how we can be winners.

Given the power of this life endeavor, how much real, ongoing feedback and guidance do we receive, especially around the two vectors of relationships and results? Not nearly enough! Often the performance feedback is, at best, limited to technical aspects of the job and does not include the impact on team, peers, and other critical relationships.

Most employees must guess how they are performing in the eyes of their managers and leaders. What usually happens is that the most intensive feedback, and in some cases, most of the feedback many of us are given, occurs in an annual performance review. So, once a year we get some sort of mark or grade, tied usually to a justification around compensation adjustments, about our performance in one of our most critical and defining life activities—an activity that consumes about half of our waking lives. There is something seriously flawed in this scenario.

A not-so-subtle message is given when the performance feedback occurs only once a year. It is a devaluation of the people doing the work. It also leads to some interesting games and acts of avoidance on the part of those providing the reviews and those receiving them.

Most employees must guess how they are performing in the eyes of their supervisors and peers. The sorry state of performance reviews reveals a glaring weakness in American management. As one manager put it, "If they don't tell us anything, we think we must be doing okay. I wish they'd tell us when we're off course—we'd make the course corrections. Often, it feels like they just don't give a damn about us!"

There is also the issue of the quality of the data shared, the way we are talked with, and the way we talk to others. The process of delivering feedback is critical. However, very few managers have ever received a really powerful and effective performance review. The vast majority of performance reviews are executed poorly, if they are executed at all. When reviews are done, it is usually because they have been mandated—not because they are valued as powerful tools that create empowered and effective employees.

At Staub-Peterson, we have helped organizations revamp and renew their feedback processes while fundamentally increasing the power and efficacy of the performance-appraisal process. We help them create a 360-degree feedback system around team performance that ties into personal goals and objectives of the individual. We also help them craft an ongoing coaching process that has quarterly mini-reviews fed by weekly or monthly coaching sessions. This is all built out of careful interviews with the senior management team and representative elements of the organization. It is tied to the values, vision, mission, and strategic objectives of the organization. This is usually integrated into a Strategic Human Systems Plan, which provides the framework for shaping and moving the entire organization down the path of excellence and powerful results.

Since many executives do not have the necessary "people skills" to provide impactful, coordinated, and comprehensive reviews, we additionally make part of the system a training process in giving and receiving effective and impactful reviews. Many supervisors have never received a good review themselves; thus they have little idea of the tremendous power at their disposal. This also applies to giving ongoing process feedback daily.

The feedback given typically lacks three things: depth, strategic guidance, and heart.

Depth

The lack of depth comes from a failure in intimacy. Most likely, the supervisor is not intimate with the work being done or with the people working with and for him or her. The reviews and feedback during the year most often consist, at best, of either simply "pats on the back" or pointing out a specific failure or problem behavior. This does not allow for real understanding and growth.

Lacking depth, the process of giving feedback becomes one of wasted opportunities. The depth experience comes when the leaders put it firmly in their minds that giving high-quality feedback is one of the most important practices they can apply.

Few things in life have more impact than sitting down eye to eye with another human being and telling him or her the truth about his or her pattern of behavior and performance. Telling them about a specific behavior, sharing the impact that behavior had on the team and the work process, and then letting them know how you feel about it is an incredible experience of depth and intimacy. This applies to both praising people and criticizing them.

Why does this work? Despite all of our complexities, we are also, in some ways, very simple. We all tend to be self-interested. We are curious and concerned about our fate, our well-being, and our happiness. We tend to respect those who show us respect and trust those who demonstrate trust in us. We tend to be suspicious of those who are suspicious of us and contemptuous of those who show us contempt. We end up reflecting the traits, qualities, assumptions, and behaviors that are demonstrated toward us from an individual as well as a system.

It is extremely powerful when someone takes the time to really let us know, with precision and attention to details, how we are doing: what they appreciate and why, what they are concerned about and why. This leaves us touched and engaged, knowing someone is really paying attention and that they care.

Strategic Guidance

Caring feedback delivered with precision is not enough. The feedback must also be strategically guided. That is, it must be delivered in a context of ongoing, focused professional and personal development. The intention of the leader is to attend to the developmental aspects of preparing others to learn and grow in both scope and effectiveness over time. Part of this strategic guidance is judgment as to what aspects to emphasize and what to target first in developing action plans for growth and improvement.

Other aspects of strategy apply to pattern identification, tie-in to the employee's aspirations and motivations, and the overlay and integration of organizational strategic needs into the guiding data given. The integration of these elements gives the supervisor a logic and focus for the feedback process. It also provides a wonderful process for embedding the values, purpose, and aspirations of the enterprise into the matrix of ongoing, everyday work in the heart and mind of the person receiving the feedback.

Heart

This is the final ingredient in creating meaningful and powerful feedback. It underpins and supports depth and strategy. Without it, there is no real personal encounter that can have much lasting impact. It is the "place we are coming from" when we talk to another. It must be inspired by the quote, "I can't hear what you are saying, because who you are is speaking so loudly."

Giving feedback without passion is ineffectual. What kind of passion do I mean? The passion to see the enterprise excel; the passion to see individuals be the best they can be; the genuine desire to personally achieve excellence; the passion to lead and make a difference. All of this requires heart.

If I am giving you feedback that is technically correct and strategically aligned, but I am disinterested and disengaged, you will pick up on that and know it at a gut level. Conversely, if I deliver the feedback with a lot of anger or judgment, you will know that, too, and feel punished, if not shamed. Either way, I have lost much of your motivation and desire to really engage with me. At best, you consider me somewhat insincere; at worst, you feel I am either simply trying to manipulate you or punish and humiliate you. When this occurs, it is tragic.

Heart is that elemental force that really drives the development of intimacy, integrity, and passion. It is the substance of meaningful relationships. It cannot be faked for long, nor can anything take its place. Feedback without engaging your heart will leave others cold. It is like professing that you care for someone and are really interested in their problems while clipping your fingernails and watching television. You have not really tuned in and encountered them.

The key to providing this powerful feedback from your heart is to demonstrate what has been called "tough love." Tough love means sharing the passion by being hard on results and performance-based issues, while being soft on the relationship or people side. How does this work? It works when you hold the line and demand accountability for results without blaming or shaming.

For example: You ensure there is follow-up and follow-through on projects and assignments. Results are tracked and responsibilities are clear with no excuses. In talking with the people involved in producing the results, however, you talk in supportive and caring ways. So, you make it clear that others are accountable for and required to get both results and commitments while dealing with the relationships in a coaching, positive manner.

The result is that the people involved feel cared for, valued, and also understand that the results and commitments are not optional. This generates a strong desire to produce and return the trust—living up to the requirements and the way they are treated. It also does something else to advance the leadership agenda: it models the desired behaviors and values, leading to a process of replicating those behaviors with customers, other departments, suppliers, teams, and so on. This is of incalculable value in driving the leadership agenda, creating a consistency of effort with greater degrees of trust, openness, and candor. This means the team and the individual can learn faster, with less resistance and barriers to the transmission of corrective feedback.

Only when you encounter and engage others through meaningful feedback do you become a leader. This means going through the personal barriers you might have to intimacy: encountering people eye-to-eye and heart-to-heart as you tell them what you deeply appreciate, or where they are weak or failing or need to grow. It requires great courage first, and then the application of a few critical skills.

Our lack of courage toward the performance-appraisal process is an American leadership tragedy. It is a failure of nerve that costs us dearly. Only when that courage is present to provide powerful feedback can we apply the skills that generate outstanding results.

EXERCISE

> On a scale from one to 10, how would you rank yourself in terms of the quality of your feedback behavior? If we surveyed your team, how would they rank you on the effectiveness, frequency, and consistency of your feedback?
>
> What is your life orientation to developing your potential and the potential of those who work with and for you? What do you really believe people are all about? Think long and hard about these questions, for they shape the quality of your interpersonal interactions.

Recent research has shown that the most common cause of failure among middle- and senior-level managers who fall by the wayside is poor interpersonal skills, not the least of which is poor feedback processes.

EXERCISE

> Ask your boss to conduct a survey of your communication and feedback processes with peers and direct reports. State that you will take a cut in pay if they do not report that you do

an outstanding job of keeping them informed and up to date
on company issues, as well as providing a clear understanding of where they stand and how they can improve.

If you are like many managers and supervisors in corporate America
today, you will never make such a commitment. The sad truth is that the
feedback most often provided to the workforce is inadequate for the highly
competitive global marketplace and the rapid pace at which we do business.

EXERCISE

Conduct a series of quality circles about the power and efficacy of the feedback processes you provide to the people around
you. Share the results with your superior, and also plan on
improving the impact of feedback provided. Create observable,
measurable criteria by which to gauge the results of such a
process over the next 12 months. Publish that plan and the measurable criteria so that all in your department can see what standard you are setting—one by which you are being evaluated.

Be aware: Without ongoing corrective and affirming feedback, any
change process will quickly wither and die. These days, that withering
will cost people jobs and can spell the difference between life or death
for a team or organization.

Feedback Skills

Keep in mind that people want to know the score. A critical aspect of
enhancing operational functioning has to do with benchmarking and
ongoing comparison against the benchmarks. People need to know what
the best-in-class performance is of the key competitors in their field or
area. They need to have developmental feedback about how they are doing
and how they can do even better. Tough love means the data can be supportive of what is best within them, inviting them to use those strengths and
qualities while challenging them to stretch, and requiring results.

What are the skills necessary to do this? The essential feedback skills are:

- Strategic identification of leverage
- Mind-setting
- Shifting contexts
- The ability to ask powerful questions
- Active listening
- Constructing confrontational and appreciative messages

- Designing action plans
- Follow-through and follow-up behaviors
- Setting up ongoing feedback loops

Strategic Identification of Leverage

This is the art and science of effectively reading others' preferred modes of learning and of absorbing information. It also includes the capacity to analyze and pick the best starting point given the situation, organizational needs, and personal issues. It is, at root, the recognition of diversity and the fact that people have different hot and cold buttons, preferences, and ways of learning. They also have a need to be appreciated as unique and valued, and to be seen for themselves.

Mind-setting

This is the powerful technique of creating a mental frame of reference for someone else in order to help her or him absorb and make sense out of what you have to say. It is the practice of generating a context within which the message can be held and understood. A mind-set is generated by laying out, up front, what you hope to accomplish, what you want the other to take away, and how you want him or her to feel, think, and make use of the information to be shared. It also reveals your hopes, aspirations, and desired outcomes in providing the feedback. This is all done before you give the feedback. It asks for buy-in to the intent of the mind-set before the message is delivered. If done well, it "frames" the message for the receiver, enabling them to hear it with less interference from their ego, fear levels, listening distortions, and past assumptions.

Shifting Contexts

This refers to the tool of moving the content of the conversation to another level or frame of reference when you run into an obstruction or difficulty in the other person's listening. It allows for flexible responsiveness and builds upon the depths of awareness demonstrated in Edwin Markham's poem in Practice 5, page 116. Example: "We seem to be stuck here. What if we step back and talk about what our vision is and what our essential purpose is all about? Tell me what you see as the vision and purpose of this work we are doing." It is moving the discussion to another frame of reference and using that reference point to break a logjam.

The Ability to Ask Powerful Questions

This builds upon the power questions outlined in Practice 4. Knowing how to ask questions that engage the interest and curiosity of others is an important skill. Examples: "If you were in my shoes and I had engaged in this behavior, what would you have to say, and how would you hope I would respond?" "Given what we are trying to accomplish here, what do you think the best approach to giving feedback would be?" "What is the best way for me to help you hear some feedback that points out how you could be performing better?"

Active Listening

This is covered in Practice 4 and basically means listening in an interactive and engaging manner, using the skills outlined in that section.

Constructing Confrontation and Appreciation Messages

This is a skill that is essential to providing powerful, impactful, and accurate feedback. It consists of four distinct steps you use when confronting and giving appreciation:

1. Write down the essence of what you want to say and what you hope to accomplish.

2. Be behavior specific. Spell out the behavior in clear, non-judgmental terms, such that anyone hearing your description would know what had been done. This is done to ensure that the behavior in question is being addressed, and not some unprovable emotional or psychological state. You want to be clear that what is being talked about is a verifiable behavior and not some interpretation.

   Examples: "When you came into the meeting 30 minutes late for the third time," not "When you show disrespect for my meetings." "When you interrupt me as I am talking," not "When you are rude and don't listen." "You turned your back on him and made a face," not "You were bored and disrespectful." "When you stayed an hour late to help us get the mailers out," not "When you were so helpful."

3. State the impact of the behavior on the team, the work effort, the customer, or you. This means you are connecting the specific behavior outlined in step two to some specific impact on the work or the people engaged in doing the work.

Example: "When you came to the meeting 30 minutes late for the third time, the impact was that several people came up to me after the meeting was over and wondered if you were committed to the project." For the appreciation message: "When you stayed an hour late to help us get the mailers out, you enabled us to meet the deadline and gave a powerful message of your commitment to the team. That left me feeling appreciative and really glad to have you on the team."

4. State the impact upon you with regard to your feelings about the incident. This helps to connect you with the issues at hand and states the impact of the behavior upon the relationship. Example: "When you came to the meeting 30 minutes late for the third time, the impact was that several people came up to me after the meeting was over and wondered if you were committed to the project. This left me feeling disappointed and raised my own questions about your commitment."

This four-step process ensures that the corrective and appreciative feedback you wish to provide is targeted, accurate, powerful, and most helpful. It makes use of the four dimensions of leadership: intimacy (in the manner of the communication and the sharing of your emotional reaction), competence (in the depth, precision, and focusing of the feedback), integrity (in the structural wholeness of what is being communicated), and passion (in the commitment and effort made to get a powerful and effective message across).

Designing Action Plans

This is the process of ensuring that there are clear action items and a plan developed for process improvements where needed. These plans should be behavior specific; focus upon measurable issues; have consequences, target dates, target levels; and be monitored. They can be for competency issues in either technical performance or in interpersonal and team performance. Without these mini and maxi action plans, feedback is only half-baked, even if delivered as powerfully as outlined above.

Follow-Through and Follow-Up

All of the plans must be reviewed and feedback has to be provided with regard to progress made or not made. Without follow-through and follow-up, plans are useless. Additionally, lack of follow-up communicates a loud message, saying "I don't take these plans or my feedback to you seriously, and neither should you."

Setting Up Ongoing Feedback Loops

Only with a series of ongoing feedback loops is it possible to provide effective coaching. This means designing and utilizing a systematic process of gathering and giving performance and behavior-specific feedback. Making this part of the everyday process of supervising and managing is the only way to provide consistency and real power in the proactive practice of providing feedback.

The great practice of giving feedback has as its essential function that of helping those around you to learn and improve; the emotional energy flow is that of caring. It is this essential emotional tone of caring and its message of concern that helps drive leadership success. It also provides for the ongoing development and process improvement of others, letting them know where they stand with regard to you and your perceptions about their performance.

Giving feedback is an essential driver in vision realization and the effective focusing of purpose. It allows for learning to occur and is the essence of successful coaching and staff development. Without effective feedback, people feel disconnected, uncared for, and cannot perform at their best. It also means that a wonderful opportunity for cohesiveness and unity of focus is squandered.

Feedback is the practice of making course corrections and helping to develop an increasingly effective workforce. Honor this practice and put it to work for you, and you will reap the rewards. Neglect it, or pay only lip service to it, and you will pay the piper in lost opportunities, decreased followership, and lower morale.

PRACTICE 10

Principled Flexibility

FLEXIBILITY

Being flexible

enables you to be

more responsive and

proactive, thus

increasing trust in

your ability to meet

your evolving needs.

One example comes to mind of the power of flexible thinking. It is a historical and famous battle that occurred in ancient Japan. In the battle of Tensho Iga No Ran (1579), a force of over 10,000 samurai troops, commanded by warlord Oda Nabuo, set upon the ninja province of Iga. Intent upon utter annihilation, Nabuo marched with "10,000 banners fluttering in the autumn breeze, and the sun's rays reflecting off the colors of the armor."

The ninja of Iga were impossibly outnumbered, perhaps as dramatically as 100 to 1. Additionally, in terms of resources, supplies, armor, weapons, and horses, they were hopelessly outclassed. But through superior leadership and flexible and creative strategies, they emerged victorious. Setting traps and employing tactics to confound and confuse the attacking samurai, they separated the vastly superior force into manageable groups and surrounded them systematically.

Stephen Turnbull in his book, *The True Story of Japan's Secret Warrior Cult*, writes: "The Ise samurai were confused in the gloom and dispersed in all directions. They were chased into muddy rice

165

fields and surrounded. Some killed each other by mistake. Others committed suicide. It is not known how many thousands were killed."

Frequently, it was the very thing the samurai believed was the source of his superior security—his impressive and very heavy armor—that afforded the ninja the critical advantages of speed, agility, and above all else, flexibility. In addition, the ninja, unlike the samurai, were not bound by prescribed, "tried and true," traditional battle processes and policies.

The danger of inflexibility and rigid boundaries, typical of a command-and-control paradigm, is that they become increasingly fatal to a leader, an organization, or even a society, as the level of complexity and the pace of change accelerates.

Leadership cannot exist without flexible thinking. Leadership is, by definition, the capacity to forge ahead, blaze new trails, open new realms. It is characterized by breaking with tradition and seizing new opportunities where others see only danger and ruin. Leaders take to heart the single Chinese character, which stands for both crisis and opportunity. They see the opportunities inherent in problems, recognizing that one person's problem is really a business opportunity for someone else. They have to be flexible or they cease seeing the possibilities around them and their teams. Leaders cherish flexibility because it keeps them nimble, quick, and strong.

For all of this, innovative and flexible thinking gets a lot of lip service, but few organizations or managers really commit to the process of creating, nurturing, honoring, and actualizing flexibility within their ranks.

This is our world: increasing levels of complexity and an exponential pace of change. Those systems that cannot adapt, that are unwilling or unable to read the new realities, will be swept aside. This will happen no matter how successful they have been historically.

But what is this thing called flexibility? The dictionary defines it as "1. the capacity to bend without breaking; not stiff or rigid. 2. adjustable to change; capable of modification."

Flexibility is the capacity to adapt, change, and bend, but not break. It requires an open mind, a resilient spirit, and the willingness to innovate. The *Tao Te Ching* puts it this way:

> *Men are born soft and supple;*
> *dead, they are stiff and hard.*
> *Plants are born tender and pliant;*
> *dead, they are brittle and dry.*

Thus whoever is stiff and inflexible
is a disciple of death.
Whoever is soft and yielding
is a disciple of life.

The hard and the stiff will be broken.
The soft and supple will prevail.

The function of this practice is to increase responsiveness and proactivity. The emotional component that goes with it is an increased level of trust. True flexibility is principled in that it is not merely being blown about by the wind, but is rooted in key values and principles.

Flexibility is the capacity to accurately assess the current reality we face and the creativity to adapt and respond to that new reality. This requires a fairly high level of applied intelligence. To be flexible in our thinking means we have developed the capacity to entertain new thoughts and concepts—to learn and to apply that learning to our lives.

What gets in the way of flexibility? What prevents an organization from learning newer and more appropriate responses? By way of answering, consider what Steve Bachand, CEO of Canadian Tire, has to say:

> You can get your organization to observe the things that need doing and are done by more successful competitors, as well as get the organization to understand what has to be done. However, it is very difficult to effectively implement what is observed and understood.
>
> In some cases, it is just the result of a lack of skills, but in most cases, it's just very difficult to break out of the old habits. Some of those habits, or constraints, are a result of the way the organization cooperates—internal processes within the company that become major inhibitors.
>
> For example, we need a sense of urgency about getting it done now, if not yesterday. That was not part of our process previously. Rather, it was, "Look, everything you do, do well. Everything you do, do perfectly. Don't make mistakes." That is too slow and doesn't fit our current reality. It's hard to shed those rules and shackles even if you understand what you're trying to accomplish.

The lack of flexibility, the being stuck in what was successful in the past, was called "hardening of the categories" by Jim Farr, an old boss of mine. This is a dangerous disease that can destroy all a leader has worked for, as well as undermine the health and vitality of a team or organization. As I write this, I think of Ken Olsen at Digital Electronic Corporation and John Ailers at IBM. Both were powerful leaders. However, they were replaced and deemed to have failed their organizations because they became somewhat rigid in their thinking and leadership and apparently lost touch with where their industries were going.

This disease is tragic in its impact, and we can see its result in the business failures and the tragic shortsightedness of companies. It is more than a little responsible for the massive layoffs of personnel in corporate America.

Leaders, those that go the distance, have acquired the capacity to learn quickly—to change what they and their systems are doing. They do this knowing it is required by the changing and evolving world around them. They have inoculated themselves against category hardening and premature stiffness by playing with ideas, exploring new aspects of themselves, and surrounding themselves with people who will challenge them. The flexibility this creates gives a tremendous strategic and tactical advantage in dealing with and responding to customers, suppliers, competitors, changing markets, fellow employees, and stockholders.

This flexibility is not simply blowing with the prevailing breeze. To be effective, it has to be principled flexibility. That is, a central core of principles gives coherence, meaning, and substance to the adaptability and creative responsiveness of the system. Lacking that inner gyroscope of meaning, there is a very real danger of wobbling off course or of creating anarchy and chaos.

Arie de Guys, former director of planning for Royal Dutch Shell, participated in creating a culture of flexible thinking through innovative, team-oriented processes. Executives would meet and participate in scenario creation and paradigm exposure. The scenario processes worked on generating creative plans around possible global events and situations. The paradigm exposure dealt with everyone on the team, exploring their different conceptual maps of reality, checking each other's assumptions and beliefs. The result was a team that could surface and challenge assumptions, fixed ideas, and hardened categories. This meant that the thinking patterns became more fluid, open, and creative. All of this rested on flexible thinking, which was disciplined by clear values, direction, and principles. The end result was that Royal Dutch Shell vaulted to the head of the pack in profits with regard to the seven global petroleum and energy companies.

This flexible thinking did not come easily for Royal Dutch Shell, nor does it for any other company or organization. There is a strong tendency in most of us (and certainly in all systems) to create a map of reality that provides predictability, coherence, structure and rules for success. This gets to be a self-referential reality that can blind us to the fact that our map no longer even closely approximates the reality of our customers, our industry, or our culture. It is this tendency that can blind very intelligent people, causing them to not see the obvious while falling behind. This is hardening of the categories. To break out of this trap, or to create a process for avoiding the trap, requires flexible thinking. However, flexible thinking requires a willingness to have our beliefs, our assumptions, and our ways of thinking and evaluating the world challenged.

Flexibility requires a creative and open mind; we must examine what might be required and how we might need to accommodate the rapidly shifting landscape of customers, competitors, technology, information generation and transmission, and so on.

An award in France, the medal of Maria Theresa, is given to the soldier or officer who, by disobeying direct orders and improvising on the scene, saves the day. It is one of the highest awards one can earn. This medal recognizes the incredible courage and resourcefulness it takes to break with a preset line of instructions, creating a new response and set of initiatives based upon the unfolding reality before someone. Winning the award requires great courage, because the consequence of disobeying direct orders in combat is usually death—because the improvisation and changes are not sure, only seemingly better than the orders given. It also requires resourcefulness, because new initiatives occur in combat, under life-and-death circumstances, and they must be accurate, results-driven, and tied into the overall strategic plan. This is, in the words of Spielberg's Indiana Jones, "making it up as we go."

The Battle of Tensho Iga No Ran
In the martial arts, as in life, the advantage lies with the individual who can remain focused while demonstrating flexibility and responsiveness in execution. Given equal skills and strategic know-how, the side with the greatest flexibility will ultimately prevail. As mentioned at the beginning of this practice, in ancient Japan the samurai warrior was the pinnacle of the martial arts tradition. He was well-provisioned, highly trained, expertly armed and armored, lavishly supported. However, the samurai turned out to be no match for the newly emerging ninja method of fighting.

The ninja were poor villagers who could not afford the armor, the horses, or the weaponry of the samurai. They did not have the traditional, powerful training and schooling opportunities that the samurai experienced. They were self-organized, self-taught, and, out of necessity, they learned to improvise, developing new strategies and approaches. They made flexibility their major weapon, and it was awesome.

The ninja outmaneuvered the samurai and outfought them, repeatedly using this weapon. The weapon had as one of its leading components the capacity to learn quickly, using and applying that knowledge in the next encounter. This process of continuous learning and applied improvements through disciplined improvisation gave them an ongoing edge in every situation they faced.

The battle highlighted at the beginning of the chapter is just one demonstration of the superior power of principled flexibility over rigid, formalistic thinking. What worked, and what still works, for the ninja also works in any enterprise. The power of principled flexibility focused upon a clear purpose is really incredible.

Generating this flexible thinking requires five things:

- An emphasis on high quality, continuous information gathering, and reality sampling.
- A set of bedrock operating principles that offer guidance and orientation while maximizing flexibility.
- An emphasis on strategic thinking that is conceptual and creative, out-thinking and out-maneuvering the competition.
- A cultural bias toward improvisation and innovation, within a framework of principles and a coherent strategy.
- A commitment to and deep valuation of continuous, ongoing learning and the willingness to apply that learning to current reality.

3M, more than any other organization in our time, has managed to create such a culture of innovation and flexibility. Their very structure demands and supports creative and flexible thinking, as well as powerful initiative at all levels. Hewlett-Packard and Rubbermaid aren't far behind in their deliberate design to foster human systems, flexibility, and continuous innovation. Unfortunately, they are the exceptions.

How many other organizations actually build in the concept and practice of flexibility within their departments and teams? How many of us have been coached and trained in flexible thinking skills? What is our commitment and that of our leadership system to continuous, lifelong learning? How frequently do we sample reality and actively encourage the people around us to challenge our assumptions and check them against what is going on and developing in the world? Are we clear on what the fundamental principles are by which we approach our work and each other? Do we value and practice strategic thinking, applying it to the challenges before us? What recognition system do we have in place to reward the flexible leaders, managers, and other employees who invent more successful means of accomplishing the organization's purpose?

The answer, tragically, is that not many organizations, managers, or would-be leaders really appreciate, understand, and value principled flexibility. Even fewer practice it.

The result? We have been blinded by our past successes and hypnotized by the mind-set that has defined our past 40 years: the command-and-control paradigm. This leaves us stiffer and more rigid, and less responsive and nimble, in seeing, responding to, and dealing with our rapidly evolving and increasingly complex world.

Yet, it is the absolute requirement of leaders today that they be flexible and principled, capable of learning quickly and of quickly letting go of past paradigms and formulas of success that no longer fit or work. Without principled flexibility, all of the other practices can sink under the unbearable burden of rigidity.

What follows are a few exercises on developing and attending to the applied practice of principled flexibility, taken from some of our work with individual leaders, teams, and organizations. The exercises are designed to help you identify areas of potential improvement as well as increase your "F.Q." (flexibility quotient). Developing strength in this practice opens the door to empowering some of the other practices by helping you to be more available to new ideas, more willing to explore new possibilities, and more capable of rapid and effective change.

Exercises to Develop Your Flexibility Quotient
Answering these questions is a critical function and duty of leadership. To fail to create and cultivate flexible thinking within yourself, the team, and the organization is a great mistake and a failure of leadership.

1. On a scale of one to 10, how flexible would you rate yourself? How easy is it for you to change and adapt? How open are you to new ideas? Can you identify and outline your basic operational principles? How actively do you seek out information about how your industry, competitors, customers, and

technology are changing? Do you think strategically and
value this as a tool for powerful change?

Now ask your direct reports and your boss to rate your flexibility using the same questions. Now try your spouse. Your
children. Your friends. Would their answers agree with yours?
Do you see the value of increasing your flexibility? How
would that be measured? What evidence would you need
to see that would let you know you are being more flexible? How are you cultivating flexible thinking and responsiveness in your followers and organization?

2. Answer the following questions to get a sense of perspec-
tive on the need for principled flexibility:
   • List the major changes that have occurred in your indus-
     try and business over the past few years.
   • What are the technological and market changes that will
     be affecting you over the next few years?
   • What impact are competitors having on your business?
   • How has the work environment changed?
   • What operational changes are necessary?
   • How is your workforce changing?
   • How has your family changed? Your city or town?
   • What changes do you think you will have to be prepared
     to face over the next five years? Ten? Twenty?

3. In a few sentences describe how you have reacted to
change in the past.
   • Have you embraced change and taken a leadership role
     in helping it occur smoothly and effectively?
   • Have you resisted change and held to the past?
   • Ask your direct reports, your boss, your peers, and your
     spouse about how you respond to change.
   • What changes do you think you will have to be prepared
     to face over the next five years? Ten? Twenty?

4. Since the one constant in our age and world is change
and accelerating change, how are you preparing yourself to respond and "ride the elephants" versus being
trampled underfoot?

If you were in charge of the organization and saw: (1)
increasing competition, (2) a need for more stringent
quality, and (3) financial pressures forcing you to make

operational and management changes, would you be pleased at the attitude and responses to change efforts of someone like you?

What would you do if you did not see flexibility or responsiveness in such an individual?

What would happen to those people in the organization who were unwilling or unable to learn and be flexible?

5. List the innovations and changes you have made over the past year. List the innovations and changes your team has made. What innovations and changes are you planning next? How do these align with the vision, mission, purpose, and goals listed earlier?

Other Exercises

- Play a different role in your next team meeting. If you talk a lot, then mostly listen. If you are usually quiet, then speak up.
- Drive to work a different way.
- Reverse or change the sequence of what you do in getting ready for work in the morning.
- Think of a new way to get your point across.
- Practice a new way of listening and responding.
- Change your morning work habits: arrive earlier or later; mingle, if a you're loner; or sit alone, if you're a mingler.
- Ask for help if you never do, and do it alone if you tend to always seek help.
- Give more genuine compliments if you tend to not give compliments.
- Imagine you are a creative genius who happens to be six years old. How would you view the work environment and what you do? What changes would you make to create a stimulating, exciting, and engaging work experience for yourself and others? How would you simplify the process? Make a list of these ideas. Now sit with your team members and ask for their help in redesigning work flow and processes to maximize involvement and enjoyment while producing even higher results.
- Play with questions such as: What have you done to help your department anticipate what will be required by your customers? How are you preparing yourself and others to be able to respond quickly and effectively to the inevitable

changes that are coming but cannot be clearly seen? How
are you organizing yourself and your team to recognize and
seize opportunity as it flies by?

We desperately need people and systems with a deep appreciation for
principled flexibility in functioning and responding. We need leadership
that consciously develops the capacity for flexibility in order to prepare
us for dealing with tomorrow.

This is one of the great practices, and much rides upon it. To fail in
this one is to court greater failure, even disaster, down the road. To cultivate it is to play in the field of possibility, creating a sense of resilien-
cy and innovation.

PRACTICE 11

Soliciting Personal Feedback

SOLICITING
FEEDBACK

Seeking personal

feedback empowers

you and ultimately

exercises your

courage.

General Douglas MacArthur was a renowned warrior and a living legend. During the Korean War, President Truman stood in MacArthur's giant shadow. The general was full of himself and considered Truman a minor functionary, who was at best an irritant and barrier to carrying out the great battle strategy. MacArthur repeatedly failed to seek Truman's feedback and concerns, even though Truman was his commander in chief.

MacArthur, unfortunately by then a legend in his own mind, advocated dropping nuclear bombs in Korea and on the Chinese border. He spoke out in spite of the public policy President Truman had put in place. Truman removed General MacArthur from command and called him back to Washington. While there was a great cry for Truman's impeachment, and although MacArthur had a hero's welcome and ticker tape parade in New York, things unraveled for the general. He failed to heed the feedback of others, and by his own words and attitude rapidly lost support. Truman, soliciting and carefully considering feedback, stood by his principles and gained in stature while MacArthur faded. MacArthur made a fatal mistake, a mistake most of us have often

175

made: not listening to or seeking out performance feedback. If not corrected, the failure to take in feedback brings down careers, destroys marriages, damages friendships, and robs us of success and joy.

The function that flows from seeking feedback is self-empowerment; self-empowerment comes through learning about your impact on others. The emotion that goes with that function is one of courage in the face of fear, probable pain, and insult to ego.

Some of the greatest courage required of a leader is found in seeking honest appraisal and feedback with regard to effectiveness and impact. This requires seeking out, listening to, and acting on what others have to say. It requires the strength to ask, "How can I improve my leadership behaviors? What do you think helps most? Least? How do I get in the way or shoot myself in the foot?" It takes the courage to say, "I screwed up," or "I was wrong," or "I'm sorry." It also means, paradoxically, rewarding people who have hurt your feelings by encouraging them to continue telling you what they think is wrong with you!

As Arie de Guys points out, the key to having a competitive edge is learning faster than the competition. To be able to learn faster requires that you get your ego out of the way in order to see and hear how you can improve in your leadership effectiveness. Ego, fear, and impatience lengthen the education time curve and slow down the process of learning. The ability to learn by seeking out, hearing, and utilizing personal leadership feedback is essential to improving your leadership effectiveness.

If there is any science to leadership, it is in leaders ensuring that they get feedback about their impact on followers. This is the golden rule of effective leadership: Do not fly blind! Know where you stand with regard to the perceptions of others. Steve Ardia expressed it this way:

> As I look at myself, I think that one of the real keys to becoming more effective is knowing more about yourself. You have to understand yourself first and realize how each of us is different from everyone else. You can increase your awareness of how you impact other people positively and negatively, and with that information, you can modify your own behavior so that you have a more positive impact more and more of the time. Slowly you build a core; you build a momentum, and the organization starts to move in that direction. I think the other thing you need is patience. It does take time. It takes much more time than I ever imagined, and patience was never one of my strong points, but you must have it.

Without an effective network and system of feedback loops, a leader is, at best, flying blind. The lack of feedback makes it impossible for leaders to develop any accurate degree of self-awareness and understanding of their impact on others and the overall team. At worst, the leader is operating from faulty assumptions and inadequate data about the concerns and followership of others. The only guide is then the ego—notorious for its unreliability.

Again, this is so axiomatic that everyone nods their heads. "Of course we want feedback as to how others see us and what they feel about our decisions and actions." Yet how many have the wherewithal to create ongoing, focused, and meaningful feedback for themselves? The answer: not many. My experience is that many leaders and managers are flying half blind, if not completely blind! Why? There are several reasons:

- Fear of what they might hear.
- A culture of fear in which employees have learned that it is not wise to point out when the emperor has no clothes.
- A prevailing command-and-control paradigm that sees asking others for personal performance feedback as a sign of weakness and a slippage of power.
- Failing to realize the importance of being self-aware and informed as to how we are perceived by potential followers.

The fear of hearing what others think about your leadership is a major barrier. It is very common and is usually covered up with other feelings and conscious rationalizations. "I'm not here to win a popularity contest" is one frequent defense against finding out what others think and feel. "As a manager I have to do unpopular things, so why give them the chance to criticize me?" is yet another argument. These statements miss the point and indicate a faulty understanding of what leadership feedback can and should do for a leader. A fragile ego can thus be buttressed by denial and rationalization without ever having to learn and grow in how to communicate, touch, and align people more effectively.

It is my observation as a student of behavioral science, a trainer, and a consultant that one of the striking problems in corporate America centers around the fragility of the executive and supervisory egos. There is a great deal of embedded fear about what others might think and feel about someone. It is largely unconscious but can surface fairly quickly. It takes courage to acknowledge the fear and then face it. It is just too easy to lie to oneself. The culture supports this process of self-description. It is really a tacit process of flying blind in order to preserve the ego!

To test this in yourself, try the following exercise.

EXERCISE

Imagine that your peers and subordinates are going to honestly evaluate your performance as a leader. They are going to write it up individually, and a report is going to be issued to you with an emphasis on your strengths, weaknesses, growth areas, potential, and reputation, as well as some advice about what you can do to improve.

Now take a sheet of paper and answer the following questions: What do you think they will advise? What will be the common themes? What will the advice say? How do you feel about what you think they'll say?

Now imagine taking this data and sharing it with others. Would you feel comfortable sharing this data with your boss? How about if it were posted in your area and you were measured publicly against it? What would you feel ashamed of? What would you be most proud of? What have you minimized that has had the most negative impact? How will you respond to the people who say the most critical things? Where will you feel most personally challenged?

At Staub-Peterson, we have conducted hundreds of leadership impact studies, gathering anonymous data from subordinates, peers, and superiors for targeted leaders—leaders in trouble, as well as real stars. Every one of them, male and female, was surprised at some of the themes that emerged. They had all underestimated the amount of frustration generated by some commonplace behaviors they had seen as trivial—behaviors others viewed as serious and problematic. Leaders were flying from either partially blind (stars) to mostly or completely blind (those in obvious trouble).

This exercise has served to underscore for me just how difficult it is to get our egos out of the way, deal with the fear of being hurt, and get at the true perceptions about our leadership performance with regard to our impact on others. It also points to the level of fear we have created such that others do not feel safe in coming to us to give their feedback.

A culture of fear is really a disease that is endemic and of epidemic proportion in many organizations. Deming, the grandfather of the quality revolution, points out that "We must drive out fear if we are to create a quality-driven enterprise." Given this, what does fear do to a culture? What creates fear, and how do we diminish it or drive it out?

Fear paralyzes communication and sows bitter seeds of mistrust. It limits the team interaction and team play that are so vital to long-term success. Further, it creates an atmosphere of doubt while fostering sub-par and grossly flawed feedback. In a culture where fear flourishes, feedback is strangled and distorted.

When fear runs as an undercurrent in an organization, leaders get blindsided. This stems from the basic human tendency to cover one's rear end and not invite criticism or curry disfavor by communicating problems about leadership performance. It also generates risk aversion as well as covering up mistakes and problems. People then do not feel they can honestly and openly point out flaws, make corrections, and learn from mistakes without being punished.

The fear runs in several channels: the fear of job action being taken, the fear of being shamed publicly, the fear of seeming wrong, foolish, or awkward. The stronger the flow, the more poison in the common well. We have also developed corporate cultures in which people feel they must be right all the time or they have failed.

What creates the fear, and how do we diminish it? Fear is generated whenever we attack the person versus the idea, whenever we ridicule or publicly berate someone, whenever we punish for mistakes made, or whenever we attack someone or brush them off when they are trying to tell us about our behavior and the consequences of our words and actions. Fear is created when we don't keep others informed about their value or we fail to consistently confront performance issues. We promote fear whenever we appropriate ideas and don't give credit. Fear is also a common outcome when we refuse to take responsibility for mistakes or model denial as the best mode of defense. We create fear whenever we stop listening and asking heartfelt questions.

What can we do about fear? A great deal, actually, from the individual leadership side, and even more from a leadership-systems perspective. As individual leaders we can demonstrate the courage to ask about our performance and then be big enough to take criticism and demonstrate appreciation to those giving it. This takes time. Most will not be forthright at first. They have been burned before and have come to believe that the person asking for feedback does not really want to hear about how they could improve. They know the fragility of management and supervisory egos when it comes to interpersonal performance feedback.

We can also set up leadership feedback loops with key players at multiple levels of the enterprise. This creates an ongoing process of eliciting and generating leadership performance data about ourselves.

We can model the desired behavior by adhering to the effective practice of giving feedback to others. Demonstrating the courage to tell the truth in a supportive manner, speaking heart to heart, is powerful medicine for an anemic, fearful culture. This anchors our commitment to the feedback process and gives credence to our asking for feedback. Walking the talk can seldom be underestimated in its power to motivate and inspire others.

Barriers to Feedback

• *A prevailing command-and-control paradigm.* This particular world view, with its assumptions, beliefs, perceptual maps, and rules for success, is one of the greatest barriers to obtaining accurate and honest read-outs from others with regard to our leadership impact and effectiveness.

The command-and-control model is really more a management orientation (with emphasis on distinct, tight structures, rules, procedures, hierarchy, and authority) versus a leadership paradigm (creating alignment, inspiring, cutting through red tape, breaking new ground, innovating).

The command-and-control model seeks to limit, direct, and restrict. It is full of assumptions about the importance of preserving hierarchical power, maintaining distance from others, and remaining in control at all times. It does not welcome criticism about personal leadership and management behaviors, seeing this as insubordinate and not properly respectful of authority. Command and control has value as a model, but only if held in the context of a larger leadership model built upon the four basic dimensions of integrity, intimacy, competence, and passion. If not held in this context, the command-and-control model severely restricts the quality and quantity of upward feedback.

The paradox, then, is that command-and-control behaviors actually lead to less control, since key performance and improvement data is being withheld. This cripples any efforts at improving quality, increasing learning opportunities, or generating more enthusiastic and proactive followership.

• *Failing to be more self-aware and well-informed about our leadership impact.* Remember the words of Sun Tzu about being self-aware and aware of others. Without a deep appreciation for the value of being aware and plugged continuously into the feedback loop, it is hard for any of us to pay the emotional price to put our egos on the line, to hear the hard news. While it may be painful at times to take a good, hard look at ourselves through the eyes of others, suspending our typical filters of denial and rationalization, it is absolutely essential if we are to really improve in our leadership abilities.

In the long run, those who will not see turn out to be unable to see. This is extremely perilous in the age of the "four elephants," the great megatrends forever changing our world and our ways of doing business. However, it has historically been true that life and enterprise are ultimately harder on those who are unaware and therefore unable to learn and evolve.

We have an exercise we put all participants through who come through our five-day High-Impact Leadership Seminar. It is about giving and receiving feedback. The exercise is designed to help them discover and experience the greatest secret about feedback.

We have each person stand, one at a time, and go around the room to every other person and give them direct feedback. The feedback is based on first impressions and some group interactional experiences. Each person follows a formula to help them focus and direct their feedback. As each person stands to receive it from the person moving around the table, they listen as two reasons for wanting to work with them are listed and then two reasons for not wanting to work with them are laid out. This always provokes anxiety because it challenges the courage, openness, and flexibility of each participant.

After everyone has given their feedback, we ask some questions of the group: What did you learn from this experience about yourself and feedback? What was hardest—giving feedback or receiving it? What are you feeling now with regard to the group? What implications for more effective leadership do you see? How honest and open were you? In what way is this like or unlike the way you handle giving and receiving feedback on the job? In your personal life?

The answers are always amazing. Everyone feels more bonded to the group and closer, even though they have all shared with each other two reasons why they wouldn't want to work with the others. The process of finding the courage to go through the experience, struggling together and all experiencing the same process, tends to unite and draw the group together. There is also a level of honesty, disclosure, and personal contact they may never have experienced in their work. This exercise demands intimacy and integrity, while pointing to the degree of commitment and competency each person has with regard to giving and receiving feedback.

After having had thousands of executives go through our leadership training, this exercise has revealed some consistent patterns and themes. It also unveils the greatest, obvious, yet unnoticed secret in the realm of human communications.

The Secret of Feedback

Everyone seems to believe that when it comes to people there are essentially two forms of feedback. One is positive, and the other is negative.

Positive feedback is characterized as the kind of data that is ego syntonic; that is, it makes us feel good, strokes our ego. Negative feedback is seen as the kind of data that is ego dystonic—hurting our feelings, puncturing our ego. Most believe that people really want to hear the positive data, but really don't like—and prefer to avoid—the negative data. Only a few of the thousands of participants have had trouble giving the "positive" feedback. Nearly all of them struggle with giving the "negative" feedback.

Almost all of the participants also own up to the fact that they seldom give feedback as directly and honestly as they have just done with a roomful of relative strangers. Nearly everyone admits to a certain level of anxiety or fear when it comes to the issues of giving direct and powerful feedback.

There is usually an audible gasp or shocked silence when it is pointed out to them that there are, in reality, no such things as positive and negative feedback. What we call positive feedback is really just the stuff we like to hear, while so-called negative feedback is the stuff we don't want to hear, making us feel hurt or uncomfortable.

There is, in reality, only one kind of feedback, and it is called "information."

What we really do is simply label information as positive or negative based on our personal preferences of what makes us feel good and what makes us feel bad. Therefore, we let our preferences get in the way of giving and receiving important information.

In essence, the only real barrier to effective feedback is our ego. We like or do not like feedback based on whether it bolsters or threatens our self-image or how we feel about ourselves.

But what is, at heart, the most valuable data we need to hear? Data that says, "You are perfectly on course," or data that says, "You're off course!" So-called negative feedback points to the areas of greatest opportunity for us. We learn where we are and what we can do to lead more effectively and with greater power.

The very data we least want to hear is precisely the data we most need to hear! And we are all in the same boat with regard to this.

The leader who is courageous enough to elicit feedback will quickly discover something of even greater value, the great secret at the heart of all human feedback. The secret lies in the fact that even though feedback concerning yourself may not always be accurate, you will always learn something about the person giving the feedback. The person giving you feedback about you may or may not be on target with regard to you, but they are always telling you about their perceptions, the way they've got it put together, their needs, values, feelings, assumptions, and beliefs!

This is a great truth that dramatically shifts the context of listening to feedback, forever eliminating the need to get defensive. It means that if I am really committed to being a powerful leader, I know I must have a handle on how the people around me see the world, my leadership, their jobs, and so on. It also means I need to understand what motivates them, what they need, like, and dislike, what they fear, and what they hope for. It means I understand that an essential key to my success as a leader is found in understanding how others have put the world together. This practice fundamentally empowers and actualizes the practice of seeking to understand others.

When someone is giving me feedback, they may or may not be giving me useful information about me; however, they are always giving me vital information about them. This is the great, obvious secret. It means that I can definitely tune in and listen, asking for clarification and amplification, while perhaps learning something of value about me, but definitely knowing that I am learning how to more effectively lead and influence people.

They are basically telling me what their needs, values, and beliefs are. This puts me in a far more powerful position from which to lead.

Knowing the importance of soliciting personal feedback, how do we learn to get our ego out of the way and really listen? The following is a four-step process for taking feedback:

• *Listen with the ear within your heart.* Listen for what the person or group is saying about what they need and are looking for from you. Hear what they are telling you about their perceptions, needs, and hot buttons. Seek to map out their motivations, interests, and needs, working to clarify those by hearing what impacts them and asking for more information around these areas.

• *Listen to discover personal meaning, and focus on what upsets you most.* Ask yourself: What do I need to discover about myself in this feedback? What am I most resistant to in this message? What is causing that resistance? What meaning does this feedback have for me with regard to being more effective in influencing and working with this individual or team? Realize that what you most resist and get upset over is probably striking some chord or aspect of yourself to which you are sensitized and protective against. Thus, resistance points to what, in all likelihood, most needs to be attended to. Use your resistance as a warning signal to pay extra-close attention.

• *Follow and reflect, clarifying and elucidating what is being said.* This is a critical part of really engaging and understanding what someone is trying to tell you. This follows from active listening skills explored in an earlier chapter.

• *Demonstrate appreciation for the courage and honesty it took to provide you the feedback.* This is essential, since it tends to invite future feedback and rewards someone for being forthright. It also sends a message that you are bigger than your ego, as well as professional and committed enough to be focused on how to improve and perform better.

Feedback Loops

To ensure you are making the feedback process part of an ongoing system of personal leadership improvement and effective course corrections, it is essential that you set up feedback loops. Feedback loops are mechanisms for ensuring that you are getting constant input and information on the impact you are having on the people driving to achieve the desired results.

A feedback loop is a process of sampling the perceptions around your leadership impact and behavioral influence. It tends to be most effective when you ask four or five specific people to be part of your loop. Usually a superior, several subordinates, and one or two peers make an excellent sample for a feedback loop. Let them know what you are trying to do—namely, to improve and enhance your leadership effectiveness by using them to give you course-correction data. Done well, this process provides invaluable data. It also helps the people involved to feel a sense of ownership in your improvement and success—they are looking to see the changes and can take some credit for helping you achieve and succeed in making changes.

For example, one way to set up a very powerful feedback process is to engage in a "two-down" format. The two-down format and process is as follows:

Two-Down Format and Process

The two-down process hits a number of key management and leadership criteria. It is strategic, operational, and tactical. It is a process that actively promotes and develops ongoing continuous coaching and mentoring for people throughout the organization. It is strategic in that it also provides a continuous sampling of climate study issues and data throughout the organization. It is operational and tactical in that it gives specific coaching information and specific coaching opportunities for an executive to develop his or her direct reports.

The two-down process is not meant to supplant the chain of command, nor is it meant to undermine the authority of a manager or supervisor. It is also not meant to be the "spine." It is a process of helping identify opportunities for growth and of providing clear coaching information to help in the development of an executive manager or supervisor. It also helps connect the senior most executive, middle managers, and supervisors into an ongoing network of relationships through a web of continuous information sampling and ongoing coaching.

These are the following points to keep in mind to help provide effective guidelines:

- Communicate to everyone that you will use a two-down process as standard operating procedure throughout the organization.

- Let everyone know it is meant to gather information in order to help in the coaching and development of everybody.

- The person conducting a two-down should never offer advice or direction to someone else's subordinates, other than the advice that the subordinate should attempt to communicate directly and work any particular issues/concerns with their direct supervisor.

- The person conducting the two-down needs to be sensitive to the fact that they are there to show support for management, for the supervisors in question, and for the individual with whom they are speaking.

- The two-down is a process of asking a powerful set of questions and listening rather than talking.

- It is important when conducting a two-down to tell someone that you are there to find out about progress, successes, the things the person feels good about, and any ideas for improvement and/or concerns.

- Always leave the encounter with encouragement and a reminder to the individual to speak more candidly and directly with their supervisor.

- It is imperative, once information has been gathered from several sources, that you seek an opportunity to meet with the supervisor, manager, or executive and provide them with an overview of your observations and question them about their understanding of the data.

- Make sure you listen to their responses and concerns, and make it clear you are there to help support them; use this as a coaching and development opportunity rather than a "gotcha."

- Also, ensure that those receiving feedback know not to go back and be angry with their direct reports about having spoken more candidly with you. Take the time to talk them through their feelings and help them see how they can positively deal with the information and use it for their development in being even more effective in their leadership.

Key Questions to Ask in a Two-Down Process (Pick the best three or four based on the situation and need.)

1. Tell me some successes or things you are feeling good about in terms of your area or department and the organization in general.

2. What progress do you think leadership and managers have made over the past three to six months?

3. If you could change just one or two things that would make a positive difference, a real difference in how we get the work done, what would it be and why?

4. What have you learned over the past quarter, and how have you applied that learning to the workplace and/or your fellow employees?

5. What skills and knowledge have you helped others gain over the past quarter? Who did you help, and what difference do you think it has made?

6. What contributions do you feel you have made to your area, team, department, or the organization in general, that have made a positive difference during the past quarter? How do you think we can measure it?

7. Do you understand what the strategic direction of the company is and how it fits into what you do in your work here?

8. What information do you need in order to be able to do your job even better, and what is the best way to get that information to you and the others around you?

9. What feedback, ideas, and thoughts can you share with me that you think will be important for me, or for the organization to be aware of?

Summary Points

- It is critical that everyone understand that the organization is to be transparent, totally open, candid, and without secrets.

- It is imperative that everyone understand that it is the direct supervisor's job to go below, to listen, and to ask questions as a way of gathering information. Make sure everyone realizes that the supervisor can provide more accurate and effective coaching to help deal with possible blind spots, and interpersonal weaknesses, as well as training or supervisory opportunities for growth.

- It is important that everyone know the process is designed to help redirect employees to their supervisors and is not meant to be an alternative command route.

- It is imperative that everyone get practiced in asking the key questions and in listening without directing. They shold be ready to provide good coaching to those individuals from which two-down data has been gathered.

- It would be very helpful for all employees to review Practice #9— Providing Feedback, particularly the concepts of giving feedback strategically, with depth and with heart.

- It would also help to have all employees review Practice #11— Soliciting Performance Based Feedback, and how to deal with ego, fear, and impatience issues.

Interpretations

Keep in mind that everything we hear and see about the world and each other is an interpretation. The universe is so vast, and what we think we know about it is such a tiny fraction of it, that for all intents and purposes, we really know nothing. No one can really explain what a thought is composed of, how we produce one, how it works. We cannot adequately explain the process by which we reach out and pick up a glass of water. We are in a vast and seemingly infinite universe, and we truly know nothing.

This means that everything we think, feel, say, and understand is really an interpretation—an interpretation based on data, experience, the filters of beliefs, assumptions, values, prejudices, and an attempt to make sense of it all. Knowing it is all an interpretation can provide a tremendous liberation and a heightened capacity to listen to feedback from others. We can choose to be generous or highly limiting in our interpretations.

What they are telling us about ourselves is their interpretation of what our behaviors and words mean to them. Our understanding of what they are telling us, and our reaction to it, is our interpretation. Therefore, our response is really an interpretation of an interpretation. Knowing this can be freeing. We don't have to automatically respond or defend. We can step back and listen, being interested and curious about their interpretations and our way of interpreting and understanding what it means to them and us.

Knowing it is an interpretation gives us a choice. We can choose to interpret their words and actions from a "generous" point of view. We can choose our perspective, getting some distance, and thus freedom, from the possible tyranny of our self-definition and ego boundaries. What that can mean is that we can begin to receive and incorporate the feedback from a more open and generous space. This gives us a chance to choose our response, freeing us up not only to learn, but also to model a more mature and professional way of taking and utilizing critical feedback.

By following the four steps and remembering it is all an interpretation, we can learn to be more effective in not only taking, but in positively seeking out and eliciting personal feedback on our leadership impact. This then models for others the way critical feedback should be handled.

It is only through a respect of, and proper attitude toward, personal feedback that we can begin to really make use of and learn from the observations and ideas of others. It also means that we vastly speed up the learning curve, empowering our own development and process improvement. This, then, helps drive the last and 12th Practice and is a consequence of adhering to it.

PRACTICE 12

Cultivating the Heart of Courage

At the heart of

leadership is courage

—the courage to do

the right thing

—which brings

satisfaction

and joy.

Leadership is about drawing a larger frame of reference. It is, at its core, a creative set of acts. We are all called, in this time of rapid change, to attend to a larger frame of reference. The old tribal mentality of "my people" versus "others" —my little circle versus the world—is the path of destruction.

Looking at it from a leadership perspective, we know we must create more inclusive images and realities. Buckminster Fuller talked about "spaceship earth." This image of a fragile, blue and green, living spaceship floating in the darkness of space is evocative. Whether we call our planet a spaceship, Gaia, or simply "mother," it is time for a wholehearted approach to leadership characterized by the courage to see more of who we are and where we stand in time and space. We can, if we choose, step into a larger space, a place of compassion.

A successful, wealthy senior executive came through a leadership training program I conducted. He looked gray and gaunt. His business was doing well, but he was distracted and bound up in knots since his family life was in shambles. He had recently experienced a bitter rupture in the

191

relationship with his 22-year-old daughter, the jewel of his heart. He was heartbroken, bitter, and grieving. They had formerly talked and spent time together several times a week. It had now been more than two months with no contact. I asked him if he had attempted to reconcile, and he replied that she was in the wrong and had sinned before God; she would need to show remorse and ask his forgiveness. After some hesitation, he shared with the group what had led to the rupture.

His daughter had come to him to share her excitement over a planned summer trip to Europe. He was less than thrilled with her traveling by herself and shared his concern for her safety. She reassured him, "Daddy, don't worry. My boyfriend will be traveling with me!" This worried him even more, "Well, sweetheart, when you travel for several months in close proximity, you might be tempted to get too close." She looked at him in surprise and then reassured him, "Don't worry, Daddy, I've been on the pill for a while." He was devastated. Up until that moment, the executive had simply assumed his daughter was a virgin and saving herself for marriage. He blew up and said things to her that brought tears to her eyes and some angry screams from her. She ran from the house, and they hadn't spoken since. What was worse, his wife blamed him for the rupture, while he was clear that it was his daughter's fault and he was in the right.

Yet, somehow being in the right brought no comfort and only a nagging pain and a sense of grief. It was affecting his work and his whole outlook on life. He kept telling the group and me how she was wrong and had sinned, violating all she had been taught and the moral code of God. He had prayed and talked to the minister of his church, and yet nothing eased his sense of anguish. He had heard that our leadership training often had a profoundly positive impact on the personal lives of those attending, as well as increasing their leadership abilities. Hoping against despair, he had come seeking some guidance and help.

I asked him which was more important to him, being right or being close to his daughter. He nearly wept as he plaintively asked, "But I can't just approve of her actions, of sex before marriage! It is wrong, and she is in a state of sin!" His sadness was palpable, and I felt the bitterness and pain within me for the times that I had hurt those I loved by either disappointing them or pushing them away with my judgments. With tenderness I spoke from that place of recognition within me and asked, "At the end of your life, what will you most value, your sense of being right or your love for your daughter?" He burst into tears and said, "My daughter, my little girl! But how can I approve of her when I feel that she is so wrong?" I took a deep breath and gently suggested, "You don't have to approve of this behavior, but can you approve of her? Can you see her separately from this set of actions?" He nodded, unable to speak. Then he found his voice. "Yes, I think what she has done is wrong, but I know she is good, and I love her."

In the end, after some talking through the issues, he opened his heart, choosing love and connection over righteousness. He hoped she would change that behavior, and he would tell her that he did not agree with it. However, he loved her and wanted her in his life. The man called her that night to apologize for the things he had said and asked her to forgive him for casting her out of his heart. His daughter forgave him and also apologized for not living up to his expectations. She also told him that she did not intend to change since she felt that her love and connection with her boyfriend was holy and good. Her beliefs and her dad's were not the same about premarital sex. They reconciled. Oddly, over the next few months, as he wrote to me later, their relationship became richer and more honest.

He had been relating to the illusion of who he thought his daughter was and not to the real flesh and blood woman she had become. They carried the sadness and the memory of the hurt they had done to each other, but it tempered their relationship and carried it to a level of openness and mature love that enriched them both. At the same time, this successful businessman came to see the ways he judged others and felt superior to them, creating a barrier and sense of separateness from them. He began to suspend some of his judging behavior and was rewarded with more creativity and productivity from his employees, while his relationship with his wife blossomed. He told me he came to experience being closer to God.

This is a story about leadership. The man had to reach deeply into himself and find what was most important and most precious. He had to have the courage to give up being right and to face his own darkness, his sense of moral superiority, and his addiction to being right. He then had to take the lead in reaching out to the daughter he had labeled and emotionally attacked. The openness and level of intimacy he was willing to develop helped him lead both his family and the people at work into a more powerful, compelling, and meaningful way of relating. The payoffs were an improved quality of experiencing life and a heightened level of performance at work. As the man changed, the people and environment around him changed. Thus, an open heart carried with integrity can change your world.

Cultivating the heart of courage is perhaps the greatest of the practices—so great that it is really a guiding principle. Someone once asked

Louis Armstrong what the real difference was between an amateur and a professional. Armstrong thought a moment and then replied, "An amateur is someone who plays well when they feel good. A professional is someone who plays well no matter how they feel."

The profound truth revealed here emerges when you consider all that has been said in the previous practices. True leaders are willing to learn, to grow, to challenge and be challenged, to let go of old patterns of success and comfortable routines, because what is required and what must be accomplished is more important and takes precedence over their own personal likes and dislikes. The critical function of this practice is that of commitment. The emotion that goes with it is a deep sense of satisfaction, even joy, at rising above personal limitations and doing what must be done.

Horst Schultze, COO of the Ritz Carlton, says:

> You are nothing unless it comes from your heart: passion, caring, really looking to create excellence. If you perform functions only, and go to work only to do processes, then you are effectively retired. And it scares me—most people I see, by age 28, are retired . . .
>
> If you go to work only to fulfill the processes and functions, then you are a machine. You have to bring passion, commitment, and caring—then you are a human being.

This takes Courage with a capital "C." We cannot be successful in any enduring way unless we are willing to engage our hearts and develop the musculature of courage. This means facing the anxiety and the fear of stepping outside our zones of comfort with regard to knowledge, past practices, habits, cognitive patterns, emotions, and behavior.

It takes courage to go beyond the edges of what we know. In the Middle Ages, cartographers drew maps of the known world. On the borders and spaces that went beyond their current knowledge they wrote, "Here be dragons," to indicate the perils of the unknown. Men and women who have the courage and resourcefulness to go to the edge of what is known, inspiring others to follow, are called leaders. It takes courage and resourcefulness to face the dragons of the unknown, to deal with the fear not only within oneself, but also to confront the fear, doubts, and nay-saying of others.

Taking a leadership role requires us to be bigger than our feelings, our preferences, our habits, our fears, and our ego. It also means engaging and challenging those around us—dealing with their fear, cynicism, ego, doubts, and resistance.

This practice—cultivating the heart of courage—is really about doing the right thing first, and only then doing things the right way—knowing that the "right" way (what is established, habitual, status quo, consensually agreed on) may be outmoded or even wrong in different settings and circumstances. It is, at heart, really about personal mastery.

It is having the heart to do what is necessary. How many of us let our emotions of the moment get in the way of doing what needs to be done? How often do we let our ego dictate a response versus using our higher judgment?

As Tom Brooks considered his stint as head of Naval Intelligence, he expressed the following thoughts:

> I should have done more nipping at the heels: the business of driving the vision home, a little extra effort to ensure that the echelons below are signed up and going strong—but more than that, actually checking the pulse of the various parts of the organization to see which ones are going 55 mph and which ones have slowed down to 10–15 mph, and then personally taking initiative to go after them.
>
> Jack Welch does a variation of that. He's out of his office all the time, taking the pulse of the organization. Everybody tells me, "Everything's great"; everybody says, "Aye, aye, sir" when I give the orders. All of my executives seem to be enthused and fired up to my vision. They all understand, they're all on board, they're out, they're charging—but is it getting down to the floor of the factory? And do they really understand it, or do I need to get out there and personally push?
>
> I have admiration for Welch. I think he's a man of great drive, a man of great vision, and a man who's able to articulate his vision. He does follow through, and he has a great faculty: his ability not only to look at things in a simple fashion, but his willingness to stand up there and say, "Hey, all this stuff really isn't as hard as people make it out to be." There are some fairly straightforward, fundamental principles of common sense involved in running a business. And you don't have to be a genius to do it. But you've got to have the drive, the push, the enthusiasm, and the fire to get out and push and make it happen.

As stated in the first chapter, seven kinds of personal courage are required of leaders if they are to be the best they can be. These form the base of personal mastery. They are:

1. The courage to dream and put forth that dream.

2. The courage to see current reality.

3. The courage to confront.

4. The courage to be confronted.

5. The courage to learn and grow.

6. The courage to be vulnerable.

7. The courage to act.

In the preceding chapters, we have laid out practices and tools that, taken together, systematically develop the courage muscle. They flesh out the seven acts of courage and, in turn, rely on them.

These acts of courage are the basis and absolute requirements if the five tasks of leadership are to be realized and if the heart of leadership is to be cultivated and developed.

To be a leader means to be a dedicated professional. We play well no matter how we feel and we do what is best for the team, the departments, and the organization, even if it makes us uncomfortable, anxious, angry, or fearful. We are open to having our paradigms of reality challenged and will actively seek out and learn more effective paradigms, even if they are initially upsetting. We have mastered or are working on mastering our personalities so that we are more objective and open to seeing the world and others—and even ourselves—without the filters of denial, projection, rationalization, justification, and blame.

Denial

Denial is the psychological term for a defensive structure of the ego that literally enables an individual to simply not "see" or be consciously aware of what is blatantly obvious to others. It is used by executives to maintain the comfort of the status quo and to uphold the illusion that they are on top of what is going on in their organization. Having conducted numerous organizational climate studies, I have found that many times the executives are unaware of the level and intensity of anger, frustration, and pain in their organizations. Denial is a powerful defense and can make you blind and deaf to the things others see. It is dangerous for a leader to remain unaware.

Projection

Projection is the psychological defense of reading your own issues, perceptions, and feelings into a situation and person—not seeing the situation or person for what it is, but coloring and distorting it. An example is that of hearing an attack and accusation in someone's feedback when it is not there. Projection is like carrying a movie inside your head and playing that movie out—projecting and imposing the images and feelings onto others and situations. It leaves us out of touch with what is really going on and can lead to interpretations of behavior and events that are widely off the mark.

Rationalization and Justification

This defensive mechanism of explaining away facts, feelings, and feedback from others is perhaps the most widely used by executive egos and in corporate settings. The more people you can get to join in the rationalizing and justifying of events and actions taken or not taken, the more compelling and powerful the collective blindness. This is a defense that allows you to continue to function as you have always functioned and never see the full consequences or pain it produces. Leaders are aware of this danger and are always willing and open to challenge the status quo and the obvious arguments and explanations.

Blame

Blame is like a powerful, addictive drug. Using the defense of either overtly or covertly blaming others, you never need face yourself and take yourself to task. Blame is addictive in its appeal. Think how seductive it is to be able to take a problem or recurring issues and see someone or something else as responsible. This leaves you in the clear and "right," making the other wrong. The problem is that it is nearly impossible, then, to really improve, grow, and become more effective, since corrective feedback is derailed. Blame also gets in the way when you apply it to yourself. The real issue for a leader is not who or what to blame, but, from a systems perspective, how have we created this problem, and how will we best address it? Blame is insidious and reinforces fear, making the culture and people in it afraid of risk. It kills the learning spirit, as Deming has demonstrated.

Leaders have the courage to stop the blame game and focus attention on the systems and overall goals—bringing a new commitment to seeing the current reality and then addressing it.

In the rapidly changing, global marketplace of today, we are all being called to go beyond the confines of our comfort zones, to stretch, to develop, and to use more of our resources. This is required of us if we are to increase the effective intelligence of our organizations. To do this necessitates creating a learning systems approach, which increases the capacity for the whole team, the whole organization, to learn faster and more thoroughly. While all of this is a necessity, it is neither comfortable nor easy. However, it is the task of true leaders.

To consider your level of professionalism—your heart of courage—versus amateurism, answer the following questions as honestly as you can. When you draw a blank, it may indicate an area where you need more input and attention. Also, to give it power, consider different ways of eliciting feedback from others.

- What are the parts of your job you enjoy the most? The least?
- What things are you avoiding?
- What one thing that you currently aren't doing could you begin to do that would make the most positive difference in your work? In your leadership? In the functioning of your team?
- What gets in the way of your doing it?
- What are you currently doing that, if you stopped doing it, would make a positive difference in your work? In your life?
- In what ways are your old habits and preferences getting in the way?
- What is your comfort zone as a leader? Can you map it?
- Do you have the courage to break out of your habitual patterns?
- How will you begin to stretch beyond the confines of your comfort zone?
- What are the implications if you continue to let your comfort zone dictate your behavior?

Your comfort zone is your habits, your routine, your habitual patterns. Suppose you are someone who doesn't like to confront. As a leader, you do not let your personal discomfort keep you from figuring out a way to go out there and confront when it is necessary. If you are somebody who likes to confront and doesn't know how to give praise and appreciation, then as a professional you must learn to do so.

We all have comfort zones. They are just like narrow spheres of behaviors within which we are comfortable. Whenever we step outside a comfort zone, we get anxious. The walls of our comfort zone are lined with the barbed, electrified wire of fear, doubt, and anxiety. We experience anxiety whenever we touch the boundaries of our habits, routines, assumptions, and patterns. We experience anxiety because we might look awkward; we might look foolish; we don't know how we will do.

If most kids were like most adults, they would get on a two-wheeler for the first time, and they'd fall off. Then they'd get back on, put down the kickstand, sit back, and look cool. People would ride by, saying, "Come on, ride with us." They'd reply, "Naw, I'm having a great time just sitting here." And they would never learn to ride the bike.

We have got to be like kids again—willing to make mistakes, to try new things, to learn. My son is six; he is learning to ride a two-wheeler. He falls—he gets on—he falls—he gets off. He cries, argues, kicks the bike. Then he gets back on it. He is learning to ride it. His persistence and willingness to be awkward mean that he is learning new skills every day. For too many adults, we let our fears, our egos, and our impatience shut us down to learning, improving, and mastering new dimensions and aspects of our lives.

Leaders are always stepping outside their comfort zones. They are always doing something awkward—always doing something that feels uncomfortable—because they realize they are professionals, having the heart to make a difference.

You can't make a difference in this world of ours, changing as fast as it is, if you acquiesce to your comfort zone. Too many have and do acquiesce. IBM did; it fell in love with its mainframes. It lost its leadership edge because it didn't have the courage. It did at one time, but it lost it in a glorification of management and culture at the expense of real leadership. IBM bet the whole company back in the '50s when it built the first mainframes. It didn't have the courage to leap from that to the next thing.

Most people I have worked with throughout corporate America let their comfort zones, habitual patterns, and personalities run them and their businesses. They are driven by forces within themselves that they do not see and attend to, let alone master. This is a great loss. It means that unconscious assumptions, beliefs, attitudes, prejudices, fears, traits, expectations, values, and needs are in the driver's seat. They do not appreciate the requirements of personal mastery. This is not professional, smart, or wise. It is automatic and involves predetermined behavioral loops, endlessly repeating themselves, slowing down and limiting the process of learning and improving.

This is tragic. It is a failure of either perspective or of nerve. It limits many of us to the sphere of what we know and have mastered. It also limits us in our flexibility and capacity to creatively respond and innovate. It means we miss the obvious and get trapped in the antique and obsolete. This is the path of the dinosaurs, and it leads to failure, if not extinction.

Steve Ardia puts it this way:

> There's one other critical part of it all—maybe it's the opposite side of fear—and that's courage. And there are definitely times when you know the organization is only doing it because you are steadfast. I don't think you want to be in that position too often or too long—but it does take courage to know you have a belief and stay by it and bring the organization through. That takes courage.

To move beyond the limited sphere of what is known and provide a powerful inspirational model for others requires the capacity and willingness to risk. We risk appearing foolish and awkward. We risk our comfort. We risk our past certainty. We risk not being "right." We risk encountering the dragons that live on the border of the familiar and known. To continue to take these risks is to initiate a process of continuous revitalization and renewal. Revitalization and renewal are at the core of leadership.

Says Ardia again:

> If you want to be a leader, you'd better start by liking people, and if you don't like people, then you should go into a technical side where you can be a single contributor. I think you've got to know yourself so you can positively impact those around you. You're constantly selling—you're selling your concepts, and you're selling yourself as a person and as an individual, in the belief that others will follow you.
>
> The old adage, that the definition of leadership is followership, is so true that it is the only definition that makes any difference. You want to set up some feedback loops; you want to stay open, because we can take any strength to excess, and it becomes a weakness. So, you also have to keep balancing yourself and how you behave.
>
> And the other part is that there's a lot of satisfaction in knowing you can make a difference in people's lives as a leader. So it's a tremendous opportunity to give to people. And along with it comes a tremendous responsibility. However, if you've got the right ingredients and the right circumstances and the courage, it can provide tremendous satisfaction and give meaning to your whole life.

Steve actually lists five key criteria for being a professional leader. They are:

- Like people
- Know yourself
- Establish feedback loops
- Stay open
- Keep balancing yourself and your life

At Staub-Peterson we also add:

- Continue to learn and seek opportunities to learn
- Think strategically
- Develop empathy and compassion

To develop and make use of the eight criteria above requires courage. How do we cultivate and find the requisite courage? We find courage by reminding ourselves of what is most important to us—what we most deeply value. As Covey has shown, the process of identifying our key values, and then daily reviewing and remembering them, is instrumental to our having the courage to bring our hearts into our lives and the decisions we face.

We find courage by associating with others of courage, or by reading and studying about them—reminding ourselves that others have preceded us.

We find courage by telling ourselves the truth about our current reality and then reminding ourselves about our vision—what we are here to accomplish, what we most desire.

We find courage by being encouraged and supported by others, by creating a network of dedicated and caring colleagues and friends.

We find courage by reminding ourselves of or discovering what matters most to us. When we lay out what is most important—what our deepest aspirations are, where our hearts are—we find the motivation to generate courage. After all, we are going after what we most deeply desire. We are being truthful with ourselves about who we are and where we want to go. This gives coherence and meaning to our risk taking, our sacrifice and efforts.

Finally, we find courage by encouraging others. The act of supporting just one person in dealing with something they fear has tremendous impact on our own psyche. It is nearly impossible to encourage others to do the right thing and face their fears and not end up feeling more encouraged ourselves.

Developing the heart of courage requires all of this as well as the commitment to periodic revitalization. Revitalization is the process of reinventing and breathing new life into our lives, the enterprise, or organization. It is the challenging and complex task of reviewing current functioning while daring to dream and envision a higher state of being and becoming.

Leaders of heart appreciate the need to go beyond their fear and comfort zone, to stretch, to recognize where they are deficient, and, based upon the needs of the team or organization, to engage in a process of learning and utilizing everyone's strengths to do what is necessary.

Leaders are the ones who have the wherewithal to put themselves in harm's way as required to help bring the vision and dream to fruition, to drive the process of getting results. Their actions serve to inspire and engage others, building relationships centered on getting things done.

As stated in the chapter about the four chambers in the heart of leadership, there are only three real barriers to more effective leadership. These barriers are:

> *Fear*—being run by our comfort zone and automatic defenses.
> *Ego*—listening to our smaller self, our old system of identification.
> *Impatience*—lack of persistence, rushing versus listening.

These three form the walls, the barred window, and the locked door of our comfort zone. The heart to do what is necessary is the crux of the matter and, in the final analysis, the most critical of the 12 practices, since it drives their utilization when the going gets tough. Without this heart there can be no true integrity, for it forms the foundation of personal and professional authenticity. It is the commitment to the vision, the aspiration, the enterprise, the people, and self that drives everything. It is rooted solidly in the dimensions of integrity and passion.

Out of this heart flows the sustaining emotional energy of courage, and it feeds back into the vision. Out of that it flows back down through the other 10 practices, driving and supporting their implementation even when it is inconvenient, difficult, or painful. It fundamentally empowers all of the other 11 practices, but needs the guidance and direction provided by the practices of vision and focusing on purpose.

Ultimately, the motive energy flowing from the practice of heart and professionalism generates a wave of organizational courage, commitment, and integrity. This wave drives the enterprise toward greater success. The resulting sense of accomplishment and personal mastery leads to an emotion of joy.

All 12 of these practices can be roughly summarized into a number of key behaviors. These behavioral elements, when you have the courage to follow them, fundamentally empower and drive results while building relationships. Your leadership impact and effectiveness increases exponentially as they are applied.

Competency

- Clarify what is required in order to be successful.
- Ensure the right competencies are present and deployed.
- "Muscle" build through common experiences and learning points.
- Coach and mentor.
- Ensure the right tools and methodologies are present and used.

Integrity

- Maintain focus on the purpose of the organization, division, team, and department.
- Tell the truth without sugar coating the current reality.
- Develop, maintain, and reinforce team agreements with regard to solution-focused behaviors.
- Articulate and then follow your operating principles and values.

Passion

- Show emotion; find and then share your enthusiasm.
- Liberate the motivation of others by encouraging them and demonstrating your commitment to them.
- Actively support others, helping to champion them and their ideas.
- Follow through and follow up on plans and actions.
- Demonstrate a sense of urgency.

Intimacy

- Take the time to connect with others.
- Seek to understand and read others.
- Stay close to the market, to the customer, to the evolving needs and forces.
- Open yourself up to feedback and proactively seek it out; make time for team-based feedback.
- Develop a personal vision, and seek the vision others have of what is possible.
- Have the courage of self-examination and the willingness to grow.

CONCLUSION

Stewardship
and Beyond

The great fallacy

about leadership is

that others will take

charge of making

things right.

The truth is,

we all have the

responsibility

to lead.

Someone once asked Freud what defined a healthy and successful person. Freud replied, "Wie man arbeiten und lieben"—how one works and loves. It is fitting to conclude this book on leadership by reflecting on this answer. It is perhaps the most succinct yet eloquent answer to a complex question.

True leaders focus on the essentials. They work and love from a center that encompasses and builds on the four essential chambers at the heart of all lasting leadership: intimacy, competence, integrity, and passion. They bring the whole of themselves to the enterprise, and they invite others to do the same. This creates an atmosphere of courage, challenge, excellence, and even transformation.

Those in the magnetic field of influence generated by a leader begin to experience a transformation of their abilities, both in what they do and how they relate and work with others. This almost invariably carries over into their personal lives. Those around a leader begin to function and show initiative, becoming more capable of demonstrating leadership themselves.

205

What is the role of leadership with regard to our future? Perhaps only to realize that there is no future without leadership. There will always be a need for strong and effective leaders. The big difference from the past centuries is that we need those leaders and their leadership at all levels and from many more of the members of our society. We need this because the world is changing and will be accelerating in those changes much too rapidly for just a few leaders. We are all called upon to help lead, first ourselves and then others. I firmly believe there is a hunger in the soul of America, in the soul of the world, in the souls of the people we interact with every day that call out to be fed with vision, hope, and courage.

Once more, John Hechinger, Jr., former CEO of a $2.5 billion company, speaking from the experience of losing the battle with Home Depot, sheds invaluable light on the challenges facing today and tomorrow's leaders:

> You need to set up in your organization a process of continual change. In any organization there is enormous inertia, because inertia is actually a more efficient and effective way of running your business. It's easier to do the same thing over and over again. You can drive your costs down; it's easier; people know what to do; you don't have to retrain people. There are lots of good reasons not to change. They make a lot of sense.
>
> You have to have outside influence somehow, either from some other part of the organization or from consultants, that continues to shake up the organization. If you don't get yourself into a mode of continual improvement and change, you find yourself in a position of having to make radical change and leapfrog significantly, which is very, very difficult to do and takes a long time. In today's competitive environment, many times it takes too much time—more time than the competition allows you to have.
>
> You need to do everything possible to have the people, yourself, and everything in the organization geared to being able to accept change, and to know what that change is going to be and have some mechanism for responding to it. The most difficult thing is playing catch-up.

Or consider the parting words of Gene Kaczmarski:

> A successful organization requires a complex and diverse set of skills that are rarely found in one individual. The most

successful leaders I know or have read about seem to be capable of accurate self-assessment. They surround themselves with others who possess traits, characteristics, and skills that complement their own. The traits that cannot be delegated or complemented are integrity and trust. You only get one shot. Once trust is lost, so is leadership. I have heard it described that trust is like a fine Waterford crystal—once it's broken, it is almost impossible to repair.

Learning something new is scary. There's always one who is willing to step out and take the lead. So you work with them, and you develop the program. If it's as successful as you think, everybody will just line up and follow suit.

We have been half asleep for far too long, letting the inertia of past success and economic dominance rule. We need to see leaders as agents of change and transformation. We have, historically, been ceding our responsibilities and our power to a favored few. That power and responsibility is a stewardship we need to reclaim—for the sake of our lives, organizations, society, children, and the habitat around us.

I chose the word "stewardship" because it indicates something we do, not own. It points to the fact that we are the caretakers for this earth, for our institutions, and for our society. We are not the owners of this earth, of our communities, or of the lives around us. We do not own our children or our mates. We do not even own our own bodies, since someday we all will have to surrender even our bodies to the universe. In all ways, we are truly stewards or caretakers, charged with the responsibility and the privilege of caring for this world and for each other.

We are the ones who will determine the quality of the world and the life we leave to our children and all future generations. This is the kind of leadership and awareness this book has been attempting to address. This is something to be passionate about: our children, making a difference, personal meaning and authenticity in our lives.

We have learned a great lie. There has been a great falsehood at the heart of our understanding of what leadership is all about. We have believed that others will save our jobs, our wildlife, our families, our society. Yet it takes all of us, pulling together, if we are to succeed. Leadership is required of all of us, and it is one part magic and six parts common sense. It is the art and science of observing and acting upon the obvious. However, as we have seen, many times the obvious is nearly impossible to see, and often overlooked. The obvious facts we must face are that our lives are increasingly characterized by change, evolution, and, more often than not, revolution.

Velocity is becoming the rule of the game. Our lives blur by and can end so quickly. The things and situations around us are changing more and more rapidly. How do we wish to live in this hectic, mile-a-second world? What will our response be? Going passive is only an obstacle and a hindrance to the effort of finding a healthy and dynamic way of living, working, and loving in this mutating, prolific world of ours. To despair and give up is to cheat the world and our fellow beings of the gifts we bring and the power we have to share. Not developing our leadership capabilities—staying mired in the command-and-control paradigm—is to waste the talents and gifts of those around us. Domination, the old leadership response, will only create resistance, resentment, and rebellion. Ultimately, it will lead to disastrous failure. Invitation, in the long run, is definitely more powerful.

How we respond makes all the difference in the world. We can be agents of growth and transformation—leading at times, following at times—as we participate in the dynamic of co-creating the world within which we must live, as well as the one our children and their children will inherit. Will we open our hearts and minds to the possibilities of co-creating our lives, our families, our organizations, our society, and our world? Or will we look for the guy or gal on the great white horse to lead us and save us?

The world is becoming too small, too interconnected, too intricate, too complex, and too fast for this old formula to work, if it ever did. The faults and the answers lie within ourselves. We are the question and the answer, and those around us contain their own vital parts of the great puzzle of living well and generating successful stewardship.

The four dimensions of leadership—integrity, intimacy, competency, and passion—are critical to being effective stewards, and they are essential if we are to feel really fulfilled and successful in our lives.

Providing a channel for the development of the four dimensions are the 12 practices, which provide action orientations—guides to developing effective leadership that stands the test of time. These practices take the seven habits Covey has outlined and provide an orientation and a framework for meaningful action and real power in our lives, at all levels of becoming, being, and doing.

The choice is ours. We can choose to be one of three kinds of people: those who watch things happen, those who wonder what happened, or those who make things happen. Leaders are those who choose to help make things happen—things they care about. This demands that we engage the commitment and energy of those last two groups.

If you choose to be a leader, you now understand the depth of the challenge. It requires challenging your comfort zone, facing your fears and anxiety, and dealing with the fear and anxiety of others. It means cultivating and developing a sense of personal mastery with a commitment to lifelong learning. It requires that you be a professional, bringing your passion, integrity, competence, and capacity for intimacy to higher levels. It requires that you develop your "heart" muscle, daring to care, to dream, to reach, to create, to support, and to be supported.

There is no greater job or challenge available today. Being a leader means realizing that you influence and work with people in a 360-degree sphere: up, down, and around. It means you are putting yourself on the line and inviting others to do the same.

It is frightening, frustrating, painful, challenging, difficult, unnerving. And it is also one of the most rewarding and vital roles you can ever play. Our industries, our country, our planet are desperate for leadership. All it takes to start, ultimately, is your courageous heart.

Let me finish with the words of Buckminster Fuller. I had the opportunity to be on a lecture circuit with Bucky about a year or two before he died. We were at the same conference. I had always admired the man and had read his book *Space Ship Earth*. I admired what he had accomplished and who he was—a true maker, a creator, a leader. I walked up to him. He was short, very rotund, with big thick glasses that looked like the bottoms of Coke bottles, and hearing aids in both ears. I walked up to him and said, "Oh Bucky, I have read your works; I admire you tremendously, and it is a great honor to meet you." Probably not the most graceful of tones, as I felt very awkward and slightly in awe. He just sort of twinkled at me.

You know people who twinkle. He just stood there and twinkled. Then he shook my hand and said, "Well, thank you very much. I appreciate that." He smiled at me, and I smiled back. He just kept smiling at me. I smiled back, and as the seconds went by my legs started to twitch a little bit. Then he leaned forward and said, "Now you go out and do your part."

I believe that is the role of leaders—to go out and do their parts in drawing other people into creating visions, listening to the visions, asking for the corrective feedback, demonstrating the capacity and willingness to be a professional—to put themselves on the line. The quality that cuts across all of that is courage. The one true requirement in terms of what it takes to be a leader is the courage to step beyond the bounds, to break out of the box, to be courageous enough to abandon ourselves to the wild ideas and strengths of other people. This creates and generates truly remarkable results.

It is important to remember that your job as a leader is not just to create followers and to influence people, but to fundamentally demonstrate courage and encourage others to step into leadership roles. Ultimately, you will be measured as a leader by your capacity and ability to develop other leaders around you. It is only through the influence of multiple sets of leaders, working in concert, that we are able to truly create meaningful and sustainable change. The following points of view will help you in cultivating your own courage, while helping to encourage others:

1. Have the courage to go more deeply into your heart, as well as the hearts of those around you. As you do, you will find a greater power coming to you, both in your ability to influence others and in your ability to generate other leaders.

2. When you have the courage to change yourself, the world around you, by definition, must change. People around you will not be able to respond or act the same way when dealing with you. (Remember what happened when Rosa Parks had the courage to step forward and fight an unjust system that said she must sit at the back of the bus. Her courageous act of defiance was also an act of leadership that was the spark that helped launch the public battle for the conscience of America in the Civil Rights Movement.)

3. Give up the need to be right, and you can accomplish anything. (General George Marshall was once asked how he was able to build America's war machine so quickly in World War II and how he was able, after the war, to persuade Congress to rebuild the war-torn economies of Japan and Germany. He replied that it was possible to do anything if you were willing to give credit, take the blame, and give up the need to be right.)

4. Never forget the back-room and day-to-day operations. Never forget the people who are behind the scenes, caught up in the daily grind, enabling the organization to succeed. Remember to go back and encourage them, to draw forth their ideas, to engage them, and to look for leaders emerging there.

5. If you give up judging and blaming and cultivate a state of curiosity, a state of seeking to understand, you will find that your influence and power grow exponentially.

6. Remember that your life is bigger than any job or any organization. This will help you maintain a sense of perspective, allowing greater innovation and creativity to flow. It also will help center you in the importance of every human life.

It is helpful to remember the last words Buddha spoke to his disciples when he was dying. They all said, "Oh, master, what shall we do without you; what shall we do?" He was silent and still for a long time. They continued to plead, "Tell us what to do. Tell us how we should live." Finally, he opened his eyes and, with his last breath, said, "Do your best."

I believe if you are going to be a true maker, a true leader, not only will you do your best, but you will enable, support, and facilitate those around you to be able and willing to do their best. You will be surprised at how many people you will find to support you and to work in helping you realize a dream if you are developing the heart with competence, integrity, intimacy, and passion. Welcome to the fellowship of courage and excellence. There are many of us to welcome you. Good luck on your journey!

The Eternal Truths of Leading

1. Leaders create other leaders: leaders have the ability to call forth the potential and ability of those around them.

2. Leadership is a 360-degree sphere of influence: you lead up, you lead down, and you lead sideways.

3. Leadership is an interactive field of influence in which the environment calls forth leaders and in which leaders reshape the environment.

4. Leadership is earned and seized, not given or bestowed.

5. Leadership is always from the inside out. (It is the tone and quality of your heart that determines the tone and quality of your leadership.)

6. Leadership is about vision, focus, and creating alignment at multiple levels.

7. The key to lasting leadership is courage: the ability to access not only your own courage, but to call forth courage in those around you.

8. Leadership is high touch: leaders focus on connecting meaningfully with other people.

9. Leaders must know how to follow if they are to continue to lead.

Bibliography

Albrecht, Karl. *The Only Thing That Matters*. New York: Harper Business.

Autry, James A. *Love and Profit*. New York: William Morrow & Company, 1991.

Bennis, Warren. *An Invented Life: Reflections on Leadership & Change*. Reading, MA: Addison Wesley, 1993.

—. *On Becoming a Leader*. Reading, MA: Addison-Wesley, 1989.

Beer, Michael. *The Critical Path to Corporate Renewal*. New York: McGraw Hill, 1990.

Bradshaw, John. *Healing the Shame That Binds You*. Deerfield Beach, FL: Health Communications, 1988.

Bridges, William. *Managing Transitions: Making the Most of Change*. Reading, MA: Addison Wesley, 1991.

Byham, William C. *Zapp! The Lightening of Empowerment*. Pittsburgh, PA: Development Dimensions International Press, 1988.

Campbell, Joseph. *Myths to Live By*. New York: Viking Press, 1972.

Card, Orson Scott. *Speaker for the Dead*. New York: T. Doherty Assoc., 1986.

—. *Red Prophet*. New York: Tor, 1988.

—. *Ender's Game*. New York: Tor, 1991.

Covey, Stephen R. *The Seven Habits of Highly Effective People*. New York: Simon & Schuster, 1989.

—. *Principle-Centered Leadership*. New York: Summit Books, 1991.

DePree, Max. *Leadership Is an Art*. New York: Doubleday, 1989.

Dickens, Charles. *A Christmas Carol*. New York: Julian Messner, 1983.

Dobyns, Lloyd and Clare Crawford-Mason. *Quality or Else: The Revolution in World Business.* Boston, MA: Houghton Mifflin. 1981.

DuPont Employees & Thaves, B. *Are We Creative Yet?* Wilmington, DE: DuPont, 1990.

Fisher, Roger and William Ury. *Getting to Yes: Negotiating Agreement Without Giving In.* Boston, MA: Houghton Mifflin, 1981.

Fritz, Robert. *The Path of Least Resistance.* New York: Fawcett Book Group, 1989.

Gleick, James. *Chaos: Making a New Science.* New York: Viking, 1987.

Goldratt, Eliyahu. *The Goal: A Process of Ongoing Improvement.* New York: North River Press, 1986.

Harvey, John B. *The Abilene Paradox and Other Meditations on Management.* San Diego, CA: University Assoc., 1988.

Heider, John. *The Tao of Leadership.* New York: Bantam, 1986.

Hyatt, Carol and Linda Gottlieb. *When Smart People Fail.* New York: Simon & Schuster, 1987.

Jampolsky, Gerald. *Love Is Letting Go of Fear.* Millbrae, CA: Celestial Arts, 1979.

Kanter, Rosabeth Moss. *The Change Masters: Innovation for Productivity in American Culture.* New York: Simon & Schuster, 1983.

—. *When Giants Learn to Dance.* New York: Simon & Schuster, 1983.

Katzenbach, James and David Smith. *The Wisdom of Teams: Creating the High Performance Organization.* Boston, MA: Harvard Business School Press, 1993.

Keyes, Ken. *Handbook to Higher Consciousness.* Coos Bay, OR: Loveline Books, 1989.

The Holy Bible. King James Version.

Kotter, John and James Heskett. *Corporate Culture and Performance.* New York: Free Press, 1992.

Laborde, Ginny. *Influencing with Integrity: Management Skills for Communication & Negotiation.* Palo Alto, CA: Science and Behavior Books, 1983.

Le Guin, Ursula. *A Wizard of Earthsea.* Berkeley, CA: Parnassus Press, 1968.

Millman, Dan. *Way of the Peaceful Warrior.* Tiburon, CA: H. J. Kramer, 1984.

Moss, Richard. *The Black Butterfly: An Invitation to Radical Aliveness.* Berkeley, CA: Celestial Arts, 1986.

Organizational Psychology. Vol. 45, No. 2. Washington, DC: American Psychological Association, 1990.

Palmer, Helen. *The Enneagram: Understanding Yourself and Others in Your Life*. San Francisco, CA: Harper Collins, 1991.

Paul, Jordan and Margaret Paul. *Do I Have to Give Up Me to Be Loved by You?* Mill Creek, MN: Hazelden, 1992.

Peterson, Kirtland C. *Mind of the Ninja*. Chicago: Contemporary Books, 1986.

Rifkin, Jeremy. *Time Wars: The Primary Conflict in Human History*. New York: Simon & Schuster, 1989.

Senge, Peter. *The Fifth Discipline: The Art and Practice of the Learning Organization*. New York: Currency Doubleday, 1990.

Seuss, Dr. *Oh, The Places You'll Go!* New York: Random House, 1990.

Siegel, Bernie. *Love, Medicine & Miracles*. Boston, MA: G. K. Hall, 1988.

Staub, Robert E. *Twelve Principles of Leadership*. Greensboro, NC: Staub-Peterson Leadership Consultants, 1990.

Tichy, Noel. *Managing Strategic Change: Technical, Political, and Cultural Dynamics*. New York: John Wiley & Sons, 1983.

Tichy, Noel and Mary Anne Devanna. *The Transformational Leader*. New York: John Wiley & Sons, 1990.

Tichy, Noel and Stratford Sherman. *Control Your Destiny or Someone Else Will*. New York: Currency Doubleday, 1993.

Tze, Sun. *The Art of War*. London: Oxford University Press, 1971.

Van Oeck, Roger. *A Whack on the Side of the Head*. New York: Warner Books, 1990.

Vogt, Judith F. and Kenneth L. Murell. *Empowerment in Organizations: How to Spark Exceptional Performance*. San Diego, CA: University Associates, 1990.

Walton, M. *Deming Management at Work*. New York: G. P. Putnam & Sons, 1990.

Watzlawick, Paul. *How Real Is Real? Confusion, Disinformation, Communication*. New York: Random House, 1977.

Watzlawick, Paul and Roger Weakland. *Change: Principles of Problem Resolution*. New York: W. W. Norton, 1974.

Weisboro, M. R. *Productive Workplaces*. San Francisco, CA: Jossey Bass, 1987.

Zaleznick, Abraham. *The Managerial Mystique*. New York: Harper & Row, 1989.

—. "Real Work." *Harvard Business Review* (Jan.-Feb. 1989): 57-64.

Index

About the Author

Robert E. "Dusty" Staub, II, is president and founder of Staub Leadership Consultants. He has spent more than 20 years working with individuals, organizations, families, and community groups to deliver effective coaching in personal and organizational leadership development. In the past 10 years, over 10,000 executives have gone through his intensive High-Impact Leadership Seminar. Dusty's material has been published or cited in many national publications, including *Fortune, Reader's Digest, Executive Excellence*, and *LeaderQuest*.

Dusty is married to Dr. Christine Staub, a licensed medical family practitioner who specializes in homeopathy. The couple resides in Greensboro, North Carolina. They have three children: Sean, Kendra, and Chamberlain. Dusty's interests include reading anything and everything, spending time with his children, taking long walks in the woods, and yoga.

Dusty is the author of a book on personal mastery, *The Seven Acts of Courage,* which focuses on helping you cultivate greater power and self-mastery through courageous action. He has just completed a children's manuscript on courageous living called "A Peril of Dragons: The Adventures of Moostaffa the Marvelous Mustached Mouse." He is also working on a novel that explores the art of relationships, entitled *Breaking the Great Spell: Relationship as Strategic Advantage.*

About Staub Leadership Consultants

Staub is a comprehensive leadership development organization dedicated to helping its clients achieve personal mastery and improve organizational effectiveness through improved leadership, empowerment, communications, and team-based creativity. The firm's approach is unique in that it combines elements of behavioral science with business-based practices to provide enduring solutions. The company partners with organizations across the spectrum of U.S. industry, ranging from *Fortune* 500 companies to mid-size and small companies, helping their partners master the challenges of leadership and achieve bottom-line, measurable results.

The company offers a wide array of tailored packages that can benefit you or your organization:

Standard programs:
• High-Impact Leadership Seminar
• Next-Step Transformative Leadership Training
• Next-Step Renewals
• The Heart of Leadership Mastery
• IF^2 Future Customer Needs Program

Customized packages:
• Team-Based Creativity
• Team Development
• Leadership 2000
• Individual Executive Development
• Climate Studies
• Facilitation Training
• 360-Degree Assessments
• Keynote Speeches

For more information about products and programs from Staub Leadership Consultants, please return the business reply card in this book, or write to:

Staub Leadership Consultants
3300 Battleground Avenue, Suite 240
Greensboro, NC 27410
Attn: Tracey B. Simmons
phone:(336) 282-0282
fax:(336) 282-6013

For information on *Executive Excellence* or *Personal Excellence* magazines, books, audio tapes, CD-ROMs, custom editions, reprints, and other programs and products, please return the business reply card in this book or call Executive Excellence Publishing at:

1-800-304-9782
or visit our Web site: **www.eep.com**